AT HOME
with the WORD
1 9 9 5

Sunday Scriptures and Reflections

Marian Bohen, OSU

Barbara Budde
Joyce Hollyday
Roy Lanham
Sherry Bitsche Lanham

LTP
LITURGY TRAINING PUBLICATIONS

Reprinting from *At Home With the Word 1995*

A parish or institution may purchase a license to reprint the Reflections (and their discussion questions), the Practices of Faith, Hope and Charity, the Prayer of the Season or the holy day boxes from *At Home With the Word 1995*. Please see page 160 for details.

If a parish or institution wishes to reproduce some or all of the scripture texts, a license must be acquired from the copyright owners. (See below.) When writing to copyright owners, state clearly which texts you wish to use, the number of copies to be made and how often you'll be using the copies. There may be a license fee.

Acknowledgments

The Sunday scripture pericopes contained herein are from the *Revised Standard Version Bible,* copyright © 1946, 1952, 1971 by the Division of Christian Education of the National Council of Churches of Christ in the U.S.A., as emended in the *Lectionary for the Christian People,* copyright © 1988 by Pueblo Publishing Company, Inc. Used with permission. All rights reserved. For information on reprint permission, write: The Liturgical Press, St. John's Abbey, Collegeville MN 56321.

Most Roman Catholic parishes proclaim the Sunday scriptures using the *New American Bible* readings from the *Lectionary for Mass,* copyright © 1970 by the Confraternity of Christian Doctrine. For information on reprint permission, write: ICEL, 1275 K Street NW, Suite 1202, Washington DC 20005.

The translations of the psalms used herein are from the *Liturgical Psalter,* copyright © 1993 by the International Committee on English in the Liturgy, Inc. (ICEL); excerpts from the English translation of *The Roman Missal,* copyright © 1973 by ICEL; the English translation of the gospel canticles ("Canticle of Zechariah," "Canticle of Mary" and "Canticle of Simeon") are copyright © 1993 by ICEL: the "Salve Regina" from *A Book of Prayers,* copyright © 1982 by ICEL. Used with permission. All rights reserved. For reprint permission, write: ICEL, 1275 K Street NW, Suite 1202, Washington DC 20005-4097.

The Prayers of the Season are by Gabe Huck.

The holy day commentaries are by Peter Mazar.

The art in this book is by Nina Morlan. The design is by Jill Smith. David A. Lysik was the editor, and Deborah Bogaert was the production editor. Typesetting was by Kari Nicholls, in Palatino and Universe. The book was printed and bound by Noll Printing, Huntington, Indiana.

At Home With the Word 1995, copyright © 1994, Archdiocese of Chicago: Liturgy Training Publications, 1800 North Hermitage Avenue, Chicago IL 60622-1101; 1-800-933-1800; FAX 1-800-933-7094. All rights reserved.

ISBN 1-56854-034-5
CODE: AHW95
$6.00

How to Use At Home With the Word

This book invites you to be at home with God's word, to live *with* the Sunday scriptures in order to live *by* them.

SCRIPTURE READINGS: These are the heart of *At Home with the Word.* To prepare for Sunday worship, you may want to read the scriptures before going to church. Better yet, to allow God's word to dwell in you, use this book to return to the Sunday scriptures again and again throughout the week after they have been proclaimed in church. This will help you gain familiarity with the books of scripture as they are set out in portions for us to feast on Sunday after Sunday.

REFLECTION: Scripture interpreter Marian Bohen asks us to mull over the readings, and there are several ways to do that. We can read the reflections to learn more background information and to consider things we've never considered before. We can also keep a journal of thoughts and discoveries. Households or small groups can meet weekly to share the readings and the reflection.

This is Year C, the year of the gospel according to Luke. Throughout Ordinary Time, we will be reading most often from this gospel. Please see Marian Bohen's introduction to the Gospel of Luke, on page 4.

PRACTICE OF FAITH: Barbara Budde presently ministers in a parish as liturgist and RCIA director. She suggests prayers, rituals and meditations that may be helpful in developing a life grounded in faith.

PRACTICE OF HOPE: As the associate editor of *Sojourners* magazine, Joyce Hollyday has traveled widely to glean stories of hope.

PRACTICE OF CHARITY: Sherry and Roy Lanham — campus ministers at Eastern Illinois University in Charleston — have compiled suggestions for living the law of love at home, at school, at work and at play.

WEEKDAY READINGS: Some people may want to read more than the Sunday scriptures. We've listed the chapters of the book of the Bible from which the first readings for daily Mass are taken each week.

At Home with the Word also includes:

MORNING, EVENING AND NIGHT PRAYER: Simple patterns of prayer for the home. They're for every day and for all ages. These prayers take five or ten minutes and are meant to be repeated every day. Don't be afraid of repetition. After all, that's one way to learn.

SEASONAL PSALMS AND PRAYERS: Each season of the year is introduced by a special page that includes an acclamation, a psalm and a short prayer. Repeating a single psalm throughout a season is a fine way to learn the psalms by heart.

SUNDAY AND FRIDAY PSALMS AND PRAYERS: Sunday is our day of feasting, Friday our day of fasting. Both days need extra prayer and acts of discipleship. Here are psalms, a Lord's Day poem by Henry Baker and a prayer for Fridays from the bishops' letter, *The Challenge of Peace.*

ORDER OF MASS: The Mass is the heart of our heritage of Sunday prayer. Individual acclamations and litanies also can be used as prayers during the week.

An Introduction to the Gospel of Luke

The Gospel of Luke forms the first portion of a two-part work, Luke-Acts, by the same late first century author. Traditions dating from the latter part of the second century attribute this work to a companion of Paul named Luke (see Colossians 4:14; 2 Timothy 4:11; Philemon 24). The date of its composition is generally placed between 80-85 CE. It is also thought that Luke may have been a Syrian from Antioch, because the writing is clearly not from Palestine and probably not from Rome.

AIM To discover why Luke-Acts was written, we have the author's own words. In the introduction to the gospel, Luke states that while many had already "taken in hand" the drawing up of a narrative of what had been passed down, he wished to write his own orderly account. He did this so that Christians of the second generation, living with the disappointment of the delay of Christ's return, might be assured of the truth and reliability of what they had been told.

GENERAL PLAN OF LUKE As in the writing of any history, the ordering and arrangement of the material, as well as the omission or the inclusion of such material, contributes to a certain interpretation and sets a particular tone. The core of the earliest Christian tradition about Jesus is contained in the passion/death/resurrection event. The events of Jesus' ministry form an outer circle around this core, and all three synoptic gospels recount a story of this ministry that is, in essence, the same. Around this, the infancy narratives of Matthew and Luke from a third circle. What makes each gospel account unique are the certain details and words introduced to intensify and fill out their thematic undertones.

As for the outermost circle—the infancy narratives—Luke's account centers on Mary and her relatives. More than the others, Luke's gsopel presents women as disciples, as important in the plan of salvation.

From Mary's Song (1:46-55) and the message to the shepherds, through to the end of his gospel, Luke highlights "the great reversal," a theme common in the Hebrew Bible that he continues: The poor and the lowly will be raised up and have the good news preached to them; the powerful, on the other hand, will be cast down.

A recurring theme in Luke is the kingdom, that world where society's values are turned upside-down. The condition for receiving Jesus as Lord and Savior — for entering this upside-down kingdom — is itself a turnaround, a *metanoia*, or conversion. But this is not a one-time or static conversion. It is a journey, like the journey of Jesus himself, an exodus into the hard climb up to Jerusalem, the center of religious and political power. At the end of the journey is the final clash between the way things are and the way God wants them to be. Salvation (liberation) lies in the direction of this journey.

LUKE'S COMMUNITY AND THE MESSAGE FOR OUR COMMUNITIES By a careful, reflective reading of the Gospel of Luke, we can discover the outlines of the community to which Luke belonged. But to comprehend what Luke means when he frequently writes of the poor, the rich, or possessions, it is necessary to understand the economic and social realities of first century Palestine.

In the Greco-Roman world of the time, a good person was a "benefactor" — a person of means who served and was beneficial to others. In Luke's gospel, the theme of beneficence is prominent, and the final irony is that Jesus — healer, teacher, benefactor — was executed as a "malefactor." In the notion of the benefactor was the idea of reciprocity. When a benefactor gave, he or she received something in return; so an invitation to dinner would result in a future return invitation (see 14:12-14). Or, the giving of alms would result in the grateful dependency of the recipient (see 16:1-13).

In Luke's gospel, Jesus is a benefactor. Luke begins with the definition of a "good person" that his community understands, but then he follows the journey of Jesus into a new definition that is enlarged and enriched by the tradition of Israel. Justice and solidarity in the real world of goods, possessions, status and power were constant themes in the prophets' proclamations. Jesus, the one sent from God to proclaim the reign of God, announced the good news to the poor (see 4:18) in the spirit of the prophets and went about doing good in a way that could be understood within the Hellenistic world.

Luke's gospel, more than any other, combines the religious vision of God's kingdom, where justice and peace are the governing principles of human life, with the cultural image of the good person who is a boon for others. In this new vision a great reversal comes about: the "other" is accepted (for example, Zacchaeus and Lazarus) and the giver expects nothing in return. This is one of the startling aspects of Jesus' dealings with others: He creates space for a free response and does not give in order to receive. He does not invite others into dependency; rather, Jesus calls and elicits a free response.

Finally, Luke's gospel is not a heavy-handed volume of moral teaching. A gifted narrator, Luke has arranged the various sources and traditions at his disposal into an intriguing series of compelling stories, unified under the theme of a journey into a world turned on its head. Luke's narrative redirects our focus away from ourselves and those like us toward a vision of a world that accepts, includes and embraces "the other" as sister and brother.

FOR FURTHER READING

Danker, Frederick W. *Luke*. Proclamation Commentaries. 2nd ed. Philadelphia: Fortress Press, 1987.

Johnson, Luke Timothy. *The Gospel of Luke*. Sacra Pagina Collegeville: The Liturgical Press/ Michael Glazier, 1991.

LaVerdiere, Eugene. *Luke*. New Testament Message 5. Wilmington, DE: Michael Glazier, 1980.

Moxnes, Halvor. *The Economy of the Kingdom: Social Conflict and Economic Relations in Luke's Gospel*. Philadelphia: Fortress Press, 1988.

The Order of Mass

INTRODUCTORY RITES

Entrance Song

A psalm or hymn may be sung.

Greeting

After the sign of the cross, the presider greets the assembly and all respond:

And also with you.

Rite of Blessing and Sprinkling Holy Water

On Sundays there may be a blessing and sprinkling of water to recall baptism. Then the penitential rite is omitted.

Penitential Rite

This rite may take many forms. It may include the "I confess" and the "Lord, have mercy":

I confess to almighty God,
and to you, my brothers and sisters,
that I have sinned through my own fault
in my thoughts and in my words,
in what I have done,
and in what I have failed to do;
and I ask blessed Mary, ever virgin,
all the angels and saints,
and you, my brothers and sisters,
to pray for me to the Lord our God.

Lord, have mercy.
Christ, have mercy.
Lord, have mercy.

Gloria

On feast days and on Sundays outside Advent and Lent, all sing:

Glory to God in the highest,
and peace to his people on earth.
Lord God, heavenly King,
almighty God and Father,
    we worship you, we give you thanks,
    we praise you for your glory.
Lord Jesus Christ, only Son of the Father,
Lord God, Lamb of God,
you take away the sin of the world:
    have mercy on us;
you are seated at the right hand of the Father:
    receive our prayer.

For you alone are the Holy One,
you alone are the Lord,
you alone are the Most High,
    Jesus Christ,
    with the Holy Spirit,
    in the glory of God the Father. Amen.

The introductory rites conclude with the opening prayer, to which all respond:

Amen.

LITURGY OF THE WORD

Reading(s)

After each reading the lector says, "The word of the Lord," and all respond:

Thanks be to God.
Then all share a moment of silent reflection.

Psalm

A psalm is sung from the psalter or the lectionary.

Gospel

The proclamation of the gospel is welcomed by singing the Alleluia or, during Lent, some other acclamation of praise.

Before the gospel, the proclaimer says, "The Lord be with you," and all respond:

And also with you.
Then the proclaimer says, "A reading from the holy gospel according to N.,"
and all respond:

Glory to you, Lord.
After the gospel, the proclaimer says, "The gospel of the Lord," and all respond:

Praise to you, Lord Jesus Christ.

Homily

After the homily, a moment of silent reflection may be shared.

Profession of Faith

On Sundays and solemnities, all say:

We believe in one God,
    the Father, the Almighty,
    maker of heaven and earth,
    of all that is seen and unseen.

We believe in one Lord, Jesus Christ,
    the only Son of God,
    eternally begotten of the Father,
    God from God, Light from Light,
    true God from true God,
    begotten, not made,
        one in Being with the Father.
Through him all things were made.
For us and for our salvation
        he came down from heaven:
by the power of the Holy Spirit
        he was born of the Virgin Mary,
        and became man.
For our sake he was crucified
        under Pontius Pilate;
        he suffered, died, and was buried.

On the third day he rose again
in fulfillment of the scriptures;
he ascended into heaven and is seated
at the right hand of the Father.
He will come again in glory
to judge the living and the dead,
and his kingdom will have no end.
We believe in the Holy Spirit, the Lord,
the giver of life,
who proceeds from the Father and the Son.
With the Father and the Son
he is worshiped and glorified.
He has spoken through the prophets.
We believe in one holy catholic
and apostolic Church.
We acknowledge one baptism
for the forgiveness of sins.
We look for the resurrection of the dead,
and the life of the world to come.
Amen.

General Intercessions

The liturgy of the word concludes with prayers of petition for our church and our world, to which the assembly may respond:

Lord, have mercy.
or:
Lord, hear our prayer.

LITURGY OF THE EUCHARIST

Preparation of the Altar and the Gifts

Gifts are collected for the poor and for the church.

If there is no music or song, prayers may be said aloud to which all respond:

Blessed be God for ever.
The assembly speaks to the presider:

May the Lord accept the sacrifice at your hands,

for the praise and glory of his name,
for our good and the good of all his Church.
The presider says the prayer over the gifts, and all respond:

Amen.

Eucharistic Prayer

Our great prayer of praise and thanksgiving begins with a dialogue between the presider and the assembly. The presider says, "The Lord be with you," to which all respond:

And also with you.
Then the presider says, "Lift up your hearts," and all respond:

We lift them up to the Lord.
Then the presider says, "Let us give thanks to the Lord our God," and all respond:

It is right to give him thanks and praise.
Then the presider offers the eucharistic prayer of the assembly, and all sing the acclamations:

PREFACE ACCLAMATION

Holy, holy, holy Lord, God of power and might,
heaven and earth are full of your glory.
Hosanna in the highest.
Blessed is he who comes in the name
of the Lord.
Hosanna in the highest.

MEMORIAL ACCLAMATION

Christ has died,
Christ is risen,
Christ will come again.
or:
Dying you destroyed our death,
rising you restored our life.
Lord Jesus, come in glory.
or:
When we eat this bread and drink this cup,
we proclaim your death, Lord Jesus,
until you come in glory.
or:
Lord, by your cross and resurrection
you have set us free.
You are the Savior of the world.

GREAT AMEN
The eucharistic prayer concludes with all singing:

Amen!

Communion Rite

LORD'S PRAYER
The presider invites the assembly to join in the Lord's Prayer, which concludes with the presider saying, "...as we wait in joyful hope for the coming of our Savior, Jesus Christ." Then all say:

For the kingdom, the power and the glory
    are yours,
now and for ever.

SIGN OF PEACE
Following a prayer, the deacon or presider says, "The peace of the Lord be with you always," and all respond:

And also with you.
Then all are invited to exchange a sign of the peace of Christ.

THE BREAKING OF THE BREAD
The holy bread is broken and the holy wine poured in preparation for communion. The following litany is sung throughout this action:

Lamb of God,
you take away the sins of the world:
have mercy on us.
The litany continues:

Lamb of God,
you take away the sins of the world:
grant us peace.

COMMUNION
The presider invites all to share in holy communion, and the assembly says:

Lord, I am not worthy to receive you,
but only say the word and I shall be healed.
The minister of communion says, "The Body of Christ" or "The Blood of Christ," and the communicant responds:

Amen.
A song or psalm is sung during communion.

All share a moment of silent reflection.

The communion rite concludes with a prayer to which all respond:

Amen.

CONCLUDING RITE

Blessing

The presider says, "The Lord be with you," and all respond:

And also with you.
The blessing may take several forms. All respond by saying:

Amen.

Dismissal

The deacon or presider invites all to go in the peace of Christ, and all respond:

Thanks be to God.

MORNING
prayer

This order of prayer may be said upon waking, or before or during breakfast.

O Lord, open my lips,
and my mouth shall declare your praise.

The Sign of the Cross

In the name of the Father
and of the Son
and of the Holy Spirit.

Psalm 63

God, my God, you I crave;
my soul thirsts for you,
my body aches for you
like a dry and weary land.
Let me gaze on you in your temple;
a vision of strength and glory.

Your love is better than life,
my speech is full of praise.
I give you a lifetime of worship,
my hands raised in your name.
I feast at a rich table,
my lips sing of your glory.

On my bed I lie awake,
your memory fills the night.
You have been my help,
I rejoice beneath your wings.
Yes, I cling to you,
your right hand holds me fast.

Let those who want me dead
end up deep in the grave!
They will die by the sword,
their bodies food for jackals.
But let the king find joy in God.
All who swear by truth be praised,
every lying mouth be shut.

*One of the seasonal psalms throughout this book
may be prayed instead of Psalm 63.*

The Canticle of Zechariah

Praise the Lord, the God of Israel,
who shepherds the people and sets them free.

God raises from David's house
a child with power to save.
Through the holy prophets
God promised in ages past
to save us from enemy hands,
from the grip of all who hate us.

The Lord favored our ancestors
recalling the sacred covenant,
the pledge to our ancestor Abraham,
to free us from our enemies,
so we might worship without fear
and be holy and just all our days.

And you, child, will be called
Prophet of the Most High,
for you will come to prepare
a pathway for the Lord
by teaching the people salvation
through forgiveness of their sin.

Out of God's deepest mercy
a dawn will come from on high,
light for those shadowed by death,
guide for our feet on the way to peace.

The Lord's Prayer

*You may join hands with others or hold your
hands with palms facing upward while praying the
Lord's Prayer.*

EVENING
prayer

This order of prayer may be said before or after dinner.

O God, come to my assistance.
O Lord, make haste to help me.

The Lighting of a Candle

A candle may be lit to welcome the evening while saying:

Jesus Christ is the light of the world,
a light no darkness can overcome.

Psalm 141:1-5, 8

Hurry, Lord! I call and call!
Listen! I plead with you.
Let my prayer rise like incense,
my upraised hands, like an evening sacrifice.

Lord, guard my lips,
watch my every word.
Let me never speak evil
or consider hateful deeds,
let me never join the wicked
to eat their lavish meals.

If the just correct me,
I take their rebuke as kindness,
but the unction of the wicked
will never touch my head.
I pray and pray
against their hateful ways.

Lord my God, I turn to you,
in you I find safety.
Do not strip me of life.

The Canticle of Mary

I acclaim the greatness of the Lord,
I delight in God my savior,
who regarded my humble state.
Truly from this day on
all ages will call me blest.

For God, wonderful in power,
has used that strength for me.
Holy the name of the Lord!
whose mercy embraces the faithful,
one generation to the next.

The mighty arm of God
scatters the proud in their conceit,
pulls tyrants from their thrones,
and raises up the humble.
The Lord fills the starving,
and lets the rich go hungry.

God rescues lowly Israel,
recalling the promise of mercy,
the promise made to our ancestors,
to Abraham's heirs for ever.

Intercession and Lord's Prayer

*At day's end we offer our petitions in Jesus' name.
We make intercession for our church, our world,
our parish, our neighbors, our family and friends
and ourselves. We seal all our prayers with the
Lord's Prayer. In conclusion, all may exchange the
sign of peace.*

SUNDAY
prayer

Sunday is our weekly feast day, our celebration of creation, liberation and resurrection.

The wedding feast of the Lamb has begun, and his bride is prepared to welcome him.

Psalm 100

Shout joy to the Lord, all earth,
serve the Lord with gladness,
enter God's presence with joy!

Know that the Lord is God,
our maker to whom we belong,
our shepherd, and we the flock.

Enter the temple gates,
the courtyard with thanks and praise;
give thanks and bless God's name.

Indeed the Lord is good,
"God is lasting love!"
faithful from age to age.

Prayer of the Day

On this day, the first of days,
God the Father's name we praise;
who, creation's Lord and Spring,
did the world from darkness bring.

On this day the eternal Son
over death the triumph won.
On this day the Spirit came
with the gift of living flame.

God, the blessed Holy One,
may thy saving work be done;
in this work our souls are free
as we rest this day with thee.

Lord, by your cross and resurrection
   you have set us free.
You are the savior of the world.

Psalm 51:3-6, 12-13

Have mercy, tender God,
forget that I defied you.
Wash away my sin,
cleanse me from my guilt.

I know my evil well,
it stares me in the face,
evil done to you alone
before your very eyes.

Creator, reshape my heart,
God, steady my spirit.
Do not cast me aside
stripped of your holy spirit.

Friday is our weekly fast day, our day of special prayer, fasting and almsgiving.

Prayer of the Day

All praise be yours, God our Creator,
as we wait in joyful hope
for the flowering of justice
and the fullness of peace.

All praise for this day, this Friday.
By our weekly fasting and prayer,
cast out the spirit of war, of fear and mistrust,
and make us grow hungry
   for human kindness,
thirsty for solidarity
   with all the people of your dear earth.

May all our prayers, our fasting and our deeds
be done in the name of Jesus. Amen.

NIGHT
prayer

This order of prayer may be said before going to sleep.

May Almighty God give us a restful night and a peaceful death.

Psalm 131

Lord, I am not proud,
holding my head too high,
reaching beyond my grasp.

See for yourself!
I am calm and tranquil
like a weaned child
resting in its mother's arms:
my whole being at rest.

Let Israel rest in the Lord,
now and for ever.

The Canticle of Simeon

Lord, let your servant
now die in peace,
for you kept your promise.

With my own eyes
I see the salvation
you prepared for all peoples:

light revealing life to the Gentiles
and glory to your people Israel.

Invocation to Mary

The final prayer of the day is customarily to Mary.

Hail, holy Queen, Mother of mercy,
our life, our sweetness, and our hope!
To you we cry, the children of Eve;
to you we send up our sighs,
mourning and weeping in this land of exile.
Turn, then, most gracious advocate,
your eyes of mercy toward us;
lead us home at last
and show us the blessed fruit of your
womb, Jesus:
O clement, O loving, O sweet Virgin Mary!

The Sign of the Cross

*We end the day the way we began it,
with the sign of the cross.*

May the almighty and merciful Lord,
the Father and the Son and the Holy Spirit,
bless and keep us. Amen.

ADVENT

Maranatha! Come, Lord Jesus!

God owns this planet
and all its riches.
The earth and every creature
belong to God.
God set the land on top of the seas
and anchored it in the deep.

Who is fit to climb God's mountain
and stand in that holy place?
Whoever has integrity:
not chasing shadows,
not living lies.
God will bless them,
their savior will bring justice.
These people long to see the Lord,
they seek the face of Jacob's God.

Stretch toward heaven, you gates,
open high and wide.
Let the glorious sovereign enter.
Who is this splendid ruler?
The Lord of power and might,
the conqueror of chaos.

Stretch toward heaven, you gates,
open high and wide.
Let the glorious sovereign enter.
Who is this splendid ruler?
The Lord of heaven's might,
this splendid ruler is God.

—Psalm 24

In the long nights of December,
we call you God of Jacob
because our ancestor Jacob
    wrestled all night long with you
and won your blessing and the name
    Israel.
Remember Jacob
who saw the ladder in the sky
and all your angels going up and down,
Jacob, who was the child
of Rebekah and Isaac,
the husband of Leah and Rachel,
the father of Joseph and Judah
and of all the tribes.
These are the tribes
that climb your mountain,
seek your face.
These are the tribes of Joseph and Mary
with whom we stand and reach up
like high, open gates
that wait for you to enter, God of Jacob,
wait for your gentleness and justice
to save us.

—Prayer of the Season

READING I *Jeremiah 33:14–16*

Behold, the days are coming, says the LORD, when I will fulfill the promise I made to the house of Israel and the house of Judah. In those days and at that time I will cause a righteous Branch to spring forth for David, who shall execute justice and righteousness in the land. In those days Judah will be saved and Jerusalem will dwell securely. And this is the name by which it will be called: "The LORD is our righteousness."

READING II *1 Thessalonians 3:12—4:2*

May the Lord make you increase and abound in love to one another and to all, as we do to you, to establish your hearts unblamable in holiness before God, our Father, at the coming of our Lord Jesus with all his saints.

Finally, my dear people, we beseech and exhort you in the Lord Jesus, that as you learned from us how you ought to live and to please God, just as you are doing, you do so more and more. For you know what instructions we gave you through the Lord Jesus.

GOSPEL *Luke 21:25–28, 34–36*

At that time Jesus said, "There will be signs in the sun and moon and stars, and upon the earth distress of nations in perplexity at the roaring of the sea and the waves, the peoples fainting with fear and with foreboding of what is coming on the world; for the powers of the heavens will be shaken. And then they will see the Man of Heaven coming in a cloud with power and great glory. Now when these things begin to take place, look up and raise your heads, because your redemption is drawing near.

"But take heed to yourselves lest your hearts be weighed down with dissipation and drunkenness and cares of this life, and that day come upon you suddenly like a snare; for it will come upon all who dwell upon the face of the whole earth. But watch at all times, praying that you may have strength to escape all these things that will take place, and to stand before the Man of Heaven."

REFLECTION

On this First Sunday of Advent, Luke presents an announcement and an exhortation. In the preceding verses of chapter 21, Jesus talked about the destruction of the Temple, calamities on earth, the persecution of the disciples and the devastation of Jerusalem under Gentile rule (see 21:5–24).

The announcement in today's gospel is of signs in the heavens and distress on the inhabited earth — indications that the parousia, the end time, is at hand. But these signs are not only for the disciples or for the people of Jerusalem; they are for all people. The horizon has been broadened to a vision of universal proportions and of a redemption (*apolutrosis,* acquittal) for all humanity. When these signs are given, all will know that the kingdom, the full dominion (*basileia*) of God, is near.

In the Christian Scriptures, the kingdom has its origin in God; it is not something that can be arranged through human efforts. Nor is this dominion territorial; potentially, it includes all who dwell upon the face of the earth. The coming of God's kingdom must be awaited and prepared for by a life lived in expectation of its arrival, a life spent in an attitude of conversion.

The exhortation, "Take heed to yourselves" not to be weighed down (*barethosin,* related to the noun *baros,* weight, an oppressive suffering, a burden), is a powerful image of oppression and heaviness. It stands in contrast to the ability to stand firm and encourages us to stand erect, for liberation is at hand. Luke's gospel shows Jesus reminding the people that the journey into the future, where God's values prevail, is one that requires alertness and a readiness to slough off oppressive burdens.

■ **Compare the opening verse of today's gospel reading with the following: Revelation 6:12–13; Isaiah 13:10; Joel 2:10; Zephaniah 1:15. All these texts contain predictions of nature in turmoil — a frightening image of the endtime. What place is there in your life for such images? Do they shake you up and frighten you? Why or why not?**

■ **When you reflect on the "coming" of God for you, what reactions do you have? How do such reactions affect your life?**

■ **In what ways are you alert to the coming of God? What burdens do you still need to cast off?**

PRACTICE OF FAITH

A NEW YEAR. Once again we have entered Advent, this season of patient waiting. We look for the days when God will fulfill the promise made to the house of Israel. We look for justice and righteousness in the land. Though it is customary to make New Year's resolutions when the secular calendar changes, use this new liturgical year and this season's call for watchfulness, justice and peace to write some different resolutions: How can I act this year to be a witness of God's justice and righteousness? What can I do this year to make love abound more fully? In the midst of the world's troubles and difficulties, how can I be a sign of Christian hope? Keep these resolutions for review throughout the year, especially as Advent approaches next year.

PRACTICE OF HOPE

ABOUND IN LOVE. One month-old Devon Cornett became ill during the great blizzard of March 1993. But the roads and airport were closed when doctors determined that he needed to be taken to Asheville, North Carolina, for emergency surgery. As his condition grew critical, a truck and an ambulance began the 35-mile trek. When visibility became impossible, an emergency medical technician got out and walked in front of the vehicles to make sure they didn't slide off the road.

A surgeon, one of the few staff members who had been able to reach the hospital, agreed to do the surgery, even though he had never attempted such a procedure alone. Devon, who went into respiratory arrest and renal failure, would die if he didn't get immediate help. Devon's life was saved by the courage of strangers. His grateful mother, Kim, said, "We put it in the hands of the Lord."

PRACTICE OF CHARITY

LOOK UP AND RAISE YOUR HEADS. How do we await the coming of God's kingdom? How do we prepare in this Advent time? We raise our heads and open our eyes to see Jesus in the homeless people on the streets of our cities, in the poor and downtrodden, in our family members and in our wealthy neighbors. Look up — the kingdom is near. Prepare ye the way!

WEEKDAY READINGS Isaiah 2:1–5; 11:1–10; Romans 10:9–18; Isaiah 26:1–6; 29:17–24; 30:19-26

READING I *Baruch 5:1–9*

Take off the garment of your sorrow and
    affliction, O Jerusalem,
and put on for ever the beauty of the glory
    from God.
Put on the robe of the righteousness from God;
put on your head the diadem of the glory of the
    Everlasting.
For God will show your splendor everywhere
    under heaven.
For your name will for ever be called by God,
    "Peace of righteousness and glory of godliness."
Arise, O Jerusalem, stand upon the height
    and look toward the east,
and see your children gathered from west to east,
    at the word of the Holy One,
    rejoicing that God has remembered them.
For they went forth from you on foot,
    led away by their enemies;
but God will bring them back to you,
    carried in glory, as on a royal throne.
For God has ordered that every high mountain and
    the everlasting hills be made low
    and the valleys filled up, to make level ground,
    so that Israel may walk safely in the glory of God.
The woods and every fragrant tree
    have shaded Israel at God's command.
For God will lead Israel with joy,
    in the light of the divine glory,
    with the mercy and righteousness that come
    from God.

READING II *Philippians 1:3–6, 8–11*

I thank my God in all my remembrance of you,
always in every prayer of mine for you all making
my prayer with joy, thankful for your partnership
in the gospel from the first day until now. And I am
sure that the one who began a good work in you
will bring it to completion at the day of Jesus
Christ. For God is my witness, how I yearn for you
all with the affection of Christ Jesus. And it is my
prayer that your love may abound more and more,
with knowledge and all discernment, so that you
may approve what is excellent, and may be pure
and blameless for the day of Christ, filled with the
fruits of righteousness which come through Jesus
Christ, to the glory and praise of God.

GOSPEL *Luke 3:1–6*

In the fifteenth year of the reign of Tiberius Caesar,
Pontius Pilate being governor of Judea, and Herod
being tetrarch of Galilee, and his brother Philip
tetrarch of the region of Ituraea and Trachonitis,
and Lysanias tetrarch of Abilene, in the high-priest-
hood of Annas and Caiaphas, the word of God came
to John the son of Zechariah in the wilderness; and
John went into all the region about the Jordan,
preaching a baptism of repentance for the forgiveness of sins. As it is written in the book of the words
of Isaiah the prophet,
    "The voice of one crying in the wilderness:
    Prepare the way of the Lord,
    make straight the paths of the Lord.
    Every valley shall be filled,
    and every mountain and hill shall be
    brought low,
    and the crooked shall be made straight,
    and the rough ways shall be made smooth;
    and all flesh shall see the salvation of God."

Thursday, December 8, 1994

THE IMMACULATE CONCEPTION OF MARY

Genesis 3:9–15, 20 *Eve is "the mother of the living."*

Ephesians 1:3–6, 11–12 *God chose us before the world began.*

Luke 1:26–38 *I am the servant of the Lord.*

Sin means separation from God. We believe Mary was
never separated from God from the moment of her
conception in her mother's womb. On this Advent
feast of Mary, her "yes" undoes Eve's "no." Mary is our
new Eve, the mother of the living God.

REFLECTION

The exhortation that concluded last Sunday's gospel is repeated today and expressed in the clear imagery of Isaiah. Although his chronology is not exact, Luke begins this third chapter, which deals with the ministry of John the Baptizer, by placing John's ministry within the political and religious context of the time.

John was in the wilderness (*eremo,* desert), an image rich in meaning in biblical tradition. The desert, or wilderness, is a place of struggle and hardship, as it was for the people who fled Egypt. It is also a place for the gracious action of God, a lonely place where God can be heard.

John went throughout the region, in the manner of the prophets, announcing the good news of the forgiveness of sins (*aphesis,* release, letting go, leaving behind). For Luke, forgiveness of sins is part and parcel of the reign of God as well as a living reality within the community. Preparation for this gift of forgiveness is an immersion *(baptisma)* in repentance — a *metanoia,* or change of mind and heart, a turnaround in one's life.

This word, this announcement by John in the wilderness, is imaged by Luke in his citation of Isaiah 40:3–5. The leveling, the straightening and the smoothing are images frequently found in the Hebrew Scriptures. The way of the Lord will be prepared by a topsy-turvy movement, a change from concave to convex, high to low, crooked to straight. As we will see, this image of reversal will be an important one in Luke's writings. The last line of the passage from Isaiah is Luke's reminder that all flesh (*sarx,* humanity in all its frailty) will see, will experience, the liberation made possible by God.

■ **Read slowly and thoughtfully as much as you can of Isaiah 40 — 66. This part of Isaiah was written to comfort the exiles in Babylon around 539 BCE. What message do you discern about the coming salvation?**

■ **Where do you experience the coming of the Lord in your life? How do you know? Are there changes from high to low, crooked to straight in your life? Are these signs of the Lord's coming for you?**

PRACTICE OF FAITH

SIGNS OF SALVATION. Luke took great pains in his gospel to show the connection between God's saving word and human history. In the midst of all the political and religious power structures of first century Palestine, God's word came to John and announced that "all flesh shall see the salvation of God." On Tuesday, December 6, we celebrate the memorial of St. Nicholas. In his time, he was an example of God's saving love through the holiness of his life and his care for the poor, especially children. We also celebrate Mary this week, who, through her openness to God's word in her own history, was a most direct instrument of God's saving plan. Do one thing this week for another person that will be a sign of the salvation of God. Visit, write or cook for someone who might need your help this week.

PRACTICE OF HOPE

SEE THE SALVATION OF GOD. On December 2, 1980, Dorothy Kazel, Jean Donovan, Ita Ford and Maura Clarke — U.S. missionaries in El Salvador — were murdered by that country's security forces. All had had fears and doubts as violence engulfed the country, but each stayed, continuing their work of feeding the hungry, sheltering the refugees and comforting those who grieved.

Maura Clarke, speaking of Salvadorans who had been tortured and killed, said: "A loving Father must have a new life of unimaginable joy and peace prepared for these precious, unknown, uncelebrated martyrs." We can trust that these four women are among them, recipients of salvation for their steadfast faith and courage.

PRACTICE OF CHARITY

PARTNERSHIP IN THE GOSPEL. By our baptism, all of us are partners with Christ in living the gospel. However, sometimes it is hard to keep this truth in focus. *Sojourners,* a monthly magazine produced by the Sojourner community in Washington, D.C., will help you stay connected to your partnership with Christ. It will help connect your faith with justice and is a great resource that can act as a catalyst for you. For $30 you receive a one-year subscription to *Sojourners* magazine, the Sojourners resource catalog, and information about opportunities to connect with other sojourners. For more information or to subscribe, write or call: Sojourners, 2401 Fifteenth Street NW, Washington DC 20077-3815; 202-328-8842.

WEEKDAY READINGS **Isaiah 35:1–10; 40:1–11; 40:25–31; (Th) The Immaculate Conception; Isaiah 48:17–19; Sirach 48:1–4, 9–11**

READING I *Zephaniah 3:14–18*

Sing aloud, O daughter Zion;
   shout, O Israel!
Rejoice and exult with all your heart,
   O daughter Jerusalem!
The Lord has taken away the judgments against
   you, and has cast out your enemies.
The Lord, the Sovereign of Israel, is in your midst;
   you shall fear evil no more.
On that day it shall be said to Jerusalem:
"Do not fear, O Zion;
   let not your hands grow weak.
The Lord, your God, is in your midst,
   a mighty one who gives victory;
the Lord will rejoice over you with gladness,
   and will renew you in love;
the Lord will exult over you with loud singing
   as on a day of festival."

READING II *Philippians 4:4–7*

Rejoice in the Lord always; again I will say, rejoice. Let every one know your forbearance. The Lord is at hand. Have no anxiety about anything, but in everything by prayer and supplication with thanksgiving let your requests be made known to God. And the peace of God, which passes all understanding, will keep your hearts and your minds in Christ Jesus.

GOSPEL *Luke 3:10–18*

The multitudes asked John, "What then shall we do?" And John answered them, "Let whoever has two coats share with those who have none; and let whoever has food do likewise." Tax collectors also came to be baptized, and said to him, "Teacher, what shall we do?" And John said to them, "Collect no more than is appointed you." Soldiers also asked him, "And we, what shall we do?" And John said to them, "Rob no one by violence or by false accusation, and be content with your wages."

As the people were in expectation, and they all questioned in their hearts concerning John, whether perhaps he were the Christ, John answered them all, "I baptize you with water; but the one who is mightier than I is coming, the thong of whose sandals I am not worthy to untie; he will baptize you with the Holy Spirit and with fire. With a winnowing fork in hand, the mighty one will clear the threshing floor and gather the wheat into the granary, burning the chaff with unquenchable fire." So, with many other exhortations, John preached good news to the people.

Monday, December 12, 1994

OUR LADY OF GUADALUPE

Zechariah 2:14–17 *Rejoice, daughter of Zion*
   or
Revelation 11:19; 12:1–6, 10 *A great sign appeared in the heavens*

Luke 1:26–38 or 1:39–47 *Blessed are you among women*

Mary appeared to Juan Diego as a poor and pregnant native woman. She is an Advent sign of things to come, an image of us nuturing the word. Whenever and wherever the word is born, the night of oppression will be shattered by the dawn of justice. Bear the word!

REFLECTION

The ministry of John the Baptizer continued beyond what is recorded in Luke's gospel, yet the incidents Luke presents give us an insight into the larger picture. Luke here speaks first of the multitudes (ochlos, crowd, throng) who came out to be baptized and make inquiries about ethical requirements. Later, Luke talks about the people (laos, people as a chosen group or unit). The use of this word—laos—is most common in Luke, who uses it to refer to ordinary people, in contrast to the leaders.

It is the ochlos, the crowd, however, that is asking the questions in verses 10–14. In keeping with the tradition of the earlier prophets, who spoke of God's concern for justice, John's answers all have to do with the questioner's treatment of others. All should share; tax collectors should not charge more than the proper rate; and those in military service should refrain from using their position for intimidation or extortion.

Luke then speaks of the people (laos) as being in expectation, being in a state of suspense and watchful waiting. Most probably, "people" here refers to the people of Israel. In their expectant state, they ask themselves if John might be the messiah. In reply, John speaks about two kinds of baptism—John baptizes with water, but the one to come will baptize with the Holy Spirit and with fire.

In the Christian Scriptures, fire almost always has to do with judgment, as it does in these verses. With the coming of the mighty one, humanity will witness one who has power, strength and the ability to judge. This one, empowered by God, will begin the work of judgment, sifting wheat from chaff. Luke presents the traditional picture of the eschatological Messiah, sent to bring life, power, the Holy Spirit and judgment.

Luke ends this section by summing up in one sentence what was no doubt a continuous ministry of John. The good news is for the community, and the work of John is intended to help the community prepare for the bearer of the good news.

■ **Read the other accounts of John's preaching in Matthew 3:1–12 and Mark 1:1–8. What similarities and what differences do you find?**

■ **If you were in the crowd that gathered to hear John the Baptizer, what questions would you have asked about the demands of the coming salvation?**

PRACTICE OF FAITH

LA SEÑORA DEL CIELO. Tomorrow we celebrate the feast of Our Lady of Guadalupe, patroness of the Americas. Given the symbolism of her appearance in 1531, it is easy to understand why so many were converted. The apparition of this native maiden to Juan Diego, another native American, took place on the hill called Tepeyac, where there was a shrine to Tanantzin, the virgin mother of the god Huitozilpochili. Mary stood on the moon, in front of the sun, and was clothed with the stars. All of this indicated that she superseded the deities of the Aztec nation. Yet her eyes were downcast, indicating that she herself was not a goddess. She appeared as a young maiden, but the black sash she wore designated maternity. Tomorrow, join with those who keep her feast, and ask our patroness to bless all who live in the Americas.

PRACTICE OF HOPE

FEAR EVIL NO MORE. Mary is a young Muslim woman who spent several months in a "rape camp" in Bosnia. She shared a room with 70 other women, where screams filled the night. She was raped several times a day; women who resisted were killed.

Mary was five months pregnant when she was released, bruised and weak. She told a friend that she was going to give birth to the child that she carried to show everyone that she can, with God's help, overcome her suffering. When she got stronger, she explained, she would make a public statement, holding her baby in her arms "as a sign to the world that love conquers evil."

PRACTICE OF CHARITY

LET WHOEVER HAS TWO COATS SHARE. Every spring most of us participate in the annual ritual of spring cleaning. At that time we often clear out some of the things we no longer use. If you want to make it easier on yourself next spring, go through your closets now and decide what you *really* need. Give the useable clothes you no longer need to local organizations that provide clothing assistance to the poor and homeless (e.g., Salvation Army, Catholic Charities, St. Vincent de Paul). See this action as a sign of hope and as a way of reminding yourself of the mandate to live simply.

WEEKDAY READINGS (Mo) Our Lady of Guadalupe; Zephaniah 3:1–2, 9–13; Isaiah 45:6–8, 18, 21–25; 54:1–10; 56:1–3, 6–8; Genesis 49:2, 8–10

READING I *Micah 5:2–4*

But you, O Bethlehem Ephrathah,
    who are little to be among the clans of Judah,
from you shall come forth for me
    one who is to be ruler in Israel,
whose origin is from of old,
    from ancient days.
Therefore they shall be given up until the time
    when she who is in labor has brought forth;
then the rest of the ruler's kin shall return
    to the people of Israel.
And the ruler shall stand and feed his flock
    in the strength of the LORD,
    in the majesty of the name of the LORD his God.
And they shall dwell secure, for now the ruler
    shall be great
    to the ends of the earth.

READING II *Hebrews 10:5–10*

Coming into the world, Christ said,

"Sacrifices and offerings you have not desired,
    but a body you have prepared for me;
    in burnt offerings and sin offerings
        you have taken no pleasure.
    Then I said, 'Lo, I have come to do your will,
        O God,'
    as it is written of me in the roll of the book."

When Christ said above, "You have neither desired nor taken pleasure in sacrifices and offerings and burnt offerings and sin offerings" (these are offered according to the law), then Christ added, "Lo, I have come to do your will." Christ abolishes the first in order to establish the second. And by that will we have been sanctified through the offering of the body of Jesus Christ once for all.

GOSPEL *Luke 1:39–45*

In those days Mary arose and went with haste into the hill country, to a city of Judah, and she entered the house of Zechariah and greeted Elizabeth. And when Elizabeth heard the greeting of Mary, the baby leaped in her womb; and Elizabeth was filled with the Holy Spirit and she exclaimed with a loud cry, "Blessed are you among women, and blessed is the fruit of your womb! And why is this granted me, that the mother of my Lord should come to me? For behold, when the voice of your greeting came to my ears, the baby in my womb leaped for joy. And blessed is she who believed that there would be a fulfillment of what was spoken to her from the Lord."

Friday, December 30, 1994

THE HOLY FAMILY

Sirach 3:2–6, 12–14 *Kindness to parents will not be forgotten.*
  or
1 Samuel 1:20–22, 24–28

Colossians 3:12–21 *Christ's peace must reign in your hearts.*
  or
1 John 3:1–2, 21–24

Luke 2: 41–52 *Jesus progressed in age and grace.*

Christmas is like a midwinter Easter. In this day's gospel, hear how they found the Lord "on the third day" while celebrating the Passover. No wonder we celebrate Christmas with greenery, flowers and lights: Our risen Lord turns December into April!

R E F L E C T I O N

Today's gospel is a treasure of messianic images in which Luke's own favored themes and words appear. This story of the two pregnant women takes place in an atmosphere filled with enthusiasm and action: Mary arises and goes with haste, the baby in Elizabeth's womb leaps, Elizabeth is filled with the Holy Spirit and exclaims with a loud cry. An action-packed scenario comes to life before our eyes; Luke conveys, by his choice of words, an excitement and expectation that heralds the beginning of some major event.

Elizabeth twice declares that Mary is "blessed." In the first instance, however, Luke uses the verb *eulogeo*: Mary is "famous" because of her being the mother of the Lord. But in the second instance, when Luke wants to praise Mary's faith in God's word, he uses *makarios*: Mary is "blessed," in the sense of the beatitudes, within the context of salvation. (This same distinction can also be found in 11:27 – 28.)

Joy is another of the favored themes Luke uses in connection with the messianic time: Elizabeth's baby leapt for joy and Mary's spirit rejoiced. The word used in both cases reflects a religious joy in the experience of God's saving action. This joy takes to the air in the image of leaping; in several places in Hebrew Scripture, animals leaped in religious joy (see Psalm 114:4; Malachi 4:2). John's leaping in Elizabeth's womb expresses the instinctive exuberance of creation in its anticipation of a new, but as yet unseen, reality.

■ Read the entire song of Mary in Luke 1:46 – 55 and compare it to Hannah's song in 1 Samuel 2:1 – 10. Both songs are prayers of thanksgiving, extolling God's power in favor of the weak of this world. In your parish community, is there concern for the powerless, the outcast and the needy? How is it expressed?

■ Read as much as you can of the prophet Micah. How does your reading change your idea of the image of God in the Hebrew Scriptures?

PRACTICE OF FAITH O ANTIPHONS. During these last days of Advent, we use special readings and prayers to help us prepare for the feast of Christmas. The O Antiphons, which are sung with the gospel Alleluia and before the Magnificat at Evening Prayer, are part of this tradition. You might already know them because they form the basis of the famous Advent hymn, "O Come, O Come Emmanuel." Add these O Antiphons to your Advent prayer this week. After each address to Christ, all may respond, "Come and save us."

December 18:	O sacred Lord of ancient Israel
December 19:	O flower of Jesse's stem
December 20:	O Key of David and Ruler of the house of David
December 21:	O Radiant Dawn, splendor of eternal light and sun of justice
December 22:	O King of all nations, the only joy of every human heart
December 23:	O Emmanuel, God who lives with us to rule and guide

PRACTICE OF HOPE MY SPIRIT REJOICES. I made my way to the inner-city clinic in Washington, D.C., where the walls were decorated with tinsel and someone had painted black the face of the plastic Santa Claus on the file cabinet. The waiting room was packed with crying children. A young Latina woman, looking weary and harried, handed me some forms to fill out. I asked her where she was from.

"El Salvador," she said, her face brightening. "If I save my money carefully, I have $30 to call home at Christmas. Three minutes' worth. Every Christmas my mother answers. Every Christmas we cry together for three minutes. Never any words." She smiled. "But it is enough."

PRACTICE OF CHARITY THE BABY IN MY WOMB LEAPED FOR JOY. What a strange and mysterious feeling it is when a mother feels the movement of her child within her body. Life in the womb is a critical time for growth, and good prenatal care is essential for healthy mothers and their babies. Call your local health department or hospital and find out if there is anything you can do to help with their prenatal care programs. There is always a need for better prenatal health care and perhaps you can help get that care to the mothers who need it most, those who live in poverty. Their babies will leap for joy!

WEEKDAY READINGS Judges 13:2 – 7, 24 – 25; Isaiah 7:10 – 14; Song of Songs 2:8 – 14 or Zephaniah 3:14 – 18; 1 Samuel 1:24 – 28; Malachi 3:1 – 4, 23 – 24; 2 Samuel 7:1 – 5, 8 – 12, 14, 16

CHRISTMASTIME

The Lord our God comes, comes to rule the earth!

Sing to the Lord a new song,
the Lord of wonderful deeds.
Right hand and holy arm
brought victory to God.

God made that victory known,
revealed justice to nations,
remembered a merciful love
loyal to the house of Israel.
The ends of the earth have seen
the victory of our God.

Shout to the Lord, you earth,
break into song, into praise!
Sing praise to God with a harp,
with a harp and sound of music.
With sound of trumpet and horn,
shout to the Lord, our king.

Let the sea roar with its creatures,
the world and all that live there!
Let rivers clap their hands,
the hills ring out their joy!

The Lord our God comes,
comes to rule the earth,
justly to rule the world,
to govern the peoples aright.

—Psalm 98

When people witness deeds like these—
mercy winning victories
and justice welcomed in the public
    places—
then the earth itself will be an orchestra
and all creatures a choir,
and we shall sing together a song
that announces you,
God of poor shepherds and stargazers.
Rehearse us now in that Christmas song:
Like those shepherds may we know where
    to look,
like the magi may we know when to listen
    to the powerful
and when to mere dreams.
Come, Lord, and lift us up in song.

—Prayer of the Season

READING I *Isaiah 52:7–10*

How beautiful upon the mountains
    are the feet of the messenger,
who publishes peace, who brings good tiding
      of good,
    who publishes salvation,
    who says to Zion, "Your God reigns."
Hark, your sentries lift up their voice,
    together they sing for joy;
for with their own eyes they see
    the return of the LORD to Zion.
Break forth together into singing,
    you waste places of Jerusalem;
for the LORD has comforted the people
    and has redeemed Jerusalem.
The holy arm of the LORD is bared
    before the eyes of all the nations,
and all the ends of the earth shall see
    the salvation of our God.

READING II *Hebrews 1:1–6*

In many and various ways God spoke of old to our forebears by the prophets; but in these last days God has spoken to us by the Son, whom God appointed the heir of all things, and through whom God also created the world. This Son reflects the glory of God and bears the very stamp of God's nature, upholding the universe by a word of power. The Son, having made purification for sins, sat down at the right hand of the Majesty on high, having become as much superior to angels as the name the Son has obtained is more excellent than theirs. For to what angel did God ever say,

    "You are my Son,
      today I have begotten you"?
Or again,
    "I will be to him as father,
      and he shall be to me as son"?
And again, bringing the first-born into the world, God says,
    "Let all God's angels worship him."

GOSPEL *John 1:1–18*

In the beginning was the Word, and the Word was with God, and the Word was God. The Word was in the beginning with God; all things were made through the Word, without whom nothing that was made was made. In the Word was life, and the life was the light of all. The light shines in the darkness, and the darkness has not overcome it.

There was sent by God a person named John. He came for testimony, to bear witness to the light, that all might believe through him. He was not the light, but came to bear witness to the light.

The true light that enlightens every one was coming into the world. The light was in the world, and the world was made through the light, yet the world knew him not. He came to his own home, and his own people received him not. But to all who received him, who believed in his name, he gave power to become children of God; who were born, not of blood nor of the will of the flesh nor of the desire of a man, but of God.

And the Word became flesh and dwelt among us, full of grace and truth; we have beheld his glory, glory as of the only Son from the Father. (John bore witness to the Word, and cried, "This is the one of whom I said, 'The one who comes after me ranks before me, for he was before me.'") And from the Son's fullness have we all received, grace upon grace. For the law was given through Moses; grace and truth came through Jesus Christ. No one has ever seen God; the only Son, who is in the bosom of the Father, has made God known.

These readings are for Christmas, Mass During the Day. Other Christmas readings are:

Vigil Mass: Isaiah 62:1–5 Our Creator will marry us; Acts 13:16–17, 22–25 With a mighty arm we are saved; Matthew 1:1–25 This is how the birth of Jesus came about . . .;

Midnight Mass: Isaiah 9:2–7 For to us a child is born; Titus 2:11–14 Gods grace has come for all; Luke 2:1–14 I bring you news of great joy for all people.

Mass at Dawn: Isaiah 62:11–12 Your savior comes; Titus 3:4–7 We are saved through new birth in the Spirit; Luke 2:15–20 Let us go to Bethlehem.

REFLECTION

For Christmas day we turn to the opening verses of the Gospel of John and find several key words: Word, light, darkness, grace and truth. In the Hellenistic world, word (*logos*) implied activity, a dynamic power that in John is linked to creation, life and light. The Word-engendered light cannot be extinguished or overcome, even by the darkness. This contrast between light and darkness is a favorite Johannine motif, and the precursor to the light, John the Baptist, stands on the threshold between the two. John the Baptist is a candle in the predawn darkness awaiting the full light of the Word.

The Word does not only shine and dispel darkness, however. This true light came to his own home (*idia*, his own possessions, property), but his own people (*idioi*), born of the flesh and blood of his ancestors, did not welcome him with open arms. So the Word then created new space, giving power (*exousia*, the right) to all who would receive him in faith. The author of this gospel, writing toward the end of the first century and having seen the spread of Christian communities outside Palestine, expresses in theological terms what had already become a reality: The Word creates new space when his own place cannot or will not receive him.

This creation of new space is made clear in the phrase, "the Word became flesh [*sarx*, humanity in all its frailty and limitation] and dwelt among us [*eskenosen*, tabernacled or pitched his tent among us]." The use of "pitched his tent" recalls the Exodus experience —that long journey of the people and God's presence among them in the moveable tabernacle.

For the author of the Gospel of John, the Word — whose light chases darkness and whose coming creates new space and a new people — is also the Word who speaks most clearly of the God revealed in the scriptures. John, like Isaiah in the first reading, proclaims that "all the ends of the earth shall see the salvation of our God." The child born to us, "close to the Father's heart," is the tent-tempered light that our eyes can sustain, showing us the glory.

■ **How do you look on the word of the scriptures: as solid, printed text or as a creative force and presence in our lives?**

PRACTICE OF FAITH

GLORY TO GOD! On this traditional day of gift-giving, share this Christmas hymn from the third or fourth century with your family and friends:

Christ is born;
  Give him glory!
Christ comes from heaven:
  Go and meet him!
Christ is on the earth:
  Rise up to heaven!
Sing to the Lord,
  all the earth!

PRACTICE OF HOPE

THE WORD DWELT AMONG US. Robert Raines's two-year-old grandson was riding in the car with his parents, drinking from his bottle. The family began singing the song "Kum Ba Yah": "Someone's crying, Lord.... Someone's praying, Lord.... Someone's singing, Lord."

Then came a little voice from the backseat: "Someone's drinking milk, Lord, Kum Ba Yah." A two-year-old understands incarnation — Emmanuel, "God With Us" — in the ordinary and the extraordinary, walking beside us in all things.

PRACTICE OF CHARITY

THE MESSENGER OF PEACE. In a world where hatred and cynicism seem to consume life, we long for words of peace. The message of Jesus is the message of compassion, non-violence and love. It is important that we echo this message. Pax Christi, the National Catholic Peace movement, publishes a wide variety of books, pamphlets and prayer cards that offer ideas on how to walk in the way of peace. Their materials present simple suggestions and thought-provoking words by well-known authors. To become a member or to receive a listing of their publications, write or call: Pax Christi, 348 East Tenth Street, Erie PA 16503; 814-453-4955.

WEEKDAY READINGS (Mo) Acts 6:8–10; 7:54–59; (Tu–Th, Sa) 1 John 1:1–2:21; (Fr) The Holy Family (see page 26).

READING I *Numbers 6:22–27*

The Lord said to Moses, "Say to Aaron and his sons,
Thus you shall bless the people of Israel: you shall
say to them,

> The LORD bless you and keep you:
> The LORD's face shine upon you, and be
>   gracious to you:
> The LORD look upon you with favor, and
>   give you peace.

"So shall they put my name upon the people of
Israel, and I will bless them."

READING II *Galatians 4:4–7*

When the time had fully come, God set forth the
Son, born of woman, born under the law, to redeem
those who were under the law, so that we might
receive adoption. And because you are adopted
children, God has sent the Spirit of the Son into our
hearts, crying, "Abba! Father!" So through God you
are no longer a slave but an adopted child, and if a
child then an heir.

GOSPEL *Luke 2:16–21*

And they went with haste, and found Mary and
Joseph, and the baby lying in a manger. And when
they saw it they made known the saying which had
been told them concerning this child; and all who
heard it wondered at what the shepherds told them.
But Mary kept all these things, pondering them in
her heart. And the shepherds returned, glorifying
and praising God for all they had heard and seen,
as it had been told them.

And at the end of eight days, when the child
was circumcised, he was called Jesus, the name
given by the angel before he was conceived in
the womb.

REFLECTION

Mary is not a goddess — although Christian piety has often made here into some superhuman sort of being. Nor is Mary the exclusive role model for women and Jesus the role model for men. This section of Luke's gospel presents Mary as a model for all who struggle with, grapple with and try to understand the things that happen in life. Mary is the mother of the child whose birth brought shepherds to the manger. And yet, as Luke tells us, Mary did not understand. Mary had to ponder in her heart the events that were still a mystery to her.

In today's second reading from Galatians, written against those who would impose the law and its observance on Gentile converts, the emphasis is on faith in Jesus as the key to understanding our part in God's saving work. In a seemingly minor reference, Paul points to the role of Mary in the drama of salvation: Mary is the willing link between humanity and God, the woman born under the law who chose to open herself to become the bearer of a freedom she could not comprehend. The Son sent by God in the fullness of time was "born of a woman." Through Mary, the Son was born human into this world. Through Mary, the Son was born "under the law" in order to expand the horizons of the covenant, creating new space, new freedom. The movement is from slavery into freedom, from the status of minors with no rights to that of children with inherited rights.

The renewed covenant will be one in which faith, not adherence to the law, constitutes humanity's bond in the relationship with God. Mary, born under the law and giving birth in the confused cloud of faith, is the model of this new covenantal bond. She believed before she really understood, and she nourished her faith throughout her life. We celebrate Mary today as Mother of God in accordance with ancient Christian tradition — as an elder sister in the journey of faith.

■ Read the infancy narrative in Matthew 1:18–23 and see how Joseph, the main figure there, is presented as a just man living by faith.

■ Why do you think Mary's identity in Catholic tradition has often assumed the character of a superhuman being — sometimes becoming the center of attention — in contrast to what we read of her in Christian Scriptures?

PRACTICE OF FAITH

PEACE IN OUR DAYS. Today, as we celebrate the solemnity of Mary, Mother of God, we also celebrate World Peace Day. Using the famous Prayer of St. Francis, pray for peace today and throughout the year:

Lord, make me an instrument of your peace:
  where there is hatred, let me sow love;
  where there is injury, pardon;
  where there is doubt, faith;
  where there is despair, hope;
  where there is darkness, light;
  and where there is sadness, joy.
O Divine Master, grant that I may not so much seek
  to be consoled as to console,
  to be understood as to understand,
  to be loved as to love.
For it is in giving that we receive,
  it is in pardoning that we are pardoned,
  and it is in dying that we are born to eternal life.

PRACTICE OF HOPE

WE ARE GOD'S CHILDREN. Albertina Sisulu is a midwife who lives in Soweto, South Africa. For 17 years she was banned — prohibited from writing or speaking publicly. She spent 10 years under house arrest and has been tried for treason and imprisoned repeatedly, once with her son. Her husband, Walter Sisulu, spent 26 years in jail.

"My hope is based on the world's history," she says. "There's nothing without an end." She has one prayer: "I pray to God that one day I will see my people free." After many years of faithful and courageous struggle, she is beginning to see her prayer come true. Slowly, the walls of apartheid are crumbling. "In the Bible there is no black and white," she says. "God calls us his children — all of us."

PRACTICE OF CHARITY

AN ADOPTED CHILD. Images of children dying of hunger, disease and war shake us to the core. What can we do? The Christian Foundation for Children and Aging is a community of faith committed to helping the poor, especially children and the elderly, in the United States as well as in developing nations. CFCA creates opportunities for people to "adopt" a child at a Catholic mission. Sponsorship is $20 a month, which helps to meet the child's most critical needs. The sponsor receives a photo and an update on a regular basis from CFCA. Even if you cannot afford to sponsor a child on a monthly basis, you can make a one-time donation. For more information, write: Christian Foundation for Children and Aging, One Elmwood Avenue, PO Box 3910, Kansas City KS 66103-9983.

WEEKDAY READINGS (Mo–Th) 1 John 2:22—3:21; (Fr–Sa) 5:5–21

READING I *Isaiah 60:1–6*

Arise, shine; for your light has come,
    and the glory of the LORD has risen upon you.
For behold, darkness shall cover the earth,
    and thick darkness the peoples;
but the LORD will arise upon you,
    and the glory of the LORD will be seen upon you.
And nations shall come to your light,
    and rulers to the brightness of your rising.
Lift up your eyes round about, and see;
    they all gather together, they come to you;
your sons shall come from far,
    and your daughters shall be carried in the arms
    of their nurses.
Then you shall see and be radiant,
    your heart shall thrill and rejoice;
because the abundance of the sea shall be turned
    to you,
    the wealth of the nations shall come to you.
A multitude of camels shall cover you,
    the young camels of Midian and Ephah;
    all those from Sheba shall come.
They shall bring gold and frankincense,
    and shall proclaim the praise of the LORD.

READING II *Ephesians 3:2–3, 5–6*

I assume that you have heard of the stewardship of God's grace that was given to me for you, how the mystery was made known to me by revelation, which was not made known to people of other generations as it has now been revealed to his holy apostles and prophets by the Spirit; that is, how the Gentiles are heirs with us, members of the same body, and partakers of the promise in Christ Jesus through the gospel.

GOSPEL *Matthew 2:1–12*

Now when Jesus was born in Bethlehem of Judea in the days of Herod the king, behold, magi from the East came to Jerusalem, saying, "Where is he who has been born king of the Jews? For we have seen his star in the East, and have come to worship him." When Herod the king heard this, he was troubled, and all Jerusalem with him; and assembling all the chief priests and scribes of the people, he inquired of them where the Christ was to be born. They told him, "In Bethlehem of Judea; for so it is written by the prophet:

    'And you, O Bethlehem, in the land of Judah,
    are by no means least among the rulers
      of Judah;
    for from you shall come a ruler
    who will govern my people Israel.'

Then Herod summoned the magi secretly and ascertained from them what time the star appeared; and he sent them to Bethlehem, saying, "Go and search diligently for the child, and when you have found him bring me word, that I too may come and worship." When they had heard the king they went their way; and lo, the star which they had seen in the East went before them, till it came to rest over the place where the child was. When they saw the star, they rejoiced exceedingly with great joy; and going into the house they saw the child with Mary his mother, and they fell down and worshiped him. Then, opening their treasures, they offered him gifts, gold and frankincense and myrrh. And being warned in a dream not to return to Herod, they departed to their own country by another way.

Monday, January 9, 1995

THE BAPTISM OF THE LORD

Isaiah 42:1–4, 6–7 *I have called you for the victory of justice.*
  or
Isaiah 40:1–5, 9–11 *The glory of the Lord shall be revealed.*

Acts 10:34–38 *God anointed Jesus with the Holy Spirit.*
  or
Titus 2:11–14; 3:4–7 *We are saved through the water of rebirth.*

Luke 3:15–16, 21–22 *The skies opened and the Spirit descended.*

Today the heavens open, the Spirit appears, the Father thunders forth, and Jesus rises from the Jordan to walk among us. Our Christmas is complete.

REFLECTION

On Christmas day, John's gospel spoke of the Word made human, pitching his tent among us, revealing in his flesh the God of benevolence and faithfulness. Today we listen to Matthew, whose infancy narrative focuses on Joseph.

Matthew presents a foretaste of what the child of Bethlehem will be: the joyful end of a long journey for some, a threat for others. Matthew's story is in keeping with his general emphasis on the regal aspect of the messiah. The wise men are astrologers, and so God reveals the presence of the child in a language that can be understood in a land where astrology is a respected science. These wise men innocently ask the whereabouts of the child "born king of the Jews." Herod's reaction is one of fear (*etarachthe*, a disturbing and upsetting fear); those in power, like Herod, and those so wedded to things as they are, are terrified at the prospect of the turnabout and leveling spoken of in the Advent readings. Matthew, quoting Micah 5:2, makes an important change: In Micah, Bethlehem is a "clan" of Judah; in Matthew's version, Bethlehem is a "ruler" of Judah, a ruler that will "shepherd the people." This textual change makes Herod's fury in Matthew 2:16 more understandable. The ruler (*hegoumenos*, governor, national leader) in Matthew's version poses a real threat to Herod and his descendants.

Today we celebrate the Epiphany (*epiphaneia*, coming, appearance) of the Lord. Matthew's gospel shows that the royal entrance of the "one who is to rule Israel" is greeted with the cheers of some and the fearful fury of others. For the Herods and for those securely nestled in their belief that things are as they should be, the coming of this child poses a threat to all that is familiar and established. To those who are alert and sensitive to the signs (recall the Advent readings), the coming of this child is an invitation to embark on a journey.

■ Does it matter that these infancy narratives did not actually happen as they are told? How do you understand the fact that deep religious truths can be revealed in stories?

■ We often see reactions of fear in the scriptures, especially when people are faced with manifestations of God's presence. See, for example, the annunciations to Zechariah (Luke 1:5–17), to Mary (Luke 1:26–33) and to the shepherds (Luke 2:8–11). Why do you think this is so? What does it teach you?

PRACTICE OF FAITH

MANY BLESSINGS. For many people, Epiphany has always been the traditional day for a yearly house blessing. Use this occasion to continue the Christmas feast by having an Epiphany party. Over the entrance to your house, or as my German friends do, over the door to every room, inscribe with chalk the initials of the three kings (Caspar, Melchior and Balthasar) along with the year:

19 + C + M + B + 95

Process through the house, sprinkling all the rooms with holy water and singing a carol that everyone knows by heart. Let the chalk markings be a blessing to all who enter your home and a reminder to all of the virtue of hospitality.

Monday we celebrate the Baptism of the Lord, which is an opportunity to remember that God's first dwelling is within us. In your blessed home, have all in the household renew their baptismal promises. If you have baptismal garments and candles, bring these out for the occasion.

PRACTICE OF HOPE

ARISE, SHINE. In a corner of inner-city Boston, Azusa Christian Community shines like a light. Most of its members are young Harvard- and MIT-educated African Americans who gave up lucrative employment and housing opportunities to try to bridge some of the estrangement between black elites and the black poor. They run a Youth Advocacy Project and an Algebra Project. But most important, they bring the good news of the gospel to the dangerous streets where they live.

"The level of violence in the inner cities requires a level of spiritual power so intense that we encourage folk who don't understand the importance of the Holy Spirit for ministry to not even bother," says Azusa founder and pastor, Eugene Rivers. The community is developing forms of evangelism that are explicitly Afrocentric. Says Rivers, "Our vision over the next five years is to evangelize 1,000 young blacks."

PRACTICE OF CHARITY

THE MAGI. There comes a time in our lives when all of us recognize that everything we have, and all that we are, has been given to us. Gratitude naturally flows from this recognition, and from this gratitude, our own self-giving will flow. Like Jesus, we will become life-giving bread for others. This week, write down the many gifts you have been given and make an accounting of everything God has done for you. Then give as a gift to others the gifts you have received.

WEEKDAY READINGS (Mo) The Baptism of the Lord; (Tu–Sa) Hebrews, chapters 2—4

WINTER ORDINARY TIME

God speaks, the ice melts; God breathes, the streams flow.

Jerusalem, give glory!
Praise God with song, O Zion!
For the Lord strengthens your gates
guarding your children within.
The Lord fills your land with peace,
giving you golden wheat.

God speaks to the earth,
the word speeds forth.
The Lord sends heavy snow
and scatters frost like ashes.
The Lord hurls chunks of hail.
Who can stand such cold?

God speaks, the ice melts;
God breathes, the streams flow.
God speaks the word to Israel,
for Israel, laws and decrees.
God has not done this for others,
no others receive this wisdom.

Hallelujah!

—Psalm 147:12–20

Shall we praise you, hail-hurling God,
in winter's splendor,
in the grace of snow
that covers with brightness
and reshapes both your creation and ours?
Or shall we curse the fierce cold
that punishes homeless people
and shortens tempers?
Blessed are you
in the earth's tilt and course.
Blessed are you in the sleep of winter
and in the oncoming lenten spring.
Now and then and always,
fill these lands with peace.

—Prayer of the Season

READING I *Isaiah 62:1–5*

For Zion's sake I will not keep silent,
    and for Jerusalem's sake I will not rest,
until its vindication goes forth as brightness
    and its salvation as a burning torch.
The nations shall see your vindication,
    and all the rulers your glory;
and you shall be called by a new name
    which the mouth of the Lord will give.
You shall be a crown of beauty in the hand
        of the Lord,
    and a royal diadem in the hand of your God.
You shall no more be termed Forsaken,
    and your land shall no more be termed Desolate;
but you shall be called My Delight,
    and your land Married;
for the Lord delights in you,
    and your land shall be married.
For as a young man marries a virgin woman,
    so shall your children marry you,
and as one rejoices in marrying the beloved,
    so shall your God rejoice over you.

READING II *1 Corinthians 12:4–11*

Now there are varieties of gifts, but the same Spirit; and there are varieties of service, but the same Lord; and there are varieties of working, but it is the same God who inspires them all in every one. To each is given the manifestation of the Spirit for the common good. To one is given through the Spirit the utterance of wisdom, and to another the utterance of knowledge according to the same Spirit, to another faith by the same Spirit, to another gifts of healing by the same Spirit, to another the working of miracles, to another prophesy, to another the ability to distinguish between spirits, to another various kinds of tongues, to another the interpretation of tongues. All these are inspired by one and the same Spirit, who chooses what to apportion to each one individually.

GOSPEL *John 2:1–12*

On the third day there was a marriage at Cana in Galilee, and the mother of Jesus was there; Jesus also was invited to the marriage, with his disciples. When the wine gave out, the mother of Jesus said to him, "They have no wine." And Jesus said to her, "O woman, what have you to do with me? My hour has not yet come." His mother said to the servants, "Do whatever he tells you." Now six stone jars were standing there, for the Jewish rites of purification, each holding twenty or thirty gallons. Jesus said to them, "Fill the jars with water." And the servants filled them up to the brim. Jesus said to them, "Now draw some out, and take it to the steward of the feast." So they took it. When the steward of the feast tasted the water now become wine, and did not know where it came from (though the servants who had drawn the water knew), the steward of the feast called the bridegroom and said to him, "Everyone serves the good wine first; and when the guests have drunk freely, then the poor wine; but you have kept the good wine until now." This, the first of the signs, Jesus did at Cana in Galilee, and manifested his glory; and his disciples believed in him.

After this he went down to Capernaum, with his mother and his brothers and his disciples; and there they stayed for a few days.

R E F L E C T I O N

Today's gospel, John's account of the miracle at Cana, reflects the ancient tradition of connecting three "epiphanies": the manifestation to the magi, the baptism of Jesus, and the first "sign" at Cana. John ends this narrative with the explicit statement that Jesus "manifested his glory" so that his disciples would believe in him.

It is no coincidence that this first sign was given at a marriage feast. The Hebrew Scriptures are filled with images of marriage, wedding feasts and human love as the most apt foreshadowings of the eschaton, the last days that begin with the coming of the messiah. The marriage feast is one of joy and hope, a celebration of human love and of family. In the culture in which Jesus lived, wine was essential to these festivities; water was for purification and preparation, but wine was for happy fulfillment.

As we look at the scene sketched by John, we notice the normal separation between Jesus and his mother, a separation that comes with the maturing of a child. Mary was already there at the feast, part of the group of women naturally expected to help with the preparations. Jesus and his disciples were invited. Here, Mary "belongs"; Jesus and the disciples are invited guests.

The next scene calls to mind the younger Jesus portrayed in Luke 2:41–51, who stays behind in the Temple, making it clear to his parents that he had a mission in life. Here at Cana, his mother asks for help, in the indirect manner of her culture, and Jesus reminds her that she is not the one to determine his "hour." However, he does work this first sign, mainly for the benefit of those who would know what had happened: the servants and his disciples. The steward, the bridegroom and the guests were given no "manifestation." This Cana story is a difficult one to understand if one looks at details. If, however, we look at the symbolism of the marriage feast and the wine within the context of the eschatological hopes of the people, it becomes clear why Jesus chose this occasion for his first sign.

■ Following the symbolism found in the Hebrew Bible, New Testament writings sometimes compare God's relationship with the people to that of a bridegroom and bride or husband and wife. The marriage feast is sometimes used as an image of the kingdom (see Matthew 22: 1–2; 25:1–13; Luke 14:16–24; John 3:29) because it describes a relationship marked by imtimacy, faithfulness, joy and fruitfulness. In what ways could you use this image to describe your parish community?

PRACTICE OF FAITH

UNITED IN CHRIST. Wednesday begins the Week of Prayer for Christian Unity. Be sure to check your parish bulletin to see if there are any special prayer services or activities planned with other Christian communities this week. *Catholic Household Blessings and Prayers* offers the following prayer for Christian unity. Pray it on each of the eight days from the 18th to the 25th.

Almighty and eternal God,
you gather the scattered sheep
and watch over those you have gathered.
Look kindly on all who follow Jesus, your Son.
You have marked them with the seal
  of one baptism,
now make them one in the fullness of faith
and unite them in the bond of love.
We ask this through Christ our Lord. Amen.

PRACTICE OF HOPE

SILENT NO MORE. In a compelling one-woman drama called "Masks and Mirrors," Roberta Nobleman shared her self-described journey "from incest victim, to courageous survivor, to joyous celebrant." She carried her audience on a tide of emotion that spanned quiet tears and boisterous laughter.

Afterward, a group from the audience formed a circle on the stage. One member of the group offered her hand to the woman next to her and said, "I am a survivor, and I offer you my hand." That woman took it, responding, "I am a survivor, and I take your hand." The relaying of trust continued around the circle in a gesture that was simple, yet profoundly moving.

The rest of the audience was invited to participate. As hands connected in circles all around the auditorium, the murmur of the declaration "I am a survivor" reached a rumble. It was a graced moment, electrified with empowerment.

PRACTICE OF CHARITY

I WILL NOT KEEP SILENT. James Taylor wrote a song, "Shed a little light," about a great man who refused to be silent in the face of injustice, a man who wanted everyone to walk hand in hand as brothers and sisters. Martin Luther King, Jr., whose memory is celebrated tomorrow, was a person who understood what it meant to walk as a child of the light. This week go to your public library and pick up a book on or by Martin Luther King, Jr. Or, find and read a copy of the texts of some of his speeches. Tomorrow, as you celebrate the holiday, take time to participate in an event commemorating Rev. King. Work to break down the walls of division and racism that still divide us.

WEEKDAY READINGS **Hebrews 5:1 — 9:14**

READING I *Nehemiah 8:2–4, 5–6, 8–10*

Ezra the priest brought the law before the assembly, both men and women and all who could hear with understanding, on the first day of the seventh month. And he read from it facing the square before the Water Gate from early morning until midday, in the presence of the men and the women and those who could understand; and the ears of all the people were attentive to the book of the law. And Ezra the scribe stood on a wooden pulpit which they had made for the purpose; Ezra opened the book in the sight of all the people, for he was above all the people; and when he opened it all the people stood. And Ezra blessed the LORD, the great God; and all the people answered, "Amen, Amen," lifting up their hands; and they bowed their heads and worshiped the LORD with their faces to the ground. And they read from the book, from the law of God, clearly; and they gave the sense, so that the people understood the reading.

And Nehemiah, who was the governor, and Ezra the priest and scribe, and the Levites who taught the people said to all the people, "This day is holy to the LORD your God; do not mourn or weep." For all the people wept when they heard the words of the law. Then he said to them, "Go your way, eat the fat and drink sweet wine and send portions to those for whom nothing is prepared; for this day is holy to our Lord; and do not be grieved, for the joy of the LORD is your strength."

READING II *1 Corinthians 12:12–14, 27*

Just as the body is one and has many parts, and all the parts of the body, though many, are one body, so it is with Christ. For by one Spirit we were all baptized into one body—Jews or Greeks, slaves or free—and all were made to drink of one Spirit. For the body does not consist of one part but of many.

Now you are the body of Christ and individually parts of it.

[Complete reading: 1 Corinthians 12:12–30.]

GOSPEL *Luke 1:1–4; 4:14–21*

Inasmuch as many have undertaken to compile a narrative of the things which have been accomplished among us, just as they were delivered to us by those who from the beginning were eyewitnesses and ministers of the word, it seemed good to me also, having followed all things closely for some time past, to write an orderly account for you, most excellent Theophilus, that you may know the truth concerning the things of which you have been informed.

Jesus returned in the power of the Spirit into Galilee, and a report concerning him went out through all the surrounding country. And he taught in their synagogues, being glorified by all.

And Jesus came to Nazareth, where he had been brought up; and he went to the synagogue, as his custom was, on the sabbath day. And he stood up to read; and there was given to him the book of the prophet Isaiah. Jesus opened the book and found the place where it was written,

"The Spirit of the Lord is upon me,
because the Lord has anointed me
to preach good news to the poor.
The Lord has sent me to proclaim release
to the captives
and recovering of sight to the blind,
to set at liberty those who are oppressed,
to proclaim the acceptable year of the Lord."

And Jesus closed the book, and gave it back to the attendant, and sat down; and the eyes of all in the synagogue were fixed on him. And he began to say to them, "Today this scripture has been fulfilled in your hearing."

REFLECTION

Today we encounter one of Luke's favorite themes: the power of the Spirit. At the beginning of chapter four, Luke says that Jesus, "full of the Holy Spirit," returned from the Jordan and was "led by the Spirit" into the wilderness. In today's reading, Jesus returns to Galilee in the power of the Spirit at a time when he seemed to be growing in popularity.

Luke makes it very clear that Jesus remains within his religious tradition. Jesus read in the synagogue many times, but Luke chooses this particular time and this particular reading from Isaiah to bring into focus what he sees as the central concern of Jesus' ministry: The good news of salvation is, above all, for the lowly, the poor, the blind, the captive and the oppressed. In the world as we know it, those who have something to give receive all the attention, not the indigent and the marginalized. But once again, Luke is echoing the message of the prophets: The day of the Lord is a day of reversal and restructuring.

The "poor" in Luke are not the *penes*, the working poor. The poor who have the good news preached to them are the *ptochoi*, the destitute, the beggars. Is Luke really saying, as Jesus reads from the prophet Isaiah, that the gospel is especially for the outcasts? Or is he pointing out that within the biblical tradition, God — and therefore Jesus — gives special attention to these insignificant members of society because, in the present order of things, few people do?

On finishing the reading, Jesus sits down to comment on the word and proclaims that this scripture is now fulfilled. Luke provides one of the many examples of the turnabout and leveling that will characterize the coming of the savior, filled as he is with the power of the Spirit to create new ways of living.

■ Read all of Isaiah 61, "translating" it into a description of your city as you experience it. In what ways do you think others experience your city as you do? Why would people's experiences differ?

■ The second reading, 1 Corinthians 12:12–30, presents Paul's way of expressing the essential unity and solidarity of all in Christ. Do you feel this solidarity with other Christians? What efforts do you make to live in solidarity with others?

PRACTICE OF FAITH

WORKS OF MERCY. Jesus, quoting Isaiah, tells the people of his home town that his mission is "to preach good news to the poor . . . to proclaim release to the captives and recovering of sight to those who are blind, to set at liberty those who are oppressed." In the Catholic tradition, one of the ways we continue this gospel mission is through the corporal works of mercy: feeding the hungry, clothing the naked, sheltering the homeless, visiting the sick, ransoming the captives and burying the dead. Find a way to practice one of these on a continuing basis through participation in your parish social action group, a shelter for the homeless, a neighborhood food bank, the diocesan prison ministry or ministry to the hospitalized and homebound.

PRACTICE OF HOPE

JOY IS YOUR STRENGTH. Lindsay Point of Columbus, Ohio, was almost four years old when she began gymnastics lessons. She became quite proficient at backbends and cartwheels. A few months later, she attended Vacation Bible School. During "graduation," each child had a line to recite. When Lindsay's turn came, she became afraid. She walked out on the stage, looked around, and did a cartwheel. She brought down the house.

When she sat back down next to her mother, she said quietly, "I forgot my lines, but I remembered the cartwheel." May we all be so full of spontaneity and grace that, when we can't remember what's next, we leap for joy anyway.

PRACTICE OF CHARITY

SEND PORTIONS TO THOSE FOR WHOM NOTHING IS PREPARED. During the autumn of 1993, 40,000 children died of starvation every day. The magnitude of this loss means that we cannot let those numbers remain just another numbing statistic. As Christians we can make a difference. First, we must adjust our patterns of living; we must begin to live more simply. Next, we must personally connect with the issue of food security. Oxfam America is dedicated to giving people in the Third World a chance to provide sustainable development for themselves and their children. For more information or to make a donation, contact: Oxfam America, PO Box 2176, Boston MA 02106-9986; 617-482-1211.

WEEKDAY READINGS (Mo–Tu) Hebrews 9:15—10:10; Acts 22:3–16 or 9:1–22; 2 Timothy 1:1–8 or Titus 1:1–5; (Fr–Sa) Hebrews 10:32—11:19

READING I *Jeremiah 1:4–5, 17–19*

Now the word of the Lord came to me saying,

"Before I formed you in the womb I knew you,
and before you were born I consecrated you;
I appointed you a prophet to the nations."

"But you, prepare yourself for action; arise, and say to them everything that I command you. Do not be dismayed by them, lest I dismay you before them. And I, behold, I make you this day a fortified city, an iron pillar, and bronze walls, against the whole land, against the rulers of Judah, its chieftains, its priests, and the people of the land. They will fight against you; but they shall not prevail against you, for I am with you, says the LORD, to deliver you.

READING II *1 Corinthians 12:31–13:13*

Earnestly desire the higher gifts. And I will show you a still more excellent way.

If I speak in human languages and in angelic tongues, but have not love, I am a noisy gong or a clanging cymbal. And if I have prophetic powers, and understand all mysteries and all knowledge, and if I have all faith, so as to remove mountains, but have not love, I am nothing. If I give away all I have, and if I deliver my body to be burned, but have not love, I gain nothing.

Love is patient and kind; love is not jealous or boastful; it is not arrogant or rude. Love does not insist on its own way; it is not irritable or resentful; it does not rejoice at wrong, but rejoices in the right. Love bears all things, believes all things, hopes all things, endures all things.

Love never ends; as for prophecies, they will pass away; as for tongues, they will cease; as for knowledge, it will pass away. For our knowledge is imperfect and or prophecy is imperfect; but when the perfect comes, the imperfect will pass away. When I was a child, I spoke like a child, I thought like a child, I reasoned like a child; when I became an adult, I gave up childish ways. For now we see in a mirror dimly, but then face to face. Now I know in part; then I shall understand fully, even as I have been fully understood. So faith, hope, love abides, these three; but the greatest of these is love.

GOSPEL *Luke 4:21–30*

Jesus began to say to them, "Today this scripture has been fulfilled in your hearing." And all spoke well of him, and wondered at the gracious words which proceeded out of his mouth; and they said, "Is not this Joseph's son?" And Jesus said to them, "Doubtless you will quote to me this proverb, Physician, heal yourself; what we have heard you did at Capernaum, do here also in your own country.'" And Jesus said, "Truly, I say to you, prophets are not acceptable in their own country. Buy in truth, I tell you, there were many widows in Israel in the days of Elijah, when the heaven was shut up three years and six months, when there came a great famine over all the land; and Elijah was sent to none of them but only to Zarephath, in the land of Sidon, to a woman who was a widow. And there were many with leprosy in Israel in the time of the prophet Elisha; and none of them was cleansed, but only Naaman the Syrian." When they head this, all in the synagogue were filled with wrath. And they rose up and put Jesus out of the city, and led him to the brow of the hill on which their city was built, that they might throw him down headlong. But passing through the midst of them Jesus went away.

Thursday, February 2, 1995

THE PRESENTATION OF THE LORD

Malachi 3:1–4 *But who can endure the day of his coming?*

Hebrews 2:14–18 *He became like us in every way.*

Luke 2:22–40 *Simeon took the child in his arms.*

The light of Christmas shone feebly at first, rising to shine brightly from a star at Epiphany. Today this light is placed in our arms. The desire of our hearts and the hope of the world now shine in our flesh and blood. Like Simeon, we are hand in hand with God.

REFLECTION

Today's gospel reading continues the narrative of Jesus' appearance in the synagogue at Nazareth. As Jesus finishes his reading, the eyes of all in the synagogue are fixed on him. But now, as Jesus proceeds with his teaching on the scripture reading, the people move from wonder to wrath. This same incident is recorded in Matthew 13:53–58 and in Mark 6:1-6. There, the event occurs some time after Jesus had begun his ministry, and the people "took offense at him" because they could not tolerate someone from their hometown teaching them.

In Luke's gospel, however, the incident occurs at the beginning of Jesus' ministry and is placed there for a reason. We noticed last week that an important theme in Luke's writings is the power of the Spirit, and that the text Jesus read in the synagogue was from Isaiah and was concerned with preaching the good news to the poor and the marginalized. In today's reading, we see Luke continue in the same vein: Jesus, like the prophets before him, meets with opposition, especially from those closest to home. The Spirit-filled prophet, speaking plainly, is not accepted by his own; he must work signs and wonders outside his home, as did the prophets of old.

The first reading describes the calling of one of those prophets, Jeremiah, and tells of the opposition he will have to face. Jeremiah and Jesus, both appointed prophets to the nations, would engage in the necessary plowing up before the planting. They would both have to tear down before building up, and in so doing would encounter strong opposition. Yet both would prevail.

Luke is clearly presenting the core of Jesus' mission as prophet: Filled with the Spirit but rejected by many of those to whom he was sent, Jesus journeys out to others who might be more receptive to the good news he brings. Jesus, like Jeremiah, speaks fearlessly of the necessary uprooting and tearing down of the old in order to prepare for the new. And for those whose lives, position and comfort are too deeply rooted, too solidly cemented in the present order, the good news comes as a threat.

■ Compare Luke's account with those of Matthew (13:53–58) and Mark (6:1–6). What are the different "flavors" of each one?

■ Read the entire first chapter of Jeremiah. Are you drawn to read more about this prophet? Why or why not?

PRACTICE OF FAITH

CANDLEMAS DAY. On Thursday of this week we observe the Feast of the Presentation of the Lord, or Candlemas day. This feast existed in Jerusalem at least by the year 386 and was brought to Rome by Pope Sergius I, a Syrian. It commemorates Jesus' presentation in the temple and the proclamation of the prophet Simeon, who called Jesus "a light to the Gentiles and the glory of your people Israel." Part of the liturgy this day includes a blessing of candles for use in the parish church during the year. (Two of these candles will be used to bless throats tomorrow on the feast of St. Blase.) Bring your table, devotional and prayer candles to church to be blessed, and use the prayer in *Catholic Household Blessings and Prayers* to receive them into your home. (A copy of this book of blessings can be ordered from LTP by calling 1-800-933-1800.)

PRACTICE OF HOPE

LOVE BEARS ALL THINGS. In Nicaragua, a military attack on a village led to a massacre. One woman lost her husband and four of her five sons. In the aftermath, the grief-stricken villagers gathered at the church for a memorial service, remembering all those who had been slain. Weeping, the woman walked to the altar and offered her prayer: "I thank you, God, for the gift of life."

PRACTICE OF CHARITY

PROPHETS ARE NOT ACCEPTED IN THEIR OWN COUNTRY. The work of charity is not so much about changing the world around us as it is about transforming our own lives. When our hearts and heads have been transformed by prayer and action, then the words of our modern-day prophets can find a home. This week and throughout the year, spend time praying for your own conversion wherever you are closed to the prophets' call. Then, start to act in charity regarding that issue. Contact your diocesan office for social concerns to find out what you can do.

WEEKDAY READINGS (Mo–We) Hebrews 11:32—12:15; (Th) The Presentation of the Lord; (Fr–Sa) Hebrews, chapter 13

READING I *Isaiah 6:1–2, 3–8*

In the year that King Uzziah died I saw the Lord sitting upon a throne, high and lifted up; and the train of the Lord's garment filled the temple. Above the Lord stood the seraphim; and one called to another and said:

"Holy, holy, holy is the LORD of hosts;
the whole earth is full of the glory of the LORD."

And the foundations of the thresholds shook at the voice that called, and the house was filled with smoke. And I said: "Woe is me! For I am lost; for I am a man of unclean lips, and I dwell in the midst of a people of unclean lips; for my eyes have seen the Sovereign, the LORD of hosts!"

Then flew one of the seraphim to me, having in its hand a burning coal which had been taken with tongs from the altar. And the seraph touched my mouth, and said: "Behold, this has touched your lips; your guilt is taken away, and your sin forgiven." And I heard the voice of the Lord saying, "Whom shall I send, and who will go for us?" Then I said, "Here am I! Send me."

READING II *1 Corinthians 15:1–11*

I would remind you, my dear people, in what terms I preached to you the gospel, which you received, in which you stand, by which you are saved, if you hold it fast—unless you believed in vain.

For I delivered to you as of first importance what I also received, that Christ died for our sins in accordance with the scriptures, that he was buried, that he was raised on the third day in accordance with the scriptures, and that he appeared to Cephas, then to the twelve. Then he appeared to more than five hundred of the community at one time, most of whom are still alive, though some have fallen asleep. Then he appeared to James, then to all the apostles. Last of all, as to one untimely born, Christ appeared also to me. For I am the least of the apostles, unfit to be called an apostle, because I persecuted the church of God. But by the grace of God I am what I am, and God's grace toward me was not in vain. On the contrary, I worked harder than any of them, though it was not I, but the grace of God which is with me. Whether then it was I or they, so we preach and so you believed.

GOSPEL *Luke 5:1–11*

While the people pressed upon Jesus to hear the word of God, he was standing by the lake of Gennesaret. And he saw two boats by the lake; but those who fished had gone out of the boats and were washing their nets. Getting into one of the boats, which was Simon's, Jesus asked Simon to put out a little from the land. And Jesus sat down and taught the people from the boat. And when he had ceased speaking, he said to Simon, "Put out into the deep and let down your nets for a catch." And Simon answered, "Master, we toiled all night and took nothing! But at your word I will let down the nets." And when they had done this, they enclosed a great shoal of fish; and as their nets were breaking, they beckoned to their partners in the other boat to come and help them. And they came and filled both the boats, so that the boats began to sink. But having seen it, Simon Peter fell down at Jesus' knees, saying, "Depart from me, for I am a sinful man, O Lord." For Simon was astonished, and all that were with him, at the catch of fish which they had taken; and so also were James and John, sons of Zebedee, who were partners with Simon. And Jesus said to Simon, "Do not be afraid; henceforth you will be catching human beings." And when they had brought their boats to land, they left everything and followed Jesus.

REFLECTION

The three synoptic gospels (Matthew, Mark and Luke) all relate this calling of the first disciples. Matthew and Mark place their emphasis on the calling, but Luke elaborates on the event in order to bring out its significance in the overall plan of his gospel. In chapter four, Luke has already presented the beginning of Jesus' ministry, his rejection by many in his hometown and the more positive reception given him outside Nazareth. Luke has been careful to mention that "Jesus continued proclaiming the message in the synagogues of Judea" (4:44).

Now, in chapter five, Jesus proclaims the message outside a synagogue, from a boat pushed away from the shore. Then, in what might be compared to the Cana sign in John's gospel, Luke shows Jesus performing a miracle for his new disciples in order to give them a glimpse of the inner power that is his. Luke also brings out the character of Simon, who acknowledges his sinfulness, as one of the "lowly." Jesus replies with words of reassurance. This echoes the pattern found in Luke's narratives of Zachary, Mary and the shepherds: The good news, given in a special way to the lowly, effects a reversal in that these unattractive ones will now attract (*zogron*, catch alive) other human beings.

The sign of the nets bursting with fish is like the burning coal of the seraphim in the first reading. And as Isaiah said, "Here am I, send me," so the amazed trio of Simon, James and John leave everything and follow Jesus. This lakeside incident contains a wealth of insight into the nature of discipleship; here we see a miraculous "sign" (the catch of fish), an awareness of lowliness, reassurance from Jesus, and a willingness to become a disciple and follow a new calling—all, by now, familiar themes of Luke.

■ **Read Isaiah 6:1–2a, 3–8, in which the prophet expresses his sense of unworthiness to accept his calling. Do you ever experience this deep sense of unworthiness, saying, "Who am I to take on this work?" No one is "worthy" to be a disciple or a prophet, but do you believe that God can work wonders, even from within your unworthiness, as was done through Isaiah?**

■ **Recall an incident in your life that may have contained the pattern found in today's gospel: a sign, lowliness, reassurance and renewed discipleship.**

PRACTICE OF FAITH

FISHING FOR PERSONS. Jesus' invitation to Peter to "catch human beings" is continuing in Catholic parishes through the Rite of Christian Initiation of Adults (RCIA). Through this rite, unbaptized persons initially learn of our gospel values and of our way of life. Later, as catechumens (meaning those who learn by word of mouth), they grow in faith through prayer, through hearing the gospel and the church's teaching and through participating in our apostolic life. Often, baptized persons who want to complete their initiation join the catechumens in these activities. These already baptized ones are called candidates and are distinguished in the public rites of the church because they already share in Christ's life through baptism. Sharing the faith and initiating others is the responsibility of the whole community. Find out how you can assist those being caught by Christ.

PRACTICE OF HOPE

BY THE GRACE OF GOD. Several years ago, I was arrested with some others for protesting at a nuclear weapons exposition in Washington, D.C. We spent a night on the concrete floor of a large holding cell, across from a cell holding women who had been swept up in a raid on a house of prostitution. In the middle of the night, a woman named Gloria began to talk about her fears and the fact that God had forgiven her and was giving her a second chance in her life.

Very early in the morning, Gloria shouted across to us, "Hey, do you all know 'Amazing grace'?" Soon, strains of the hymn thundered through the long corridor. A brusque male guard came back to find out what all the commotion was. Gloria jumped up, pressed her face against the bars, and said to him, "It's only the gospel." She was right—she was a woman who recognized good news.

PRACTICE OF CHARITY

THEY LEFT EVERYTHING AND FOLLOWED JESUS. Strong words. Surely the evangelist got this wrong. Everything? We might think that the disciples of Jesus' time must have had an easier time of this than we would, because they did not have much to leave. And yet, that is not what the gospel says. They left everything. Are we challenged to do the same? St. Francis of Assisi and Dorothy Day thought so. They left everything and responded with total commitment to God. What is our response? This week, evaluate your needs and your lifestyle. Take some time to read about St. Francis of Assisi or Dorothy Day, and see how your own lifestyle might be changed so that you too can follow Jesus more readily.

WEEKDAY READINGS **Genesis 1:1 — 3:24**

READING I *Jeremiah 17:5–8*

Thus says the LORD:

"Cursed is the one who trusts in humankind
   and relies on mortal flesh,
     whose heart turns away from the LORD.
Such a one, like a shrub in the desert,
    shall not see any good come,
      but shall dwell in the parched places of the
      wilderness,
     in an uninhabited salt land.
Blessed is the one who trusts in the LORD,
    whose trust is in the LORD.
Such a one is like a tree planted by water,
    that sends out its roots by the stream,
   and does not fear when heat comes,
    for its leaves remain green,
   and it is not anxious in the year of drought,
    for it does not cease to bear fruit."

READING II *1 Corinthians 15:12, 16–20*

If Christ is preached as raised from the dead, how can some of you say that there is no resurrection of the dead? For if the dead are not raised, then Christ has not been raised. If Christ has not been raised, your faith is futile and you are still in your sins. Then those also who have fallen asleep in Christ have perished. If for this life only we have hoped in Christ, we are of all humankind most to be pitied.

But in fact Christ has been raised from the dead, the first fruits of those who have fallen asleep.

GOSPEL *Luke 6:17, 20–26*

Jesus came down and stood on a level place, with a great crowd of his disciples and a great multitude of people from all Judea and Jerusalem and the seacoast of Tyre and Sidon.

And Jesus lifted up his eyes on his disciples, and said:

"Blessed are you poor, for yours is the dominion of God.

"Blessed are you that hunger now, for you shall be satisfied.

"Blessed are you that weep now, for you shall laugh.

"Blessed are you when you are hated, and when they exclude you and revile you, and cast out your name as evil, on account of the Man of Heaven! Rejoice in that day, and leap for joy, for behold, your reward is great in heaven; for so their forebears did to the prophets.

"But woe to you that are rich, for you have received your consolation.

"Woe to you that are full now, for you shall hunger.

"Woe to you that laugh now, for you shall mourn and weep.

"Woe to you, when everyone speaks well of you, for so their forebears did to the false prophets."

R E F L E C T I O N

Luke brings us his version of the beatitudes in a series of vivid images, all echoing themes dear to him. The reading begins by noting that Jesus came down from the mountain with his disciples and stood with them on a level place. If the mountain is the place for prayer, seclusion and visions, the level plain is, for Luke, the appropriate site for Jesus to teach about the kingdom. And though the teaching here is directed primarily toward the disciples, it does not exclude those in the multitude willing to listen in.

Luke presents four "blesseds" and four "woes." (Matthew 5:1–12 has nine "blesseds.") The paradoxes set forth by Luke are clear examples of the upending of normal human ways of looking at society. In God's kingdom, it is the poor (*ptochoi*, the economically destitute and the marginalized) who "own" the kingdom of God. Those who hunger (*peinontes*, those who lack the necessities, are deprived of the fruits of their labor) will be filled. Those who weep now, who accept God's judgment on their sinfulness, will later laugh with the joy of victory (see Psalm 126:2). The real meaning of this laughter is made clear in the subsequent blessing of those who are hated, excluded and reviled: They should rejoice (*charete*, see Luke 1:28) and "leap for joy" (*skirtesate*, see Luke 1:44). This leaping for joy is a prefiguration of the eschatological dance of the cast-out prophets, the excluded poor, the hungry and the weeping.

The four woes parallel the four blesseds. One point to notice, however, is the meaning of "laugh" in the phrase, "Woe to you that laugh"; it means laughter that derides and makes fun of. Luke's account of Jesus' teaching on blessedness and woe presents one more vibrant image of the world turned on its head by the good news.

■ Compare Luke's version of the beatitudes, which is focused on the practical, this-worldly reversal, to Matthew's (5:1–12), which is longer and emphasizes a more personal, spiritual blessedness. What emphasis has helped form your idea of Christian blessedness? Which do you find more attractive? Why?

■ Do you believe that being on the side of the poor, the hungry, the sorrowing and the marginalized is a cause for rejoicing? Why or why not?

PRACTICE OF FAITH

BEATITUDES. Take time this week to let the rhythm of Luke's blessings and woes speak to your heart. Notice if any feelings of resistance surface. These are often the places where God is calling us to grow. We live in a society that mocks the values presented in the gospel, and we should not be surprised if we are drawn to those things so valued by the world: wealth, power, prestige and happiness. Look back to the listing of the corporal works of mercy from three weeks ago and renew your efforts to practice one of them.

PRACTICE OF HOPE

BLESSED ARE THE POOR. Rev. Ron Del Bene, an Episcopal priest, tells that when he was growing up, his mother, a nurse, had a thing about cleanliness. She told him to push open a door with his fist, or pull it with his little finger, to avoid germs and dirt. At age 48, he proclaimed, "I probably had the strongest little finger in America."

One evening, while he was serving chili and bread at a homeless shelter, a bedraggled man with dirt and dried blood on his hands approached him. The man clasped Del Bene's hands in both of his and said, "Brother, I love you. Thanks for being here." Awhile later, Del Bene accidentally spilled chili on his hand and reflexively licked it off. At that moment, he said, the light of awareness came to him. Jesus was no longer the handsome man he had always pictured: "I had just served him chili and bread."

PRACTICE OF CHARITY

LIKE A TREE PLANTED BY WATER. Two of the greatest gifts God has given us in creation are water and trees. We all have moments when we experience the beauty of a mountain stream, the serenity of a lake, the coolness of a shade tree or the vivid colors of autumn leaves. It is frightening to learn that our forests are dying and our rivers and lakes are being polluted. We can be good stewards; we can make choices that say "yes" to God's creation. First, we can make changes in our consumption of water and paper products. There are companies, like Seventh Generation, that offer more environmentally friendly products. Second, we can give to the National Tree Society, a group concerned about the maintenance and planting of trees. Finally, we can work for making our local recycling efforts more effective. For a catalog, contact: Seventh Generation, Colchester VT 05446-1672; 1-800-456-1139. For more information contact: National Tree Society, Inc., PO Box 10808, Bakersfield CA 93389; 805-589-6912.

WEEKDAY READINGS (Mo–Fr) Genesis 4:1 — 11:9; (Sa) Hebrews 11: 1–7

READING I *1 Samuel 26:2, 7–9, 12–13, 22–23*

Saul arose and went down to the wilderness of Ziph, with three thousand chosen men of Israel, to seek David in the wilderness of Ziph.

David and Abishai went to the army by night; and there lay Saul sleeping within the encampment, with his spear stuck in the ground at his head; and Abner and the army lay around him. Then said Abishai to David, "God has given your enemy into your hand this day; now therefore let me pin Saul to the earth with one stroke of the spear, and I will not strike him twice." But David said to Abishai, "Do not destroy him; for who can put forth a hand against the LORD's anointed, and be guiltless?" So David took the spear and the jar of water from Saul's head; and they went away. No one saw it, or knew it, nor did any awake; for they were all asleep, because a deep sleep from the Lord had fallen upon them.

Then David went over to the other side, and stood afar off on the top of the mountain, with a great space between them. And David said, "Here is the spear, O king! Let one of the youths come over and fetch it. The LORD rewards a man for his righteousness and faithfulness; for the LORD gave you into my hand today, and I would not put forth my hand against the LORD's anointed."

READING II *1 Corinthians 15:45–49*

Thus it is written, "The first Adam became a living being"; the last Adam became a life-giving spirit. But it is not the spiritual which is first but the physical, and then the spiritual. The first human being was from the dust of the earth; the second human being is from heaven. As was the one made of dust, so are those who are made of dust; and as is the one of heaven, so are those who are of heaven. Just as we have borne the image of the one made of dust, we shall also bear the image of the one of heaven.

GOSPEL *Luke 6:27–38*

[At that time Jesus said,]

"I say to you that hear, love your enemies, do good to those who hate you, bless those who curse you, pray for those who abuse you. When someone strikes you on the cheek, offer the other also; and when someone takes away your cloak do not withhold even your tunic. Give to every one who begs from you; and when some one takes away your goods do not ask for them again. And as you wish that others would do to you, do so to them.

"If you love those who love you, what credit is that to you? For even sinners love those who love them. And if you do good to those who do good to you, what credit is that to you? For even sinners do the same. And if you lend to those from whom you hope to receive, what credit is that to you? Even sinners lend to sinners, to receive as much again. But love your enemies, and do good, and lend, expecting nothing in return; and your reward will be great, and you will be children of the Most High, who is kind to the ungrateful and the selfish. Be merciful, even as your Father is merciful.

"Judge not, and you will not be judged; condemn not, and you will not be condemned; forgive, and you will be forgiven; give, and it will be given to you; good measure, pressed down, shaken together, running over, will be put into your lap. For the measure you give will be the measure you get back."

R E F L E C T I O N

The reversal of familiar value systems is spelled out in Luke's collection of Jesus' sayings. We may divide this passage into three sections, each one presenting examples and a summary statement.

The first section (verses 27–30) is about treating others the way we wish others would treat us. The examples here have to do with actions that go against behavioral norms: loving enemies, blessing those who curse, being ready to let go of things taken away.

The statement summarizing the second section, "Be merciful even as your Father is merciful" (*oiktirmon*, sympathetic, compassionate), enters more deeply into the heart of the messianic reversal. Luke deliberately uses the word translated as "credit" (*charis*), with its usual religious meaning of "thanks," three times in this section in order to emphasize his point. To those who love, do good and lend only to those who are well-disposed toward them, no thanks are due: colloquially, "big deal!"

The one to emulate is the Father, who is kind (*chrestas*, decent, honest, good-hearted) toward the ungrateful (*acharistous*) and the selfish. Jesus' teaching calls for an overturning of usual human behavior. No matter what others do, the disciple should respond like the Father — with sympathy and decency, even toward those who are evil or ungrateful.

The final section (verses 37–38) deals with the themes of judgment and forgiveness. Judgment here means passing judgment on others, and condemnation (*katadikazo*) means passing a sentence. This is made clear by Luke in his choice of the word *apolyein*, translated as "forgiveness" but which has the stronger meaning of "acquittal." The meaning, then, is that if we refrain from passing judgment on others and sentencing them, if we are ready to acquit others, then there is no way the Father will be inclined to sentence us.

■ **Carefully reflect on today's second reading in the light of today's gospel reading, remembering that "body" means unredeemed, sinful humanity (body and soul) and that "spirit" means the renewed, whole human being.**

■ **Do you most often forgive but not forget? Under what circumstances is it difficult for you to acquit others?**

PRACTICE OF FAITH

BE MERCIFUL. As followers of Christ, we are called to live the standard of love that he set: love even of our enemies. Here is an ancient text from the Visigoth liturgy to use when praying for this conversion of heart and mind:

> Lord God, out of your great love for the world, you reconciled earth to heaven through your only-begotten Son, our Savior. In the darkness of our sins, we fail to love one another as we should; please pour your light into our souls and fill us with your tenderness, that we may embrace our friends in you and our enemies for your sake, in a bond of mutual affection.

PRACTICE OF HOPE

LOVE YOUR ENEMIES. Sarah Corson was doing mission work in a remote area of South America when soldiers stormed the village. As the commander marched most of the men to a camp, she talked to him about the Sermon on the Mount. He insisted on attending the mission church on Sunday.

It was a custom to greet visitors during the service. Trembling, a man came forward, embraced the commander, and said, "Brother, this is the house of God, and God loves you, so you are welcome here." The others followed.

Risking his own life, the commander disobeyed orders to take the village women. The imprisoned men were eventually released. "I could have fought any amount of guns you might have had," said the commander, "but there is something here I cannot understand. I cannot fight it."

PRACTICE OF CHARITY

THE MEASURE YOU GIVE WILL BE THE MEASURE YOU GET BACK. We all know how good it feels to give money to worthy causes during the Christmas season or to take canned goods to the local food pantry. But can you imagine helping to purchase livestock for a family in rural Africa, where the ownership of a single cow quadruples a family's income? Or can you imagine supplying food-producing animals to families in this and other countries so that they can always provide for their needs? Heifer Project International is dedicated to the vision of eliminating hunger by making people self-sustaining. For more information, write: Heifer Project International, International Headquarters, P.O. Box 808, Little Rock AR 72203. Or call 1-800-422-0474.

WEEKDAY READINGS Sirach 1:1–10; 2:2–11; 1 Peter 5:1–4; Sirach 5:1–8; 6:5–17; 17:1–15

READING I *Sirach 27:4–7*

When a sieve is shaken, the refuse remains;
  when people speak, their filth appears.
The kiln tests the potter's vessels;
  so the test of human beings is in their
    conversation.
The fruit discloses the cultivation of a tree;
  so the expression of a thought discloses
    the cultivation of one's mind.
Do not praise others before you hear them reason,
  for this is the test of humankind.

READING II *1 Corinthians 15:54–58*

When the perishable puts on the imperishable, and the mortal puts on immortality, then shall come to pass the saying that is written:

  "Death is swallowed up in victory."
  "O death, where is your victory?
  O death, where is your sting?"

The sting of death is sin, and the power of sin is the law. But thanks be to God, who gives us the victory through our Lord Jesus Christ.

Therefore, my beloved ones, be steadfast, immovable, always abounding in the work of the Lord, knowing that in the Lord your labor is not in vain.

GOSPEL *Luke 6:39–45*

Jesus told the people a parable: "Can one who is blind lead another who is blind? Will they not both fall into a pit? A disciple is not above a teacher, but when fully taught, each disciple will be like the teacher. Why do you see the speck that is in someone else's eye, but do not notice the log that is in your own eye? Or how can you say to your brother or sister, 'Let me take out the speck that is in your eye,' when you yourself do not see the log that is in your own eye? You hypocrite, first take the log out of your own eye, and then you will see clearly to take out the speck that is in someone else's eye.

"For no good tree bears bad fruit, nor again does a bad tree bear good fruit; for each tree is known by its own fruit. For figs are not gathered from thorns, nor are grapes picked from a bramble bush. Out of the heart's good treasure the good person produces good, and out of an evil treasure the evil person produces evil; for out of the abundance of the heart the mouth speaks."

Wednesday, March 1, 1995

ASH WEDNESDAY

Joel 2:12–18 *Proclaim a fast. Rend your hearts.*

2 Corinthians 5:20 — 6:2 *Now is the time to be reconciled.*

Matthew 6:1–6, 16–18 *Pray, fast and give alms.*

The Spirit urges us into the desert discipline of the lenten spring. For 40 days we will strip away everything that separates us from God, beginning today, as we are marked with a cross of ashes: death and life in a single sign!

R E F L E C T I O N

The first section of today's gospel (verses 39–42) continues the theme of last Sunday's reading. Although the text says that "Jesus told the people a parable," this is really not a parable but a series of figures of speech that serve to illustrate the teaching. One figure is that of blindness in a teacher, in one who is supposed to enlighten and guide safely. But sight is often impeded by foreign matter in the eye. Luke sketches for us the image of the seemingly considerate, solicitous person with a huge blind spot bending over to brush away a speck of dust from the eye of a slightly myopic brother or sister.

The use of the word "hypocrite" is less frequent in Luke than in Matthew, yet both gospels use it in the negative way common in religious parlance. Actually, the word *hypokrites* meant "actor" and was used in the Greek world to describe one skilled in the theatrical arts. As used here, Jesus is saying: "Stop the pretense and the acting as if you were better than others; be more concerned with your own blind spots than with the specks in someone else's eye."

The second series of images (verses 44–45) has to do with the opposite of hypocrisy—uprightness and openness. In this section, Luke highlights another of the motifs repeated in the teaching of Jesus: Religiousness is to be found in the heart, in an inner attitude, not in the exact adherence to ritual and law. In verse 44, the images are agricultural: good fruit (*kalon*, fitting, appropriate), bad fruit (*sapron*, rotten, worthless), figs from fig trees and grapes from vines. In the last verse, the teaching is summarized with a threefold repetition of the word "good": The heart's goodness animates the good person to do good deeds. Luke uses *agathos* (upright, just) for "good" and *poneros* (wicked, sinful) for "evil." Luke is saying that one may try to pretend, to act, to produce what is not inside one to produce, but words eventually will reveal the heart.

■ **Take time to examine your patterns of speech and action, asking yourself where they come from. Do your words and actions really reflect who you are inside?**

PRACTICE OF FAITH

ELECTION. Next Sunday (or sometime during next week) your diocese will celebrate the rite of election with the catechumens. In this rite, the church discerns that certain catechumens have grown in the faith and have been "elected," or chosen by God, to receive the Easter sacraments. The yearly rite gives those of us who are already fully initiated an opportunity to reflect on our own faithfulness to the gospel. If possible, plan to attend this rite with the catechumens from your parish, and let them be an inspiration to you to spend this upcoming Lent renewing your own commitment to the gospel.

Remember that we do not use the word "Alleluia" during Lent. Sometime this week make an Alleluia banner and bury it until Easter.

PRACTICE OF HOPE

KNOWN BY ITS FRUIT. When Cesar Chavez died in April 1993, the world lost a good soul. For more than 40 years, he upheld the dignity of migrant farm workers. In 1966, he set out with 70 strikers on a 300-mile march to Sacramento. By the time they arrived on Easter Sunday, 10,000 people had joined them, and Chavez won a first-of-a-kind agreement with a grower to negotiate with farm workers for better working conditions.

The strike, "La Huelga," eventually brought many of California's largest grape growers to sign contracts with workers. Chavez' last fight was against indiscriminate use of pesticides in the fields. His motto lives on: *"Si, se puede*—Yes, it can be done."

PRACTICE OF CHARITY

THE TEST OF HUMAN BEINGS IS IN THEIR CONVERSATION. As Lent draws near, now is a good time to decide what to do for that season of fasting, prayer and almsgiving. Usually, almsgiving is understood as dropping coins into the rice bowl or milk carton on the dining room table. This is a fine practice. However, we suggest that you take almsgiving a step further this year. Let this season of Lent be one of affirmation. The power to affirm, while it does not alleviate poverty or hunger, does nourish our family, friends and coworkers. People are strengthened when we are willing to listen to them and affirm them for their abilities. Hopefully, when we come to the end of Lent, we will not only have a rice bowl full of money but also a community transformed by our willingness to affirm.

WEEKDAY READINGS **Sirach 17:19–24; 35:1–12; (We) Ash Wednesday; Deuteronomy 30:15–20; (Fr–Sa) Isaiah, chapter 58**

LENT

Wash away my sin.
Cleanse me from my guilt.

You see me for what I am,
a sinner before my birth.

You love those centered in truth;
teach me your hidden wisdom.
Wash me with fresh water,
wash me bright as snow.

Fill me with happy songs,
let my bruised bones dance.
Shut your eyes to my sin,
make my guilt disappear.

Save me, bring back my joy,
support me, strengthen my will.
Then will I teach you way
and sinners will turn to you.

Help me, stop my tears,
and I will sing your goodness.
Lord, give me words
and I will shout your praise.

When I offer a Holocaust,
the gift does not please you.
So I offer my shattered spirit;
a changed heart you welcome.

—Psalm 51:7 – 11, 14 – 19

Like a gift we only want to want,
these forty days surround us once more
and you set about washing us, God.
Scrub and scour these stubborn ashes.
Separate what we are
from what we are not
and so bring on the lenten ordeal:
the prayer by day and night,
the fast that clears our sight,
the alms that set things right.
At the end, when we have lost again,
you alone make dry bones come together
and bruised bones dance
round the cross where sinners live
now and for ever.

—Prayer of the Season

READING I *Deuteronomy 26:4–11*

Moses said to the people, "The priest shall take the basket from your hand, and set it down before the altar of the LORD your God.

"And you shall make response before the LORD your God, 'My forebear was a wandering Aramean, who went down into Egypt and sojourned there, few in number, and there became a nation, great, mighty, and populous. And the Egyptians treated us harshly, and afflicted us, and laid upon us hard bondage. Then we cried to the LORD the God of our forebears, and the LORD heard our voice, and saw our affliction, our toil, and our oppression; and the LORD brought us out of Egypt with a mighty hand and an outstretched arm, with great terror, with signs and wonders; and the LORD brought us into this place and gave us this land, a land flowing with milk and honey. And behold, now I bring the first of the fruit of the ground, which you, O LORD, have given me.' And you shall set it down before the LORD your God, and worship before the LORD your God; and you shall rejoice in all the good which the LORD your God has given to you and to your house, you, and the Levite, and the sojourner who is among you."

READING II *Romans 10:8–13*

What does the scripture say? The word is near you, on your lips and in your heart (that is, the word of faith which we preach); because, if you confess with your lips that Jesus is Lord and believe in your heart that God raised him from the dead, you will be saved. With the heart one believes, and so is justified, and with the lips one confesses and so is saved. The scripture says, "No one who believes in the Lord will be put to shame." For there is no distinction between Jew and Greek; the same Lord is Lord of all, who bestows riches on all who ask for help. For, "everyone who calls upon the name of the Lord will be saved."

GOSPEL *Luke 4:1–13*

Jesus, full of the Holy Spirit, returned from the Jordan, and was led by the Spirit for forty days in the wilderness, tempted by the devil. And he ate nothing in those days; and when they were ended, he was hungry. The devil said to Jesus, "If you are the Son of God, command this stone to become bread." And Jesus answered the devil, "It is written, 'Not by bread alone shall one live.'" And the devil took Jesus up, and showed him all the dominions of the world in a moment of time, and said to him, "To you I will give all this authority and their glory; for it has been delivered to me, and I give it to whom I will. If you, then, will worship me, it shall all be yours." And Jesus answered the devil, "It is written,

'You shall worship the Lord your God;
the Lord alone shall you serve.'"

And the devil took Jesus to Jerusalem, and set him on the pinnacle of the temple, and said to him, "If you are the Son of God, throw yourself down from here; for it is written,

'God will give you into the angels' charge,
to guard you,' and
'On their hands they will bear you up,
lest you strike your foot against a stone.'"

And Jesus answered the devil, "It is said, 'You shall not tempt the Lord your God.'" And having ended every temptation, the devil departed from Jesus until an opportune time.

REFLECTION

On this First Sunday of Lent, we are presented with Luke's version of an incident also recorded in Matthew 4:1–11 and Mark 1:12–13. In chapter three, Luke described Jesus' baptism by John and then traced Jesus' lineage through Joseph back to "Adam, son of God" (3:38). Whereas Matthew's geneology (1:1–17) places Jesus within the line of Abraham, thereby pointing to Jesus' Jewishness, Luke has broadened the horizon to show Jesus as truly and authentically human.

The dialogue between Jesus and the devil reminds us more of primal humanity and the conversation between the woman and the serpent than it reminds us of Jewish identity and the 40 years of wandering in the wilderness. Not that the serpent in the Genesis story was "Satan"; rather, the parallel here lies in the dialogue between humanity and the opponent. In Luke's account of the temptation, we see Jesus facing the accuser, the *diabolos,* in the name of us all. Jesus, full of the Holy Spirit and weakened by hunger, faces the arguments of the accuser much the same way that the woman faced the clever conversation of the mythical serpent in Genesis. The reference to stone being turned into bread recalls the Exodus experience (see Deuteronomy 8:3).

The second temptation presents the *diabolos* as one with authority over the inhabited earth (*oikoumene,* the social, political order), and Jesus is offered power in that world if only he would prostrate himself before the *diabolos.* In reply, Jesus quotes Deuteronomy 6:13 — reverence and worship are due God alone.

The third test contains a challenge to take a fool-hardy risk, to tempt God's providence (the Greek word means "overtempt," to go too far) and expect to come out safely. Luke ends this narrative with the departure of the *diabolos.* But we know this is but Act One because Luke tells us that Jesus will face more opposition at a subsequent "opportune time."

■ Compare this narrative with that in Genesis 3:1–6, the dialogue between the woman and the serpent. In both accounts, the "tempter" is a personification of all that would take us away from our calling. Do you sometimes blame a satan or evil spirit for your own wrongdoings, avoiding responsibility for your actions? What "satan" do you most often blame, and why?

■ Do you find it difficult to accept the fact that to be human is to be flawed and that God is not surprised by this, even if we are?

PRACTICE OF FAITH

THE SACRED TRIPOD. The season of Lent has its historical roots in the catechumenate, the time for initiating people into the church and a gospel way of life. Those elected by the church on the First Sunday of Lent begin an intense period of preparation for baptism, confirmation and eucharist called the period of purification and enlightenment. Those who are already fully initiated walk in solidarity with them by renewing their own faith commitment through prayer, feasting and almsgiving. These three disciplines, called the sacred tripod, have been practiced by Christians as a reminder that power, fame and fortune were rejected by Jesus in the desert and are not to be sought by his followers today.

PRACTICE OF HOPE

NOT BY BREAD ALONE. Mary Etta Perry was called to Florida to be with her 79-year-old mother, who suffered congestive heart failure. Doctors expected this to be a last visit. Eventually her mother, still weak, was moved home. Mary Etta had to return north, and no one could be found to care for her mother.

Her father finally said, "I believe I could take care of your mama. Just one thing I don't know how to do — make biscuits." That evening, her mother feebly dictated directions for biscuit-making while Mary Etta wrote them down. The next morning, her mother was alert and hungry. She said she had had a dream, which reminded her that she had promised the Lord that she would take care of her husband as long as he lived. "I don't think he can make biscuits right," she said. He died three years later; she lived two more after that.

PRACTICE OF CHARITY

NOW I BRING THE FIRST OF THE FRUIT. The church often speaks of the need to tithe. We are encouraged to give from the three "Ts": time, treasure and talent. It is an invitation to give back to God in gratitude what we have received. The most difficult of these is the tithing of money. Yet there is a need to give some of our treasure back to the church and to the human community. The decision to tithe is not an easy one to make, but it does bring a certain freedom. It slowly gives you a sense of detachment from things and of attachment to people. You may not feel that you are able to give 10%, but decide on some percentage. It is wonderful and strange to see what happens. Consider tithing. Pray about it as you continue your journey of Lent.

WEEKDAY READINGS Leviticus 19:1–2, 11–18; Isaiah 55:10–11; Jonah 3:1–10; Esther C:12–16, 23–25; Ezekiel 18:21–28; Deuteronomy 26:16–19

READING I *Genesis 15:5–12, 17–18*

The LORD brought Abram outside and said, "Look toward heaven, and number the stars, if you are able to number them." Then the LORD said to him, "So shall your descendants be." And Abram believed the LORD; and the LORD reckoned it to him as righteousness.

And the LORD said to Abram, "I am the LORD who brought you from Ur of the Chaldeans, to give you this land to possess." But Abram said, "O LORD God, how am I to know that I shall possess it?" The LORD said to Abram, "Bring me a heifer three years old, a goat three years old, a ram three years old, a turtledove, and a young pigeon." And Abram brought the LORD all these, cut them in two, and laid each half over against the other; but he did not cut the birds in two. And when birds of prey came down upon the carcasses, Abram drove them away.

As the sun was going down, a deep sleep fell on Abram; and lo, a dread and great darkness fell upon him.

When the sun had gone down and it was dark, behold, a smoking fire pot and a flaming torch passed between these pieces. On that day the LORD made a covenant with Abram, saying, "To your descendants I give this land, from the river of Egypt to the great river, the river Euphrates."

READING II *Philippians 3:17—4:1*

My dear people, join in imitating me, and mark those who so live as you have an example in us. For many, of whom I have often told you and now tell you even with tears, live as enemies of the cross of Christ. Their end is destruction, their god is the belly, and they glory in their shame, with minds set on earthly things. But our commonwealth is in heaven, and from it we await a Savior, the Lord Jesus Christ, who will change our lowly body to be like his glorious body, by the power which enables him even to the subjection of all things.

Therefore, my dear people, whom I love and long for, my joy and crown, stand firm thus in the Lord, my beloved.

GOSPEL *Luke 9:28–36*

Jesus took with him Peter and John and James, and went up on the mountain to pray. And as he was praying, the appearance of his countenance was altered, and his raiment became dazzling white. And behold, two men talked with him, Moses and Elijah, who appeared in glory and spoke of his departure, which he was to accomplish at Jerusalem. Now Peter and those who were with him were heavy with sleep, and when they wakened they saw his glory and the two men who stood with him. And as the men were parting from him, Peter said to Jesus, "Master, it is well that we are here; let us make three booths, one for you and one for Moses and one for Elijah" — not knowing what he said. As he said this, a cloud came and overshadowed them; and they were afraid as they entered the cloud. And a voice came out of the cloud, saying, "This is my Son, the chosen one; listen to him!" And when the voice had spoken, Jesus was found alone. And they kept silence and told no one in those days anything of what they had seen.

R E F L E C T I O N

After the encounter with the opposition recorded in last Sunday's gospel reading, we are given today a glimpse of the glory that belongs to Jesus. All three synoptic gospels relate this transfiguration incident, each one with minor differences. All three synoptics are clear, however, on the main point: Peter, James and John were privileged and frightened witnesses to the vision of Jesus' glory. They were chosen to hear the proclamation that Jesus is Son, chosen and beloved.

Luke narrates the event in a way reminiscent of earlier intimations of glory in the history of the people. But only Luke mentions that Jesus went up to the mountain "to pray" and that it was during his prayer that he was transfigured. Only Luke mentions what Moses, Elijah and Jesus were discussing: Jesus' departure (exodus), which he was to accomplish at Jerusalem.

The details added by Luke remind us that even in this foretaste of future glory, there was the underlying presence of the journey to Jerusalem, the exodus from this world. The sleep-heavy disciples awake to this dazzling vision, and Peter, often singled out by Luke, speaks without thinking: "Let us make three booths." These temporary shelters (skenes, tabernacles), like the cloud that overshadowed the mountain, are images taken from the Exodus event, images representing a very special presence of God. While the disciples are described as being fearful in all three synoptic accounts, it is Luke who adds that their fear came as they entered the cloud, as they were immersed in the divine presence. Their reaction was that of the religious person in the face of mystery: "They kept silence."

This incident occurs in Luke's gospel after there had been speculation about Jesus' identity (9:7–9, 18–20) and after his words about the suffering and death that awaited him (9:22). In last week's gospel, Luke outlined the opposition that every prophet can expect to face. This Sunday, we see that suffering and glory go hand in hand. Jesus, like the prophets before him, undertakes the journey to Jerusalem aware that the "glory road" is not a smooth one. The glory, after all, is not in the road; the glory is hidden in the cloud of this seemingly ordinary rabbi who goes on ahead of us.

■ **Our culture seems dedicated to avoiding facing up to our mortality. Does the gospel tell us something different about suffering and death? How do you deal with pain and suffering, especially with the terminal illness of someone you love?**

PRACTICE OF FAITH

PENITENCE. In addition to the catechumens who were declared "elect" last week, most parishes also have candidates in their midst. These candidates already share baptism with us but either come from other Christian traditions or need further catechesis. Since these candidates are already baptized, they will not celebrate the upcoming scrutinies with the unbaptized elect. However, parishes have an opportunity to celebrate a penitential rite with the candidates this Sunday. As one of the baptized, support the candidates with your prayers.

PRACTICE OF HOPE

STAND FIRM IN THE LORD. Mrs. Valearia Latham lived in a low-income tenement for the elderly in New Haven, Connecticut, where I served as a chaplain. A rotund black woman with pepper-and-salt hair, she was the mother of 13 children and grandmother of 104.

Whenever I came to visit, she always had her family Bible open in her lap. She told me one day, "I've got a feeling someday real soon the good Lord's gonna show himself to me real plain. But until he does, I'm gonna keep looking for him in here." Her Bible was her constant companion on her journey of faith. "Keep in mind," she used to tell me, "that standing fast in the Lord is not the same as standing still in the the Lord."

PRACTICE OF CHARITY

THEY WERE AFRAID. The United States is the only western democracy to allow the death penalty. The U.S. Catholic Conference, in its 1980 *Statement on Capital Punishment,* declared: "Abolition [of the death penalty] sends a message that we can break the cycle of violence, that we need not take life for life." It is the special responsibility of the church to be an example of Jesus, "who both taught and practiced the forgiveness of injustice." We must continue to work for more humane and hopeful responses to the growth of violent crime. The National Coalition to Abolish the Death Penalty works to end capital punishment in the United States. If you would like to work with them or find out more about the death penalty, write: National Coalition to Abolish the Death Penalty, 1325 G Street, Lower Level B, Washington DC 20005; or call, 202-347-2411.

WEEKDAY READINGS Daniel 9:4–10; Isaiah 1:10, 16–20; Jeremiah 18:18–20; Jeremiah 17:5–10; Genesis 37:3–4, 12–13, 17–28; Micah 7: 14–15, 18–20

READING I *Exodus 3:1–6*

Moses was keeping the flock of his father-in-law, Jethro, the priest of Midian; and he led his flock to the west side of the wilderness, and came to Horeb, the mountain of God. And the angel of the LORD appeared to Moses in a flame of fire out of the midst of a bush; and he looked, and lo, the bush was burning, yet it was not consumed. And Moses said, "I will turn aside and see this great sight, why the bush is not burnt." When the LORD saw that he turned aside to see, God called to him out of the bush, "Moses, Moses!" And he said, "Here am I." Then God said, "Do not come near; put off your shoes from your feet, for the place on which you are standing is holy ground." And God said, "I am the God of your father, the God of Abraham, the God of Isaac, and the God of Jacob." And Moses hid his face, for he was afraid to look at God.

[Complete reading: Exodus 3:1–8, 13–15]

READING II *1 Corinthians 10:1–4, 5–6, 10*

I want you to know, my dear people, that our forebears were all under the cloud, and all passed through the sea, and all were baptized into Moses in the cloud and in the sea, and all ate the same supernatural food and all drank the same supernatural drink. Nevertheless with most of them God was not pleased; for they were overthrown in the wilderness.

Now these things are warnings for us, not to desire evil as they did. We must not grumble, as some of them did and were destroyed by the Destroyer.

[Complete reading: Corinthians 10:1–6, 10–12]

GOSPEL *Luke 13:1–9*

There were some present at that very time who told Jesus of the Galileans whose blood Pilate had mingled with their sacrifices. And Jesus answered them, "Do you think that these Galileans were worse sinners than all the other Galileans, because they suffered thus? I tell you, No; but unless you repent you will all likewise perish. Or those eighteen upon whom the tower in Siloam fell and killed them, do you think that they were worse offenders than all the others who dwelt in Jerusalem? I tell you, No; but unless you repent you will all likewise perish."

And Jesus told this parable: "There was a fig tree planted in a vineyard; and the owner came seeking fruit on it and found none. And the owner said to the vinedresser, 'Lo, these three years I have come seeking fruit on this fig tree, and I find none. Cut it down; why should it use up the ground?' And the vinedresser answered, 'Let it alone, sir, this year also, till I dig about it and put on manure. And if it bears fruit next year, well and good; but if not, you can cut it down.'"

[At liturgies celebrating the First Scrutiny, the readings from Year A found on page 60 are used.]

Monday, March 20, 1995

JOSEPH HUSBAND OF THE VIRGIN MARY

2 Samuel 7:4–5, 12–14, 16 *I will make David's throne endure.*

Romans 4:13, 16–18, 22 *He is father of us all.*

Matthew 1:16, 18–21, 24 *Joseph, Son of David, fear not!*
  or
Luke 2:41–51

In the Book of Genesis, Joseph is "the dreamer of dreams." In the Gospel of Matthew, Joseph dreamed of the coming kingdom. Then he awoke to find himself the father of the king.

Saturday, March 25, 1995

THE ANNUNCIATION OF THE LORD

Isaiah 7:10–14 *A virgin will bear a child.*

Hebrews 10:4–10 *I come to do God's will.*

Luke 1:26–38 *Rejoice, O highly favored daughter!*

Because pregnancy without marriage was punishable by death, Mary's yes to the angel is acceptance of death. But in this death, the risen Spirit conquers death. Mary's mortal body conceives the Immortal One.

R E F L E C T I O N

This rather strange excerpt from Luke' gospel should be seen for what it is — two swatches cut out of a larger cloth. In order to understand this passage, it is necessary to read chapter 12 and chapter 13:1–30. The message is, "unless you repent." The call to repentance is central to the good news. Luke uses the verb *metanoeo* to express a breaking away from sin, which is quite different from simple regret or remorse.

Some of those present in the crowd told Jesus of the death of some Galileans, expecting, perhaps, that Jesus would refer to their deaths as punishment for sin — thus echoing the common belief that suffering and calamities were God's way of punishing the sinner. Instead, Jesus reiterates that his message is about repentance and change of heart, not about trying to figure out why people suffer.

In the parable of the fig tree, Luke gives a different spin to the parable than that given in Matthew 21: 18–20 and Mark 11:12–14, 20–21. In Luke's version, the message is repentance. Even after years of not bearing fruit, the fig tree is given yet another chance, another year in which to bear fruit and break away from its unproductive past.

Finally, Luke may well be pointing to the coming encounter between the innocent Galilean, Jesus, and the Roman official, Pilate. In short, Jesus is emphatically laying to rest the traditional teaching that one suffers calamities because of one's sins. Jesus gives no answer to the "why" of suffering; rather, he proclaims the urgent necessity of turning away from sin in order to bear fruit.

■ There is still a common belief that God sends illness, setbacks or natural disasters as punishment for sin. Why do you think this belief persists?

■ Read the parable of the fig tree in Matthew 21:18–20 and Mark 11:12–14, 20–21. Do you think these are two separate parables? What is the lesson you draw from the Matthew/Mark parable?

PRACTICE OF FAITH

HOLY PARENTS. This week the church celebrates two feasts, one of Joseph and one of Mary. Throughout this week, remember your own parents and all those who taught, nurtured and sustained you through life. Pray this prayer, or ever better, make up one of your own:

Loving and nurturing Lord, I thank and praise and bless you for all those who you have graciously sent into my life to guide, teach, protect and nourish me in my live. I thank you first for my parents. Bless them and keep them in your care. I thank you too for all others who have helped me to become the person you desire me to be. Lord God, bless all you have sent to teach me to love you so well. I ask this in the name of Jesus, your beloved Son. Amen.

PRACTICE OF HOPE

I HAVE HEARD THEIR CRY. Olongapo, the city outside the U.S. Subic Naval Base in the Philippines, has been called "Sin City." More than 18,000 women have worked at hundreds of sex bars frequented by U.S. sailors. Some were sold by their desperately poor parents; others were lured by the dream of marrying an American sailor; and many were deceived by being promised jobs as waitresses and dancers. Once they got to Olongapo, they realized that they were trapped.

Brenda Stoltzfus, who worked with the Mennonite Central Committee, began "buying" time with the women just as customers did — only she sat down with them and listened. She helped to establish a support center. As the naval base has closed, the center has offered a foundation for empowering women for a new future.

PRACTICE OF CHARITY

HOLY GROUND. The image of "holy ground" is a powerful one. For centuries, spiritual writers have contemplated the deep significance of holy ground. Native Americans consider the earth to be holy since it came from the hands of the Creator. Native American cultures — and the tremendous amount of wisdom they embody — are in danger of vanishing. The American Indian College Fund works to keep the traditions alive. The 27 tribal colleges not only strive to provide sound academic grounding but strive also to revitalize native cultures. If you would like to help, write or call: American Indian College Fund, 21 West 68th Street, Suite 1F, New York NY 10023-5312; 212-787-6650.

WEEKDAY READINGS (Mo) Joseph, Husband of Mary; Daniel 3:25, 34–43; Deuteronomy 4:1, 5–9; Jeremiah 7:23–28; Hosea 14:2–10; (Sa) The Annunciation of the Lord

The following readings from Year A are used at liturgies when the First Scrutiny is celebrated.

READING I *Exodus 17:3–7*

The people thirsted for water, and the people murmured against Moses, and said, "Why did you bring us up out of Egypt, to kill us and our children and our cattle with thirst?" So Moses cried to the LORD, "What shall I do with this people? They are almost ready to stone me." And the LORD said to Moses, "Pass on before the people, taking with you some of the elders of Israel; and take in your hand the rod with which you struck the Nile, and go. Behold, I will stand before you there on the rock at Horeb; and you shall strike the rock, and water shall come out of it, that the people may drink." And Moses did so, in the sight of the elders of Israel. And Moses called the name of the place Massah and Meribah, because of the faultfinding of the children of Israel, and because they put the LORD to the proof by saying, "Is the LORD among us or not?"

READING II *Romans 5:1–2, 5–8*

Since we are justified by faith, we have peace with God through our Lord Jesus Christ, through whom we have obtained access to this grace in which we stand, and we rejoice in our hope of sharing the glory of God. And hope does not disappoint us, because God's love has been poured into our hearts through the Holy Spirit which has been given to us.

While we were still weak, at the right time Christ died for the ungodly. Why, one will hardly die for a righteous person — though perhaps for a good person one will dare even to die. But God's own love is shown for us in that while we were yet sinners Christ died for us.

GOSPEL *John 4:5–15, 19–26*

Jesus came to a city of Samaria, called Sychar, near the field that Jacob gave to his son Joseph. Jacob's well was there, and so Jesus, wearied from the journey, sat down beside the well. It was about the sixth hour.

There came a woman of Samaria to draw water. Jesus said to her, "Give me a drink." For his disciples had gone away into the city to buy food. The Samaritan woman said to Jesus, "How is it that you, a Jewish man, ask a drink of me, a woman of Samaria?" For Judeans have no dealings with Samaritans. Jesus answered the woman, "If you knew the gift of God, and who it is that is saying to you, 'Give me a drink,' you would have asked him, and he would have given you living water." The woman said to him, "Sir, you have nothing to draw with, and the well is deep; where do you get that living water? Are you greater than our father Jacob, who gave us the well, and drank from it himself, and his children, and his cattle?" Jesus said to her, "Everyone who drinks of this water will thirst again, but those who drink of the water that I shall give them will never thirst; the water that I shall give them will become in them a spring of water welling up to eternal life." The woman said to Jesus, "Sir, give me this water, that I may not thirst, nor come here to draw.

I perceive that you are a prophet. Our forebears worshiped on this mountain; and you say that in Jerusalem is the place where it is proper to worship." Jesus said to her, "Woman, believe me, the hour is coming when neither on this mountain nor in Jerusalem will you worship the Father. You worship what you do not know; we worship what we know, for salvation is from the Jews. But the hour is coming, and now is, when the true worshipers will worship the Father in spirit and truth, for such worshipers the Father seeks. God is spirit, and those who worship God must worship in spirit and truth." The woman said to Jesus, "I know that Messiah is coming (the one who is called Christ); when that one comes, he will show us all things." Jesus said to her, "I who speak to you am the one."

[Complete reading: John 4:5–42]

REFLECTION

This is a familiar story, rich in meaning and capable of inspiring deep reflection. Within the context of John's gospel, which focuses on Jesus' mission as the one sent by the Father, this narrative reveals Jesus as the source of living water, as the Messiah and as boundary-breaker and repairer of breaches. In this narrative of the woman at the well, John spotlights the Jesus through whom "we have peace with God" (Romans 5:1), and so, with one another.

Jesus comes in the heat of the day to sit by Jacob's well, near the piece of land given by Jacob to Joseph (Genesis 33 – 35, 48 – 49; Joshua 24:32). While Jews and Samaritans alike honored Jacob and revered the well, the two groups had nothing else in common but mutual distrust. In Genesis 33 we are told of the origin of this enmity — the rape of Dinah and the subsequent deceit of Jacob's sons toward the Samaritans. At Jacob's well, Jesus begins to heal the breach by initiating a conversation with a Samaritan woman. The woman is surprised at this breaking down of a traditional barrier, yet she continues the conversation; she does not walk away.

Jacob drank from this well, as did his sons and his cattle. But Jesus says that everyone who drinks of the wellwater will be thirsty; only those given the living water will never thirst. It was the coming of Jesus' disciples that prompted the woman to leave, to go and tell the people in Sychar that there was someone they should meet. Many Samaritans believed in Jesus because of the woman's testimony, an important point because while Samaritans would accept the testimony of a woman, the Jews would not.

The final sentence in this segment contains John's conclusion about the uniqueness of Jesus as boundary-breaker and restorer of ruptured relationships. Many believed in Jesus because of the woman's witness; many more believed because of the words of Jesus, a Jew. Thus, John portrays the Samaritans as people who understood that the Messiah was not only for the Jews — he was truly the Savior of the whole world.

■ **Read Genesis 33—35, 48—49 and Joshua 24:32. These passages give us an understanding of why Jacob's well was important to both Jews and Samaritans. Are there places in your life that can be occasions for significant encounters? What are they?**

■ **What do you think John is telling us in this narrative about "keeping to our own kind," not making an effort to approach those who are different?**

PRACTICE OF FAITH

SCRUTINIES. The word "scrutiny" tends to frighten us. It evokes images of being a specimen under a microscope. When the church uses this word, it has a very different meaning. Scrutinies are rites during which the community prays over the elect, asking that God send the Holy Spirit to strengthen in them all that is good and holy and to heal those places in their lives where sin may be at work. Beginning this week, and for the next two Sundays, parishes will be celebrating the scrutinies for their elect. Find out when the scrutinies will be celebrated in your parish so that you can attend. Pray for the elect and for everyone in the church, since we are all in need of strengthening, healing and conversion.

PRACTICE OF HOPE

HOPE DOES NOT DISAPPOINT. In August 1993, the Sojourners Neighborhood Center in inner-city Washington, D.C. marked its 10th anniversary. Sojourners Community took a burned-out shell of a building and turned it into a place of ministry and learning. Its children's program has become a "freedom school" where young African Americans are taught their rich heritage and are mentored by neighborhood adults. Food programs, computer training and suppport groups also take place during the course of a week. According to co-executive director Barbara Tamialis, "We have felt God's call in our life deeply rooted in walking with marginalized and oppressed people — not as solution bearers, but as fellow travelers."

PRACTICE OF CHARITY

GIVE ME A DRINK. "Get it yourself!" is one possible response to someone who asks for a favor. If we fill our lives with innumerable activities and demands, there is often little room left when someone calls upon us for a simple act of charity. And yet, requests for small acts of kindness are often invitations to conversion. This week and throughout the rest of the Lenten season, welcome requests for favors into your life. Behind them, you will find the face of Jesus.

WEEKDAY READINGS (Mo) Joseph, Husband of Mary; Daniel 3:25, 34 – 43; Deuteronomy 4:1, 5 – 9; Jeremiah 7:23 – 28; Hosea 14:2 – 10; (Sa) The Annunciation of the Lord

READING I *Joshua 5:9, 10–12*

The LORD said to Joshua, "This day I have rolled away the reproach of Egypt from you."

While the people of Israel were encamped in Gilgal they kept the passover on the fourteenth day of the month at evening in the plains of Jericho. And on the morrow after the passover, on that very day, they ate of the produce of the land, unleavened cakes and parched grain. And the manna ceased on the morrow, when they ate of the produce of the land; and the people of Israel had manna no more, but ate of the fruit of the land of Canaan that year.

READING II *2 Corinthians 5:17–21*

Any one who is in Christ is a new creation; the old has passed away, behold, the new has come. All this is from God. By God through Christ, we have been reconciled to God, who gave us the ministry of reconciliation; that is, God was in Christ, reconciling the world to God, not counting their trespasses against them, and entrusting to us the message of reconciliation. So we are ambassadors for Christ, God appealing through us. We beseech you on behalf of Christ, be reconciled to God. For our sake God made to be sin the one who knew no sin, so that in Christ we might become the righteousness of God.

GOSPEL *Luke 15:1–3, 11–32*

The tax collectors and sinners were all drawing near to hear Jesus. And the Pharisees and the scribes murmured, saying, "This man receives sinners and eats with them."

So Jesus told them this parable, saying: "A certain man had two sons; and the younger of them said to his father, 'Father, give me the share of property that falls to me.' And the father divided his living between them. Not many days later, the younger son gathered all he had and journeyed into a far country, and there squandered his property in loose living. And when he had spent everything, a great famine arose in that country, and he began to be in want. So he went and joined himself to one of the citizens of that country, who sent him into his fields to feed swine. And he would gladly have fed on the pods that the swine ate; and no one gave him anything. But when he came to himself he said, 'How many of my father's hired servants have bread enough and to spare, but I perish here with hunger! I will arise and go to my father, and I will say to him, "Father, I have sinned against heaven and before you; I am no longer worthy to be called your son; treat me as one of your hired servants.'" And he arose and came to his father. But while he was yet at a distance, his father saw him and had compassion, and ran and embraced and kissed him. And the son said to him, 'Father, I have sinned against heaven and before you; I am no longer worthy to be called your son.' But the father said to his servants, 'Bring quickly the best robe, and put it on him; and put a ring on his hand, and shoes on his feet; and bring the fatted calf and kill it, and let us eat and make merry; for this my son was dead, and is alive again; he was lost, and is found.' And they began to make merry.

"Now the elder son was in the field; and as he came and drew near to the house, he heard music and dancing. And he called one of the servants and asked what this meant. And the servant said to him, 'Your brother has come, and your father has killed the fatted calf, because he has received him safe and sound.' But the elder brother was angry and refused to go in. His father came out and entreated him, but the elder son answered his father, 'Lo, these many years I have served you, and I never disobeyed your command; yet you never gave me a kid, that I might make merry with my friends. But when this son of yours came, who has devoured your living with prostitutes, you killed for him the fatted calf!' And the father answered, 'Son, you are always with me, and all that is mine is yours. It was fitting to make merry and be glad, for this your brother was dead, and is alive; he was lost, and is found.'"

[At liturgies celebrating the Second Scrutiny, the readings from Year A found on page 64 are used.]

REFLECTION

The opposition that Jesus faces appears again at the beginning of today's reading and in the person of the elder brother in the parable. Luke ended chapter 14 with a familiar refrain: "The one having ears to hear, let him hear" (14:35). In the beginning of today's gospel, Luke shows that tax collectors and sinners — the outcasts — were the ones drawing near to hear Jesus. The "lowly," the sinners, were ready to listen, while the scribes and Pharisees — the leaders — were murmuring (the verb *diagongyzo* used here connotes dissatisfaction). For those eager to hear, as well as for those who were dissatisfied with Jesus' choice of dinner companions, Jesus spoke in parables. (The parables of the lost sheep and the missing drachma precede this long and beautiful narrative of the forgiving father.)

Today's long narrative is of a certain man who had two sons. The younger son first gathered his property and then squandered it in loose living. The portrayal of this son's repentance is not that of a deeply religious conversion; the son was hungry and counted on his father's goodness to appease that hunger. His rehearsed speech was in fact cut short by the father's joy and his desire for an immediate celebration.

Enter the elder son, who resents the party, feeling that he has slaved (the word used for "served" is from the verb *douleuo*, to be a slave) while his brother has devoured their father's property by living with prostitutes (verse 30). This accusation was not exact, because the father had already divided the inheritance. The elder brother is so angry that he refers to his brother as "your son," and it is the father who reminds him that the returned son is "this, your brother." The father addresses the elder brother as "son" (*teknon*, flesh of my flesh), and in calling his son *teknon*, the father reminds the elder son of the bond that exists between the two brothers — a bond of solidarity that the elder son is attempting to ignore.

Luke's narrative sheds light on Jesus' message of repentance, the assurance of forgiveness and the persistent human reluctance to accept the repentant sinner as blood brother or blood sister. As Jesus grows in favor among the lowly, opposition to him builds up among those who feel they have served God long and well.

■ **Re-read this parable slowly. Reflect on our society's attitude toward ex-convicts and toward the marginalized of our communities. Reflect on your own feelings as well.**

PRACTICE OF FAITH

AMBASSADORS OF RECONCILIATION. People have many reasons for leaving the church community, and often all they need is some encouragement and an invitation to return. Find out if your parish has a way to reach out to inactive Catholics and see how you can be of assistance. If your parish does not have such a process, gather information about what programs do exist elsewhere. Your diocesan offices of worship or education would be good resources. Most of all, decide to be an ambassador of reconciliation in the workplace and in your neighborhood so that others will know the healing grace and power of Christ.

PRACTICE OF HOPE

A NEW CREATION. Two young men from rival street gangs — one a Crip and one a Blood — came together at the altar of a Baptist church. Confessing that they had been trying to kill each other for more than a year, they embraced one another, tears welling in their eyes.

Their reconciliation was only one of many such events at a "Gang Summit" in Kansas City in the spring of 1993. Disappointed in establishment leadership, young people from the ghettos and barrios decided to pursue a truce among gangs across the country. The feeling of unity was profound. "We would rather live than die," said one teenage gang member. "It's as simple as that."

PRACTICE OF CHARITY

HIS FATHER SAW HIM AND HAD COMPASSION. Charity outside the home can be rather enjoyable; people are usually grateful that we were there, and at the end of our commitment, we can hop in the car and be home in time for supper. It is strange that sometimes we can be quicker to show compassion to those we don't know than to our spouse, our children or our siblings. At times it seems that when we deal with our own, our love has conditions. It is not unheard of that family members have not spoken to one another for years because each one was afraid to show compassion, afraid of being taken advantage of, too angry, or too hurt to reach out again in love. The forgiving father has much to teach us. This week, consider making amends with a family member who has wronged you. Or show compassion if a family member approaches you for forgiveness. Let the forgiving Father be your guide.

WEEKDAY READINGS Isaiah 65:17–21; Ezekiel 47:1–9, 12; Isaiah 49: 8–15; Exodus 32:7–14; Wisdom 2:1, 12–22; Jeremiah 11: 18–20

The following readings from Year A are used at liturgies when the Second Scrutiny is celebrated.

READING I *1 Samuel 16:1, 6–7, 10–13*

The LORD said to Samuel, "Fill your horn with oil, and go; I will send you to Jesse the Bethlehemite, for I have provided for myself a king among his sons."

When Jesse and his sons came, Samuel looked on Eliab and thought, "Surely here before the LORD is the LORD's anointed one." But the Lord said to Samuel, "Do not look on his appearance or on the height of his stature, because I have rejected him; for the LORD sees beyond human sight; mortals look on the outward appearance, but the LORD looks on the heart." And Jesse made seven of his sons pass before Samuel. And Samuel said to Jesse, "The LORD has not chosen these." And Samuel said to Jesse, "Are all your sons here?" And Jesse said, "There remains yet the youngest, but behold, he is keeping the sheep." And Samuel said to Jesse, "Send and fetch him; for we will not sit down till he comes here." And he sent, and brought him in. Now he was ruddy, and had beautiful eyes, and was handsome. And the LORD said, "Arise, anoint him; for this is the one." Then Samuel took the horn of oil, and anointed him in the midst of his brothers; and the Spirit of the Lord came mightily upon David from that day forward.

READING II *Ephesians 5:8–14*

Once you were darkness, but now you are light in the Lord; walk as children of light (for the fruit of light is found in all that is good and right and true), and try to learn what is pleasing to the Lord. Take no part in the unfruitful works of darkness, but instead expose them. For it is a shame even to speak of the things that they do in secret; but when anything is exposed by the light it becomes visible, for anything that becomes visible is light. Therefore it is said,

"Awake, O sleeper, and arise from the dead, and Christ shall give you light."

GOSPEL *John 9:1, 6–9, 13–17, 34–39*

Passing by, Jesus saw someone who was blind from birth. Jesus spat on the ground and made clay of the spittle and anointed the man's eyes with the clay, saying to him, "Go, wash in the pool of Siloam" (which means Sent). So he went and washed and came back seeing. The neighbors and those who had seen him before as a beggar said, "Is not this the person who used to sit and beg?" Some said, "It is he"; others said, "No, but he is like him." He said, "I am the one."

They brought to the Pharisees the one who had formerly been blind. Now it was a sabbath day when Jesus made the clay and opened his eyes. The Pharisees again asked him how he had received his sight. And he said to them, "He put clay on my eyes, and I washed, and I see." Some of the Pharisees said, "This man is not from God, for he does not keep the sabbath." But others said, "How can a sinner do such signs?" There was a division among them. So they again said to the blind man, "What do you say about him, since he has opened your eyes?" He said, "He is a prophet."

They answered him, "You were born in utter sin, and would you teach us?" And they cast him out.

Jesus heard that they had cast him out, and having found him, Jesus said, "Do you believe in the Man of Heaven?" He answered, "And who is the Man of Heaven, sir, that I may believe in him?" Jesus said to him, "You have seen him: the one speaking to you is the one." He said, "Lord, I believe"; and he worshiped Jesus. Jesus said, "For judgment I came into this world, that those who do not see may see, and that those who see may become blind."

[Complete reading: John 9:1–41]

REFLECTION

John's account of the man born blind is one of the most compelling narratives of the signs worked by Jesus. The story highlights Jesus' role as the one sent from God to be the catalyst that precipitates a situation of crisis, a moment of decision. This is brought out by John through the images of blindness and sight. The man born blind eventually sees clearly and stands up for what is clear to him. The "seers," the leaders and teachers who think they see clearly, in reality wear blinders of their own making. The focus of this brief reflection, however, will be on what Jesus does in this passage.

A common belief at the time was that physical defects were punishment for sin. But Jesus contradicts that belief; he uses the man's blindness as an opening for the manifestation of God's work within the harsh reality of the human situation. Jesus speaks of "works" and "work," words that in the scriptures often refer to God's work of salvation. Then Jesus begins to act: He spits on the ground and makes clay. The word used here for "made" is *epoiesen,* a form of the verb that refers to creative activity, action flowing from creative potential. John presents Jesus literally "creating sight" in a way that evokes the image of Genesis 2:2–3, the image of the Creator God forming *adam* (earthling) out of *adamah* (earth/dust).

For the man born blind, the sign of his healing is a clear indication of the origin of Jesus' creative power: Jesus is a prophet, one who fears God, a Man of Heaven. To some of the religious leaders, Jesus' creative work and his activity of healing were merely the actions of a sinner, transgressions against the Sabbath rest. To others, Jesus' actions posed a question. John delineates in this narrative the division, the crisis, brought about by the presence and works of Jesus. The signs were done to reveal the creative work of salvation, and those who want to see, those who acknowledge their blindness, will believe and will acknowledge Jesus as the one from heaven.

■ **Light and darkness, sight and blindness are favorite themes of John. What meanings do the images have for you?**

■ **Re-read the entire passage of today's gospel as if you were producing it as a "made-for-TV" movie. Does this help you to understand the passage?**

PRACTICE OF FAITH

HOLY OIL. Samuel anointed David as king, and for centuries afterward Jews looked for the coming of the Messiah, the Anointed One. Anointing has long been one of the sacramental symbols used in baptism, confirmation, ordination and the anointing of the sick. Every year, the bishop of the diocese blesses new oil for the use of the church that year. That blessing takes place during the liturgy known as the Chrism Mass, held sometime during Holy Week. Find out when the Chrism Mass will be celebrated in your diocese and, if possible, make plans to attend.

PRACTICE OF HOPE

BEYOND HUMAN SIGHT. "Why does Molly's head keep getting littler and littler?" seven-year-old Peter wanted to know. His mother suppressed a laugh. Molly, the family's cat, was pregnant. As her body swelled over the weeks with the new life growing inside her, her head appeared to be shrinking.

For us humans, choosing new life — perhaps after a time of suffering, confusion, or despair — can be similar. It's often easy to see what we're losing and difficult to see new life on the other side of painful choices. But, as Peter unwittingly remind us, it's all a matter of perspective. Life looks different when we see with the eyes of hope.

PRACTICE OF CHARITY

CHRIST WILL GIVE YOU LIGHT. As those in the RCIA process continue their 40-day retreat, we are reminded of the powerful image of Christ as the light of the world. In a world where darkness seems to get the most print, it is important for us to be mindful of the light that dispels the darkness. The Quakers use the phrase, "mind the light." This phrase expresses the need people have to experience and share their inner light, Christ. The American Friends Service Committee is about minding the light. They sponsor over 150 humanitarian aid programs around the globe, affirming hope and light in a world filled with famine, fighting and disease. If you would like to help, contact: American Friends Service Committee, 1501 Cherry Street, Philadelphia PA 19102.

WEEKDAY READINGS Isaiah 65:17–21; Ezekiel 47:1–9, 12; Isaiah 49: 8–15; Exodus 32:7–14; Wisdom 2:1, 12–22; Jeremiah 11: 18–20

READING I *Isaiah 43:16 – 21*

Thus says the LORD,
   who makes a way in the sea,
   a path in the mighty waters,
who brings forth chariot and horse,
   army and warrior;
they lie down, they cannot rise,
   they are extinguished, quenched like a wick:
"Remember not the former things,
   nor consider the things of old.
Behold, I am doing a new thing;
   now it springs forth, do you not perceive it?
I will make a way in the wilderness
   and rivers in the desert.
The wild beasts will honor me,
   the jackals and the ostriches;
for I give water in the wilderness,
   rivers in the desert,
to give drink to my chosen people,
   the people whom I formed for myself
that they might declare my praise."

READING II *Philippians 3:8 – 14*

I count everything as loss because of the surpassing worth of knowing Christ Jesus my Lord, for whose sake I have suffered the loss of all things, and count them as refuse, in order that I may gain Christ and be found in him, not having a righteousness of my own, based on law, but that which is through faith in Christ, the righteousness from God that depends on faith; that I may know Christ and the power of his resurrection, and may share his sufferings, becoming like Christ in his death, that if possible I may attain the resurrection from the dead.

   Not that I have already obtained this or am already perfect; but I press on to make it my own, because Christ Jesus has made me his own. My dear people, I do not consider that I have made it my own; but one thing I do, forgetting what lies behind and straining forward to what lies ahead, I press on toward the goal for the prize of the upward call of God in Christ Jesus.

GOSPEL *John 8:1 – 11*

Jesus went to the Mount of Olives. Early in the morning he came again to the temple; all the people came to him, and he sat down and taught them. The scribes and the Pharisees brought a woman who had been caught in adultery, and placing her in the midst they said to Jesus, "Teacher, this woman has been caught in the act of adultery. Now in the law Moses commanded us to stone such women. What do you say about her?" This they said to test Jesus, that they might have some charge to bring against him. Jesus bent down and wrote with his finger on the ground. And as they continued to ask him, he stood up and said to them, "Let the one who is without sin among you be the first to throw a stone at her." And once more he bent down and wrote with his finger on the ground. But when they heard it, they went away, one by one, beginning with the eldest, and Jesus was left alone with the woman standing before him. Jesus looked up and said to her, "O woman, where are they? Has no one condemned you?" She said, "No one, Lord." And Jesus said, "Neither do I condemn you; go, and from now on sin no more."

[At liturgies celebrating the Third Scrutiny, the readings from Year A found on page 68 are used.]

REFLECTION

This incident was not included in many ancient manuscripts of the Fourth Gospel. It was also placed in various locations within John, and some ancient authorities even placed this passage after Luke 21:38. But despite the question of textual authority, the incident itself has the earmarks of a genuine event.

This story illustrates the growing opposition to Jesus on the part of the scribes and Pharisees, who here attempt to entrap him. We notice the use of the generic "woman," a nameless accused. One nagging question always arises from a reading of this incident: If the woman had been caught in the act of adultery, why is she the only one accused?

As the scene opens, Jesus comes to the temple and sits down in the traditional way of the teacher. There, scribes and Pharisees address Jesus as "teacher" (*didaskale*) as they set out to draw him into what they hope will be a conflict with the great teacher and law-giver, Moses. The vivid description of the scene highlights the actions of standing and bending down: The scribes and Pharisees bring the woman and "stand her" in their midst, as if she were some thing. Jesus, presumably still seated, bends down and writes in the earth. The scribes and Pharisees continue their testing, and then Jesus stands up and reminds all of them that no one is without sin. Then he stoops down again and writes in the earth (perhaps as a reminder that all humans are of this same earth, this *humus*) until the accusers have the honesty to slip away. The final scene has Jesus, still bent to the earth, looking up to the accused woman and removing the stigma of condemnation.

Today's gospel illustrates that the good news of the forgiveness of "public sinners" often meets with opposition. But Jesus reminds his audience of their solidarity in sin as members of the human race. We cannot condemn others because we cannot separate ourselves from the human condition.

■ **Read this gospel again in the light of the day's first and second readings. In Isaiah we hear the Lord declare, "Behold, I am doing a new thing," and Philippians praises the righteousness that comes from God in Christ, who did a new thing in defending the sinner. How deeply aware are you that you are one with other human beings, sharing in some way in their goodness and their sinfulness?**

PRACTICE OF FAITH

A SHOWER OF BLESSINGS, NOT STONES. Anger, impatience and frustration are all a part of human life, and it is easy to act on those emotions. But we, who know ourselves to be sinners in need of God's mercy and forgiveness, also know that we cannot be stone throwers. Instead, we are encouraged to practice compassion, mercy and forgiveness. In addition to the corporal works of mercy, listed earlier this year, the church gives us spiritual works of mercy: instructing the ignorant, correcting sinners, advising the doubtful, bearing wrongs patiently, forgiving others, comforting the afflicted and praying for the living and the dead. During the rest of this Lenten season, find ways to shower many with blessings by practicing these works of mercy.

PRACTICE OF HOPE

SUFFER TO GAIN CHRIST. At two o'clock in the morning, there was a knock on the door where Victoria Diaz Carro lived. Her father, head of a union, was taken by 25 members of the militia to the torture chambers of a Chilean prison. He was never heard from again. Diaz Carro and other relatives of the "disappeared" began creating *arpilleras*—"embroideries of life and death"—in response to their tragedy.

With sorrow and hope, these women began weaving the stories of their lives. Their colorful artwork was begun as a means of supporting their families, but it took on political and spiritual significance as well because it helped the women lose their sense of isolation.

These women are disturbing the fabric of their country with cloth and thread. Their work is considered dangerous, and many *arpilleras* have been confiscated. But hands still continue to craft stories of faith and hope.

PRACTICE OF CHARITY

NEITHER DO I CONDEMN YOU. A survey of those in prison showed that inmates want the same things most of us have: housing, employment, health care and a family. We could be cynical and think, "I would say that, too, if I were doing jail time." Or, we could think instead that many of our criminal offenders need another option; they need a chance to change the direction of their lives. Unfortunately, once someone has been in prison, we find it difficult to give them a second chance. One way to begin giving prisoners a second chance is to reach out to them. Contact your diocesan office for social concerns and learn more about prison ministry in your area and how you might contribute your support.

WEEKDAY READINGS Daniel 13:1 – 62; Numbers 21:4 – 9; Daniel 3:14 – 20, 91 – 92, 95; Genesis 17:3 – 9; Jeremiah 20:10 – 13; Ezekiel 37: 21 – 28

The following readings from Year A are used at liturgies when the Third Scrutiny is celebrated.

READING I *Ezekiel 37:12–14*

"Thus says the LORD GOD: Behold, I will open your graves, and raise you from your graves, O my people; and I will bring you home into the land of Israel. And you shall know that I am the LORD, when I open your graves, and raise you from your graves, O my people. And I will put my Spirit within you, and you shall live, and I will place you in your own land; then you shall know that I, the LORD, have spoken, and I have done it, says the LORD."

READING II *Romans 8:8–11*

Those who are in the flesh cannot please God.

But you are not in the flesh, you are in the Spirit, if in fact the Spirit of God dwells in you. Anyone who does not have the Spirit of Christ does not belong to Christ. But if Christ is in you, although your bodies are dead because of sin, your spirits are alive because of righteousness. If the Spirit of the one who raised Jesus from the dead dwells in you, the one who raised Christ Jesus from the dead will give life to your mortal bodies also through this Spirit dwelling in you.

GOSPEL *John 11:3–7, 17, 20–27, 33–45*

The sisters [of Lazarus] sent to Jesus, saying, "Lord, he whom you love is ill." But when Jesus heard it he said, "This illness is not unto death; it is for the glory of God, so that the Son of God may be glorified by means of it."

Now Jesus loved Martha and her sister and Lazarus. So when Jesus heard that Lazarus was ill, he stayed two days longer in the place where he was. Then after this he said to the disciples, "Let us go into Judea again."

Now when Jesus came, he found that Lazarus had already been in the tomb four days. When Martha heard that Jesus was coming, she went and met him, while Mary sat in the house. Martha said to Jesus, "Lord, if you had been here, my brother would not have died. And even now I know that whatever you ask from God, God will give you." Jesus said to her, "Your brother will rise again." Martha said to Jesus, "I know that he will rise again in the resurrection at the last day." Jesus said to her, "I am the resurrection and the life; they who believe in me, though they die, yet shall they live, and whoever lives and believes in me shall never die. Do you believe this?" She said to him, "Yes, Lord; I believe that you are the Christ, the Son of God, the one who is coming into the world."

Jesus was deeply moved in spirit and troubled, and said, "Where have you laid him?" They said to him, "Lord, come and see." Jesus wept. So the Jewish people said, "See how he loved him!" But some of them said, "Could not the one who opened the eyes of the blind man have kept this man from dying?"

Then Jesus, deeply moved again, came to the tomb; it was a cave, and a stone lay upon it. Jesus said, "Take away the stone." Martha, the sister of the deceased, said to Jesus, "Lord, by this time there will be an odor, for he has been dead four days." Jesus said to her, "Did I not tell you that if you would believe you would see the glory of God?" So they took away the stone. And Jesus lifted up his eyes and said, "Father, I thank you that you have heard me. I knew that you hear me always, but I have said this on account of the people standing by, that they may believe that you sent me." Having said this, Jesus cried with a loud voice, "Lazarus, come out." The dead man came out, his hands and feet bound with bandages, and his face wrapped with a cloth. Jesus said to them, "Unbind him, and let him go."

Many of the Judeans therefore, who had come with Mary and had seen what Jesus did, believed in him.

[Complete reading: John 11:1–45]

R E F L E C T I O N

This is the last of what the Gospel of John often calls the "signs" worked by Jesus. It is also the longest uninterrupted account and the one that leads directly into John's passion narrative. The theme here is life and death, and the true life given to those who believe. Lazarus is the first of all those who will hear the voice of the Son of God (see John 5:25) and be freed from the bindings that preserve the dead.

With this sign, John gives us a deeper insight into the humanness of Jesus as well as an insight into Jesus' awareness of his calling. Because Jesus loved his friends, he risked a trip into Judea, delaying the trip only so that he might work this greatest of signs. When he did arrive and he witnessed the grief that death brings, Jesus was disturbed and moved in spirit (*enebrimesato to pneumati,* groaned in his spirit, was angry). And he wept. Jesus was again deeply moved as he came to the tomb, and he cried out with a loud voice. This is no imperturbable, deeply peaceful Jesus but a man stirred by profoundly disturbing feelings. In his praying aloud, Jesus wishes to make clear to those around him that it is the power of God at work, not any human power.

The last section of the narrative (see John 11:46–57) brings into sharp focus once more the division caused by this sign: "Many" believed and "some" reported the incident to the authorities. The words put into the mouth of the high priest are John's way of concluding the ministry of Jesus as it progresses toward its final hour. John's theme of gathering into one what has been scattered is one he will express eloquently as he records the last discourse of Jesus.

John concludes this narrative by highlighting the growing opposition to Jesus and the plot of the religious leaders to kill him. Jesus' outrage and groaning in the face of the death of a friend will soon enter into his prayer in the garden, as he faces his own imminent death at the hands of his enemies.

■ **Are you given "signs" in your life? Do you expect extraordinary signs, or are you alert to the signs buried within the reality of your own life? Are signs given only to comfort, or are they also given to wake us up, to set off the spark of conversion? How do you react to such signs?**

■ **Why do you think Jesus met with such opposition from the religious leaders of his own people?**

PRACTICE OF FAITH

LORD'S PRAYER. It is recommended that sometime during this week the church pass on to the elect the Lord's Prayer. The *Kaddish* is a Jewish prayer that Jesus grew up praying and is considered by many to be the inspiration for the Lord's Prayer. Let this prayer deepen your appreciation of our prayer tradition and its Jewish roots.

May the Lord's great name be magnified and sanctified in the world that God created according to God's good pleasure! May the Lord's reign prevail during your life and during your days, and during the life of the entire house of Israel at this very moment and very soon.
   And let them say: Amen!
May the name of the Lord—blessed by the Lord—be blessed, praised, glorified, extolled, exalted, honored, magnified and hymned!
It is above and beyond any blessing, hymn, praise or consolation that all utter in this world.
   And let them say: Amen!

PRACTICE OF HOPE

LIVE IN YOUR OWN LAND. Development on Daufuskie Island, one of the Sea Islands off the coast of South Carolina, threatens the way of life of the native islanders. Farming and oyster harvesting, sharing faith as well as resources and living with respect for the land mark a culture that has survived since the days when their ancestors were slaves.

In 1984, Melrose Corporation bought up 720 acres of the island for $6.5 million. Melrose Plantation Resort—whose memberships start at $50,000—put up fences, took over the road leading to the best beach and built its "welcome center" over one of the native cemeteries. Seventy-four-year-old Louise Wilson and her daughter joined with others in a lawsuit that many saw as a losing battle. But in 1993, Melrose Corporation agreed to move its welcome center and pay damages to the native islanders—a significant victory for people who made their voices heard.

PRACTICE OF CHARITY

JESUS CAME TO THE TOMB. It is strange how people remember who was present to them during times of sorrow. When someone visits the sick in the hospital or spends time with bereaved family members or friends, a lasting impression is made. When we pray our Sunday intercessions for those who are sick or for those who have recently died, we should also be moved to action. Consider joining your parish ministry of consolation or the pastoral team that visits the sick.

WEEKDAY READINGS **Daniel 13:1–62; Numbers 21:4–9; Daniel 3:14–20, 91–92, 95; Genesis 17:3–9; Jeremiah 20:10–13; Ezekiel 37:21–28**

READING I *Isaiah 50:4–7*

The Lord GOD has given me
>   the tongue of those who are taught,
that I may know how to sustain with a word
>   those who are weary.
Morning by morning the Lord God wakens,
>   wakens my ear,
>   to hear as those who are taught.
The Lord GOD has opened my ear,
>   and I was not rebellious,
>   I turned not backward.
I gave my back to the smiters,
>   and my cheeks to those who pulled out my
>   beard;
I hid not my face
>   from shame and spitting.
For the Lord GOD helps me;
>   therefore I have not been confounded;
therefore I have set my face like a flint,
>   and I know that I shall not be put to shame.

READING II *Philippians 2:5–11*

Have this mind among yourselves, which is yours in Christ Jesus, who, being in the form of God, did not count equality with God a thing to be grasped, but gave it up, taking the form of a servant, being born in human likeness. And being found in human form he humbled himself and became obedient unto death, even death on a cross. Therefore God has highly exalted him and bestowed on him the name which is above every name, that at the name of Jesus every knee should bow, in heaven and on earth and under the earth, and every tongue confess that Jesus Christ is Lord, to the glory of God, the Father.

GOSPEL *Luke 22:14 — 23:49*

And when the hour came, Jesus sat at table, and the apostles with him. And he said to them, "I have earnestly desired to eat this passover with you before I suffer; for I tell you I shall not eat it until it is fulfilled in the dominion of God." And he took a cup, and having given thanks said, "Take this, and divide it among yourselves; for I tell you that from now on I shall not drink of the fruit of the vine until the dominion of God comes."

And he took bread, and having given thanks broke it and gave it to them, saying, "This is my body which is given for you. Do this in remembrance of me." And likewise the cup after supper, saying, "This cup which is poured out for you is the new covenant in my blood. But behold the hand of the one who betrays me is with me on the table. For the Man of Heaven goes as it has been determined; but woe to that one by whom he is betrayed." And they began to question one another, which of them it was that would do this.

A dispute also arose among them, which of them was to be regarded as the greatest. And Jesus said to them, "The rulers of the Gentiles are domineering, and those in authority over them are called benefactors. But not so with you; rather let the greatest among you become as the youngest, and the leader as one who serves. For which is the greater, one who sits at table, or one who serves? Is it not the one who sits at table? But I am among you as one who serves.

"You are those who have continued with me in my trials; and I assign to you, as my Father assigned to me, a dominion, that you may eat and drink at my table in my dominion, and sit on thrones judging the twelve tribes of Israel.

"Simon, Simon, behold, Satan demand to have you, in order to sift you like wheat, but I have prayed for you that your faith may not fail; and when you have turned again, strengthen the community." And Peter said to Jesus, "Lord, I am ready to go with you to prison and to death." Jesus said, "I tell you, Peter, the cock will not crow this day, until you three times deny that you know me."

And Jesus said to them, "When I sent you out with no moneybag of pack or sandals, did you lack anything?" They said, "Nothing." He said to them, "But now, let whoever has a moneybag take it, and likewise a pack. And let him who has no sword sell his cloak and buy one. For I tell you that this scripture must be fulfilled in me, 'And he was reckoned with transgressors'; for what is written about me has it fulfillment." And they said, "Look, Lord, here are two swords." And Jesus said to them, "It is enough."

And Jesus came out, and went, as was his custom, to the Mount of Olives; and the disciples followed him. And coming to the place Jesus said to them, "Pray that you many not enter into temptation." And he withdrew from them about a stone's throw, and knelt down and prayer. "Father, if you are willing, remove this cup from me; nevertheless not my will, but yours, be done." And rising from prayer, he came to the disciples and found them sleeping for sorrow, and he said to them, "Why do you sleep? Rise and pray that you may not enter into temptation."

While Jesus was still speaking, there came a crowd, and one of the twelve called Judas was leading them. He drew near to Jesus to kiss him; but Jesus said to him, "Judas, would you betray the Man of Heaven with a kiss?" And when those who were about Jesus saw what would follow, the said, "Lord, shall we strike with the sword?" And one of them struck the slave of the high priest and cut off his right ear. But Jesus said, "No more of this!" And Jesus touched the slave's ear and healed him. Then Jesus said to the chief priests and officers of the temple and elders, who had come out against him. "Have you come out as against a robber, with swords and clubs? When I was with you day after day in the temple, you did not lay hands on me. But this is your hour, and the power of darkness."

Then they seized Jesus and led him away, bringing him into the high priest's house. Peter followed at a distance; and when they had kindled a fire in the middle of the courtyard and sat down together, Peter sat among them. Then a maid, seeing Peter as he sat in the light and gazing at him, said, "This man also was with Jesus." But Peter denied it, saying, "Woman, I do not know him." And a little later some one else saw Peter and said, "You also are one of them" But Peter said, "Man, I am not." And after

an interval of about an hour still another insisted, saying, "Certainly, this man also was with Jesus; for he is a Galilean." But Peter said, "Man, I do not know what you are saying." And immediately, while he was still speaking, the cock crowed., And the Lord turned and looked at Peter. And Peter remembered the word of the Lord, who had said to him, "Before the cock crows today, you will deny me three times." And Peter went out and wept bitterly.

Now the men who were holding Jesus mocked and beat him; they blindfolded him and asked him, "Prophesy! Who is it that struck you?" And they spoke many other words against him, reviling him.

When day came, the assembly of the elders of the people gathered together, both chief priests and scribes; and they led Jesus away to their council, and they said, "If you are the Christ, tell us." But he said to them, "If I tell you, you will not believe; and if I ask you, you will not answer. But from now on the Man of Heaven shall be seated at the right hand of the power of God." And the all said, "Are you the Son of God, then?" And Jesus said to them, "You say that I am." And they said, "What further testimony do we need? We have heard it ourselves from his own lips."

Then the whole company of them arose, and brought Jesus before Pilate. And they began to accuse him, saying, "We found this man perverting our nation, and forbidding us to give tribute to Caesar, and saying that he himself is Christ a king." And Pilate asked Jesus, "Are you the King of the Jews?" And Jesus answered him, "You have said so." And Pilate said to the chief priests and the multitudes, "I find no crime in this man." But they were urgent, saying, "He stirs up the people, teaching throughout Judea, from Galilee even to this place."

When Pilate heard this, he asked whether the man was a Galilean. And when he learned that Jesus belonged to Herod's jurisdiction, Pilate sent Jesus over to Herod, who was himself in Jerusalem at the time. When Herod saw Jesus, he was very glad. He had long desired to see Jesus, having heard about him, and hoping to see some sign done by him. So Herod questioned Jesus at some length;

71

but Jesus made no answer. The chief priests and the scribes stood by, vehemently accusing him. And Herod with his soldiers treated Jesus with contempt and mocked him; the, arraying him in gorgeous apparel, Herod sent Jesus back to Pilate. And Herod and Pilate became friends with each other that very day, for before this they had been at enmity with each other.

Pilate then called together the chief priests and the rulers and the people, and said to them, "You brought me this person as one who was perverting the people; and after examining him before you, I did not find this many guilty of any of your charges against him; neither did Herod, who sent him back to us. Behold, nothing deserving death has been done by him; I will therefore chastise and release him."

But they all cried out together, "Away with this man, and release to us Barabbas," (some one who had been thrown into prison for an insurrection started in the city, and for murder). Pilate addressed them once more, desiring to release Jesus; but they shouted out, "Crucify, crucify him!" A third time Pilate said to them, "Why, what evil has he done? I have found in him no crime deserving death; I will therefore chastise and release him." But they were urgent, demanding with loud cries that Jesus should be crucified. And their voices prevailed. So Pilate gave sentence that the demand should be granted. He released the one who had been thrown into prison for insurrection and murder, whom they asked for; but Jesus he delivered up to their will.

And as they led Jesus away, they seized on Simon of Cyrene, who was coming in from the country, and laid on him the cross to carry it behind Jesus. And there followed Jesus a great multitude of the people, and of women who bewailed and lamented him. But Jesus turning to them said, "Daughters of Jerusalem, do not weep for me, but weep for yourselves and for your children. For behold, the days are coming when they will say, 'Blessed are the barren, and the wombs that never bore, and the breasts that never gave suck!' Then they will begin to say to the mountains, 'Fall on us'; and to the hills, 'Cover us.' For if they do this when the wood is green, what will happen when it is dry?"

Two other also, who were criminals, were led away to be put to death with Jesus. And when the came to the place which is called The Skull, there they crucified him, and the criminals, one on the right and one on the left. And Jesus said, "Father, forgive them; for they know not what they do." And they cast lots to divide Jesus' garments. And the people stood by, watching; but the rulers scoffed at him, saying, "He saved others; let him save himself, if he is the Christ of God, the Chosen One!" The soldiers also mocked Jesus, coming up and offering him vinegar, and saying, "If you are the King of the Jews, save yourself!" There was also an inscription over him, "This is the King of the Jews."

One of the criminals who were hanged railed at Jesus, saying, "Are you not the Christ? Save yourself and us!" But the other rebuked him, saying, "Do you not fear God, since you are under the same sentence of condemnation? And we indeed justly; for we are receiving the due reward of our deeds; but this man has done nothing wrong." And he said, "Jesus, remember me when you come into your kingdom." And Jesus said to him, "Truly, I say to you, today you will be with me in Paradise."

It was now about the sixth hour, and there was darkness over the whole land until the ninth hour, while the sun's light failed; and the curtain of the temple was torn in two. Then Jesus, crying out with a loud voice, said, "Father, into your hands I commit my spirit!" And having said this he breathed his last. Now the centurion, seeing what had taken place, praised God and said, "Certainly this man was innocent!" And all the multitudes who assembled to see the sight, when they saw what had taken place, returned home beating their breasts. And all his acquaintances and the women who had followed him from Galilee stood at a distance and saw these things.

[Complete reading: Luke 22:14 — 23: 56]

REFLECTION

At the Passover meal—which Luke links with the "hour"—Jesus mentions a betrayer and the apostles ask *each other* who it might be. They do not ask Jesus (as they do in Matthew 26:22–25, Mark 14:17–20 and John 13:21–27), and thus effectively cut him out of the conversation. The apostles continue their own talk, arguing over their relative importance. Jesus joins the conversation to forewarn Simon of his coming denial and to speak of his own coming death; he is met with a lack of understanding. In the lonely prayer in the garden, Jesus finds the apostles sleeping, "because of grief." This section ends as Jesus is apprehended in the garden, gamely defended by one of the disciples. The journey of his ministry ends with Jesus' healing of the servant's ear.

The second phase of the journey, the "hour" of the power of darkness, begins with Peter's denial and with Jesus who "turned and looked at Peter" (the word used implies a piercing, straightforward look). Then Jesus is led to stand alone to face the mockery of the guards and the contempt and forked-tongue questions of the religious councillors, whose final question Jesus answers with an equivocation. He is then moved to face alone the sincere waffling of Pilate and the mockery and contempt of Herod, who was cheered on by the chief priests and scribes. Finally, Jesus stands alone as Pilate yields to the pressure of the crowd incited to action.

It is only during the final stage of his journey that some others attempted to side with Jesus: "A great number of the people" (*laos*, ordinary people), including women who expressed their grief, followed Jesus. As Jesus is stretched out on the cross, one criminal (*kakourgos*, a common felon) approached in faith. And at the end, a member of the occupying army, a dissenting member of the religious council and the women from Galilee were the only ones who recognized Jesus. Luke, the master storyteller, has etched in bold colors the story of the prophet-savior, who came to proclaim the good news to the lowly—but completed his journey experiencing firsthand the depth of lowliness.

■ **In the light of this passion narrative, slowly read Isaiah 50:4–7. Isaiah's text presents what may be described as Jesus' inner attitude in the face of suffering and false accusations. When you see others accused or slandered, do you attempt to understand what they may be going through?**

PRACTICE OF FAITH

HOSANNA TO THE KING. It is right that every parish begin at least one Mass this day with a procession. This week, which we call holy, is a week filled with processions. Today we process with palms, on Thursday we carry gifts for the poor, on Friday we carry the cross and on Saturday we process with the candle and the elect to the baptismal bath. Romano Guardini, a spiritual writer and liturgist whose work was instrumental in preparing for the liturgical reforms of the Second Vatican Council, reminds us that processions are never just about moving from place to place but are a reminder to all that God is with us and always moving among us. During this week's processions, look for the presence of our Lord and King, and breathe again a hosanna to the Son of David.

PRACTICE OF HOPE

TAKING THE FORM OF A SERVANT. Rodney Roberson was working at a homeless shelter in Marin County, California. When Bobbie, a black woman who had worked late, arrived at the shelter, she discovered that there was no sleeping mat for her. She and others began accusing the staff of being prejudiced.

While they shouted, a man named Jose fell on a mat in the center of the shelter in a drunken stupor. The stench of his feet filled the air, and the complaints and profanity from the others escalated. Roberson couldn't rouse him or carry him to the shower. He went to the kitchen, returned with a bowl and dishwashing liquid, and knelt to wash Jose's feet. The complainers grinned, and Bobbie, with tears in her eyes, stepped forward and kissed his soapy hands.

PRACTICE OF CHARITY

I AM AMONG YOU AS ONE WHO SERVES. "Sing Hosanna to our King!" But always remember that the King we salute is a humble servant. As Lent ends and Holy Week begins, it is a good time to remember this; Jesus is among us as one who serves. The call to be disciples of Jesus the servant compels us to make choices. Are you willing to act in humility and compassion? Are you willing to become one who serves? Take time to answer these questions with acts of charity. Make the choice to live as a follower of Christ.

WEEKDAY READINGS **Isaiah 42:1–7; 49:1–6; 50:4–9; 61:1–9; Triduum**

PASCHAL TRIDUUM

Holy is God! Holy and Strong!
Holy, immortal One, have mercy on us!

All you sheltered by the Most High,
who live in Almighty God's shadow,
say to the Lord, "My refuge, my fortress,
my God in whom I trust!"

God will free you from the hunter's snares,
will save you from deadly plague,
will cover you like a nesting bird.
God's wings will shelter you.

No nighttime terror shall you fear,
no arrows shot by day,
no plague that prowls the dark,
no wasting scourge at noon.

You have only to open your eyes
to see how the wicked are repaid.
You have the Lord as refuge,
have made the Most High your stronghold.

No evil shall ever touch you,
no harm come near your home.
God instructs angels
to guard you wherever you go.

"I deliver all who cling to me,
raise the ones who know me,

answer those who call me,
stand with those in trouble.
These I rescue and honor,
satisfy with long life,
and show my power to save."

—Psalm 91: 1–6, 8–11, 14–16

Holy God,
praise be yours for this tree of Paradise,
this tree that made Noah's saving Ark,
this tree whose branches embraced Jesus
and so shade and shelter us all.
Here may all the weary rest
these holy days,
hungry and thirsty for your word,
eating and drinking only your word
until, in the darkness between
Saturday and Sunday,
Heaven and earth shall here be wed.
Then drowning waters shall be
waters of life
and the Savior's blood a banquet.
Holy God, praise be yours.

—Prayer of the Triduum

APRIL 13, 1995
HOLY THURSDAY

READING I *Exodus 12:1–8, 11–14*

The Lord said to Moses and Aaron in the land of Egypt, "This month shall be for you the beginning of months; it shall be the first month of the year for you. Tell all the congregation of Israel that on the tenth day of this month they shall each take a lamb according to their ancestors' houses, a lamb for a household; and if the household is too small for a lamb, then neighbors shall take according to the number of persons; according to what each can eat you shall make your count for the lamb. Your lamb shall be without blemish, a male a year old; you shall take it from the sheep or from the goats; and you shall keep it until the fourteenth day of this month, when the whole assembly of the congregation of Israel shall kill their lambs in the evening. Then they shall take some of the blood, and put it on the two doorposts and the lintel of the houses in which they eat them. They shall eat the flesh that night, roasted; with unleavened bread and bitter herbs they shall eat it. In this manner you shall eat it: your loins girded, your sandals on your feet, and your staff in your hand; and you shall eat it in haste. It is the LORD's passover. For I will pass through the land of Egypt that night, and I will smite all the firstborn in the land of Egypt, both human and animal; and on all the gods of Egypt I will execute judgments: I am the LORD. The blood shall be a sign for you, upon the houses where you are; and when I see the blood, I will pass over you, and no plague shall fall upon you to destroy you, when I smite the land of Egypt.

"This day shall be for you a memorial day, and you shall keep it as a feast to the LORD; throughout your generations you shall observe it as an ordinance forever."

READING II *1 Corinthians 11:23–26*

For I received from the Lord what I also delivered to you, that the Lord Jesus on the night when he was betrayed took bread, and having given thanks, broke it, and said, "This is my body which is for you. Do this in remembrance of me." In the same way also the cup, after supper, saying, "This cup is the new covenant of my blood. Do this, as often as you drink it, in remembrance of me." For as often as you eat this bread and drink the cup, you proclaim the Lord's death until he comes.

GOSPEL *John 13:1–15*

Now before the feast of the Passover, when Jesus knew that his hour had come to depart out of this world to the Father, having loved his own who were in the world, he loved them to the end. And during supper, when the devil had already put it into the heart of Judas Iscariot, Simon's son, to betray him, Jesus, knowing that the Father had given all things into his hands, and that he had come from God and was going to God, rose from supper, laid aside his garments, and girded himself with a towel. Then he poured water into a basin, and began to wash the disciples' feet, and to wipe them with the towel with which he was girded. Jesus came to Simon Peter; and Peter said to him, "Lord, do you wash my feet?" Jesus answered him, "What I am doing you do not know now, but afterward you will understand." Peter said to him, "You shall never wash my feet." Jesus answered him, "If I do not wash you, you have no part in me." Simon Peter said to him, "Lord, not my feet only but also my hands and my head!" Jesus said to him, "Those who have bathed do not need to wash, except for their feet, but they are clean all over; and you are clean, but not every one of you." For Jesus knew who was to betray him; that was why he said, "You are not all clean."

When Jesus had washed their feet, and taken his garments, and resumed his place, he said to them, "Do you know what I have done to you? You call me Teacher and Lord; and you are right, for so I am. If I then, your Lord and Teacher, have washed your feet, you also ought to wash one another's feet. For I have given you an example, that you should do as I have done to you."

APRIL 14, 1995
GOOD FRIDAY

READING I *Isaiah 52:13 — 53:12*

Behold, my servant shall prosper,
   shall be exalted and lifted up,
   and shall be very high.
As many were astonished at the one
   whose appearance was so marred, beyond
     human semblance,
   and whose form was beyond that of humanity,
so shall my servant startle many nations;
   rulers shall shut their mouths because of him;
for that which has not been told them they shall see,
   and that which they have not heard
     they shall understand.
Who has believed what we have heard?
   And to whom has the arm of the LORD
     been revealed?
For the servant grew up before the LORD
   like a young plant,
   and like a root out of dry ground,
having no form or comeliness for us to behold,
   and no beauty for us to desire.
He was despised and rejected by men and women,
   a man of sorrows, and acquainted with grief;
and as one from whom people hid their faces
   He was despised, and we esteemed him not.
Surely he has borne our griefs
   and carried our sorrows;
yet we esteemed him stricken,
   smitten by God, and afflicted.
But he was wounded for our transgressions,
   and was bruised for our iniquities;
the chastisement that made us whole was upon
     him,
   by whose stripes we are healed.
All we like sheep have gone astray;
   we have turned each one to our own way,

and the LORD has laid on this servant
   the iniquity of us all.
This servant was oppressed and was afflicted,
   yet opened not his mouth;
like a lamb that is led to slaughter,
   and like a ewe that before her shearers is dumb,
   so he opened not his mouth.
By oppression and judgment
   the servant was taken away;
   and as for his generation, who considered
that he was cut off out of the land of the living,
   stricken for the transgression of my people?
He was given a grave with the wicked,
   and was with the rich in death,
although having done no violence,
   having never spoken deceit.
Yet it was the will of the LORD to bruise this servant;
   the LORD has put him to grief;
making himself an offering for sin,
   the servant shall see offspring
   and shall prolong his days;
the will of the LORD shall prosper
   in the hand of the servant,
who shall see the fruit of the travail of his soul
   and be satisfied;
by his knowledge shall the righteous one, my
   servant,
   make many to be accounted righteous;
   my servant shall bear their iniquities.
Therefore I will divide a portion with the great
   for my servant
who shall divide the spoil with the strong;
because my servant poured out his soul to death,
   and was numbered with the transgressors;
yet he bore the sin of many,
   and made intercession for the transgressors.

READING II *Hebrews 4:14 – 16; 5:7 – 9*

Since then we have a great high priest who has passed through the heavens, Jesus, the Son of God, let us hold fast our confession. For we have not a high priest who is unable to sympathize with our weaknesses, but one who in every respect has been tempted as we are, yet without sin. Let us then with confidence draw near to the throne of grace, that we may receive mercy and find grace to help in time of need.

In the days of his flesh, Jesus offered up prayers and supplications, with loud cries and tears, to the one who was able to save him from death, and for being God-fearing Jesus was heard. Although being a Son, Jesus learned obedience through what he suffered; and being made perfect Jesus became the source of eternal salvation to all who obey him.

GOSPEL *John 18:1 — 19:42*

When Jesus had spoken these words, he went forth with his disciples across the Kidron Valley, where there was a garden, which he and his disciples entered. Now Judas, who betrayed him, also knew the place; for Jesus often met there with his disciples. So Judas, procuring a band of soldiers and some officers from the chief priests and the Pharisees, went there with lanterns and torches and weapons. Then Jesus, knowing all that was to befall him, came forward and said to them, "Whom do you seek?"

They answered him, "Jesus of Nazareth."

Jesus said to them, "Here I am."

Judas, who betrayed Jesus, was standing with them. When Jesus said to them, "Here I am," they drew back and fell to the ground. Again Jesus asked them, "Whom do you seek?"

And they said, "Jesus of Nazareth."

Jesus answered, "I told you here I am, so, if you seek me, let these others go."

This was to fulfill the word which Jesus had spoken, "Of those whom you gave me I lost not one." Then Simon Peter, having a sword, drew it and struck the high priest's slave and cut off his right ear. The slave's name was Malchus. Jesus said to Peter, "Put your sword into its sheath; shall I not drink the cup which the Father has given me?"

So the band of soldiers and their captain and the officers of the Judeans seized Jesus and bound him. First they led him to Annas, the father-in-law of Caiaphas, who was high priest that year. It was Caiaphas who had given counsel to the Judeans that it was expedient that one person should die for the people.

Simon Peter followed Jesus, and so did another disciple. Being known to the high priest, that disciple entered the court of the high priest along with Jesus, while Peter stood outside at the door. So the other disciple, who was known to the high priest, went out and spoke to the maid who kept the door, and brought Peter in. The maid who kept the door said to Peter, "Are you not also one of this man's disciples?"

He said, "I am not."

Now the servants and officers had made a charcoal fire, because it was cold, and they were standing and warming themselves; Peter also was with them, standing and warming himself.

The high priest then questioned Jesus about his disciples and his teaching. Jesus answered the high priest, "I have spoken openly to the world; I have always taught in synagogues and in the temple, where all the Judeans come together; I have said nothing secretly. Why do you ask me? Ask those who have heard me, what I said to them; they know what I said."

When he had said this, one of the officers standing by struck Jesus with his hand, saying, "Is that how you answer the high priest?"

Jesus answered the officer, "If I have spoken wrongly, bear witness to the wrong; but if I have spoken rightly, why do you strike me?"

Annas then sent Jesus bound to Caiaphas the high priest. Now Simon Peter was standing and warming himself. They said to Peter, "Are you not also one of his disciples?"

He denied it and said, "I am not."

One of the servants of the high priest, a relative of the man whose ear Peter had cut off, asked, "Did I not see you in the garden with him?"

Peter again denied it, and at once the cock crowed.

Then they led Jesus from the house of Caiaphas to the praetorium. It was early. They themselves did not enter the praetorium, so that they might not be defiled, but might eat the passover. So Pilate went out to them and said, "What accusation do you bring against this man?"

They answered Pilate, "If this man were not an evildoer, we would not have handed him over."

Pilate said to them, "Take him yourselves and judge him by your own law."

The Judeans said to him, "It is not lawful for us to put any one to death."

This was to fulfill the word which Jesus had spoken to show by what death he was to die.

Pilate entered the praetorium again and called Jesus, saying, "Are you King of the Jews?"

Jesus answered, "Do you say this of your own accord, or did others say it to you about me?"

Pilate answered, "Am I Jewish? Your own nation and the chief priests have handed you over to me; what have you done?"

Jesus answered, "My kingship is not of this world; if my kingship were of this world, my servants would fight, that I might not be handed over to the Judeans; but my kingship is not from this world."

Pilate said to him, "So you are a king?"

Jesus answered, "You say that I am a king. For this I was born, and for this I have come into the world, to bear witness to the truth. Everyone who is of the truth hears my voice."

Pilate said to Jesus, "What is the truth?"

Having said this, Pilate went out to the Judeans again, and told them, "I find no crime in him. But you have a custom that I should release one person for you at the Passover; will you have me release for you the King of the Jews?"

They cried out again, "Not this man, but Barabbas!"

Now Barabbas was a robber.

Then Pilate took Jesus and scourged him. And the soldiers plaited a crown of thorns, and put it on his head, and arrayed him in a purple robe; they came up to Jesus, saying, "Hail, King of the Jews!" and struck him with their hands. Pilate went out again, and said to them, "See, I am bringing him out to you, that you may know that I find no crime in him."

So Jesus came out, wearing the crown of thorns and the purple robe. Pilate said to them, "Behold the man."

When the chief priest and the officers saw him, they cried out, "Crucify him, crucify him!"

Pilate said to them, "Take him yourselves and crucify him, for I find no crime in him."

The Judeans answered him, "We have a law, and by that law he ought to die, because he has made himself the Son of God."

When Pilate heard these words, he was the more afraid, he entered the praetorium again and said to Jesus, "Where are you from?"

But Jesus gave no answer. Pilate therefore said to him, "You will not speak to me? Do you know that I have the power to release you, and the power to crucify you?"

Jesus answered him, "You would have no power over me unless it had been given you from above; therefore the one who delivered me to you has the greater sin."

Upon this Pilate sought to release him, but the Judeans cried out, "If you release this man, you are not Caesar's friend; everyone who makes himself a king sets himself against Caesar."

When Pilate heard these words, he brought Jesus out and sat down on the judgment seat at a place called The Pavement, and in Hebrew, Gabbatha. Now it was the day of Preparation of the Passover; it was about the sixth hour. He said to the Judeans, "Behold your king!"

They cried out, "Away with him, away with him, crucify him."

Pilate said to them, "Shall I crucify your king?"

The chief priest answered, "We have no king but Caesar."

Then Pilate handed Jesus over to them to be crucified.

So they took Jesus, and he went out, bearing his own cross, to the place called the place of a skull, which is called in Hebrew Golgotha. There they crucified him, and with him two others, one on either side, and Jesus between them. Pilate also wrote a title and put it on the cross; it read, "Jesus of Nazareth, the King of the Jews." Many of the Judeans read this title, for the place where Jesus was crucified was near the city; and it was written in Hebrew, in Latin and in Greek. The chief priests then said to Pilate, "Do not write, 'The King of the Jews,' but 'This man said, I am King of the Jews.'"

Pilate answered, "What I have written I have written."

When the soldiers had crucified Jesus they took his garments and made four parts, one for each soldier; also the tunic. But his tunic was without seam, woven from top to bottom; so they said to one another, "Let us not tear it, but cast lots for it to see whose it shall be."

This was to fulfill the scripture, "They parted my garments among them, and for my clothing they cast lots."

So the soldiers did this. But standing by the cross of Jesus were his mother, and his mother's sister, Mary the wife of Clopas, and Mary Magdalene. When Jesus saw his mother, and the disciple whom he loved stand near, he said to his mother, "Woman, behold your son!" Then he said to the disciple, "Behold, your mother!"

And from that hour the disciple took her to his own home. After this Jesus, knowing that all was not finished, said (to fulfill the scripture), "I thirst."

A bowl of vinegar stood there; so they put a sponge full of vinegar on hyssop and held it to his mouth. Having received the vinegar, Jesus said, "It is finished"; and he bowed his head and gave over the spirit.

Since it was the day of Preparation, in order to prevent the bodies from remaining on the cross on the sabbath (for that sabbath was a high day), the Judeans asked Pilate that their legs might be broken, and that they might be taken away. So the soldiers came and broke the legs of the first, and of the other who had been crucified with him; but when they came to Jesus and saw that he was already dead, they did not break his legs. But one of the soldiers pierced his side with a spear, and at once there came out blood and water. He who saw it, whose testimony is true, and who knows that he tells the truth, has borne witness that you also may believe. For these things took place that the scripture might be fulfilled, "Not a bone of him shall be broken." And again another scripture says, "They shall look upon the one whom they have pierced."

After this Joseph of Arimathea, who was a disciple of Jesus, but secretly, for fear of the Judeans, asked Pilate that he might take away the body of Jesus, and Pilate gave him leave. So Joseph came and took away Jesus' body. Nicodemus also, who had at first come to Jesus by night, came bringing a mixture of myrrh and aloes, about a hundred pounds' weight. They took the body of Jesus, and bound it in linen cloths with the spices, as is the Jewish burial custom. Now in the place where Jesus was crucified there was a garden, and in the garden a new tomb where no one had ever been laid. So because of the Jewish day of Preparation, as the tomb was close at hand, they laid Jesus there.

APRIL 15, 1995
THE EASTER VIGIL

READING | *Genesis 1:1 — 2:3*

In the beginning God created the heavens and the earth. The earth was without form and void, and darkness was upon the face of the deep; and the Spirit of God was moving over the face of the waters.

And God said, "Let there be light"; and there was light. And God saw that the light was good; and God separated the light from the darkness. God called the light Day, and the darkness God called Night. And there was evening and there was morning, one day.

And God said, "Let there be a firmament in the midst of the waters, and let it separate the waters from the waters." And God made the firmament and separated the waters which were under the firmament from the waters which were above the firmament. And it was so. And God called the firmament Heaven. And there was evening and there was morning, a second day.

And God said, "Let the waters under the heavens be gathered together in one place, and let the dry land appear." And it was so. God called the dry land Earth, and the waters that were gathered together God called Seas. And God saw that it was good. And God said, "Let the earth put forth vegetation, plants yielding seed, and fruit trees bearing fruit in which is their seed, each according to its kind, upon the earth." And it was so. The earth brought forth vegetation, plants yielding seed according to their own kinds, and trees bearing fruit in which is their seed, each according to its kind. And God saw that it was good. And there was evening and there was morning, a third day.

And God said, "Let there be lights in the firmament of the heavens to separate the day from the night; and let them be for signs and for seasons and for days and years, and let them be lights in the firmament of the heavens to give light upon the earth." And it was so. And God made the two great lights, the greater light to rule the day, and the lesser light to rule the night; God made the stars also. And God set them in the firmament of the heavens to give light upon the earth, to rule over the day and over the night, and to separate the light from the darkness. And God saw that it was good. And there was evening and there was morning, a fourth day.

And God said, "Let the waters bring forth swarms of living creatures, and let birds fly above the earth across the firmament of the heavens." So God created the great sea monsters and every living creature that moves, with which the waters swarm, according to their kinds, and every winged bird according to its kind. And God saw that it was good. And God blessed them, saying, "Be fruitful and multiply and fill the waters in the seas, and let birds multiply on the earth." And there was evening and there was morning, a fifth day.

And God said, "Let the earth bring forth living creatures according to their kinds: cattle and creeping things and beasts of the earth according to their kinds." And it was so. And God made the beasts of the earth according to their kinds and the cattle according to their kinds, and everything that creeps upon the ground according to its kind. And God saw that it was good.

Then God said, "Let us make humankind in our image, after our likeness; and let them have dominion over the fish of the sea, and over the birds of the air, and over the cattle, and over all the earth, and over every creeping thing that creeps upon the earth." So God created humankind in the divine image; in the image of God humankind was created; male and female God created them. And God blessed them, and God said to them "Be fruitful and multiply, and fill the earth and subdue it; and have dominion over the fish of the sea and over the birds of the air and over every living thing that moves upon the earth." And God said, "Behold, I have given you every plant yielding seed which is upon the face of all the earth, and every tree with seed in its fruit; you shall have them for food.

"And to every beast of the earth, and to every bird of the air, and to everything that creeps on the earth, everything that has the breath of life, I have given every green plant for food." And it was so. And God saw everything that had been made, and behold, it was very good. And there was evening and there was morning, a sixth day.

Thus the heavens and the earth were finished, and all the host of them. And on the seventh day God finished the work which had been done, and God rested on the seventh day from all the work which God had done in creation.

READING II *Genesis 22:1–18*

After these things God tested Abraham, and said to him, "Abraham!" And he said, "Here am I." God said, "Take your son, your only son Isaac, whom you love, and go to the land of Moriah, and offer him there as a burnt offering upon one of the mountains of which I shall tell you." So Abraham rose early in the morning, saddled his donkey, and took two of his servants with him, and his son Isaac; and he cut the wood for the burnt offering, and arose and went to the place of which God had told him. On the third day Abraham lifted up his eyes and saw the place afar off. Then Abraham said to his servants, "Stay here with the donkey; I and the lad will go yonder and worship, and come again to you." And Abraham took the wood of the burnt offering, and laid it on Isaac his son; and he took in

his hand the fire and the knife. So they went both of them together. And Isaac said to his father Abraham, "My father!" And he said, "Here am I, my son." Isaac said, "Behold, the fire and the wood, but where is the lamb for a burnt offering?" Abraham said, "God will provide the lamb for a burnt offering to God, my son." So they went both of them together.

When they came to the place of which God had told him, Abraham built an altar there, and laid the wood in order, and bound Isaac his son and laid him on the altar, upon the wood. Then Abraham put forth his hand, and took the knife to slay his son. But the angel of the LORD called to him from heaven, and said, "Abraham, Abraham!" And he said, "Here am I." The angel said, "Do not lay your hand on the lad or do anything to him; for now I know that you fear God, seeing you have not withheld your son, your only son, from me." And Abraham lifted up his eyes and looked, and behold, behind him was a ram, caught in a thicket by its horns; and Abraham went and took the ram, and offered it up as a burnt offering instead of his son. So Abraham called the name of that place The LORD will provide, as it is said to this day, "On the mount of the LORD it shall be provided."

And the angel of the Lord called to Abraham a second time from heaven, and said, "By myself I have sworn, says the LORD, because you have done this, and have not withheld your son, your only son, I will indeed bless you, and I will multiply your descendants as the stars of heaven and as the sand which is on the seashore. And your descendants shall possess the gate of their enemies, and by your descendants shall all the nations of the earth bless themselves, because you have obeyed my voice."

READING III *Exodus 14:15 — 15:1*

The LORD said to Moses, "Why do you cry to me? Tell the people of Israel to go forward. Lift up your rod, and stretch out your hand over the sea and divide it, that the people of Israel may go on dry ground through the sea. And I will harden the hearts of the Egyptians so that they shall go in after them, and I will get glory over Pharaoh and all his host, his chariots, and his charioteers. And the Egyptians shall know that I am the LORD, when I have gotten glory over Pharaoh, his chariots, and his charioteers."

Then the angel of God who went before the host of Israel moved and went behind them; and the pillar of cloud moved from before them and stood behind them, coming between the host of Egypt and the host of Israel. And there was the cloud and the darkness; and the night passed without one coming near the other all night.

Then Moses stretched out his hand over the sea; and the LORD drove the sea back by a strong east wind all night, and made the sea dry land, and the waters were divided. And the people of Israel went into the midst of the sea on dry ground, the waters being a wall to them on their right hand and on their left. The Egyptians pursued, and went in after them into the midst of the sea, all Pharaoh's horses, his chariots, and his charioteers. And in the morning watch the LORD in the pillar of fire and of cloud looked down upon the host of the Egyptians, and discomfited the host of the Egyptians, clogging their chariot wheels so that they drove heavily; and the Egyptians said, "Let us flee from before Israel, for the LORD fights for them against the Egyptians."

The LORD said to Moses, "Stretch out your hand over the sea, that the water may come back upon the Egyptians, upon their chariots, and upon their charioteers." So Moses stretched forth his hand over the sea, and the sea returned to its wonted flow when the morning appeared; and the Egyptians fled into it, and the LORD routed the Egyptians in the midst of the sea. The waters returned and covered the chariots and the charioteers and all the host of Pharaoh that had followed them into the sea; not so much as one of them remained. But the people of Israel walked on dry ground through the sea, the waters being a wall to them on the right hand and on their left.

Thus the LORD saved Israel that day from the hand of the Egyptians; and Israel saw the Egyptians dead upon the seashore. And Israel saw the great work which the LORD did against the Egyptians, and the people feared the LORD; and they believed in the LORD and in Moses, the servant of the LORD.

Then Moses, Miriam and the people of Israel sang this song to the LORD, saying,

"I will sing to the LORD who has triumphed gloriously; the horse and its rider have been thrown into the sea."

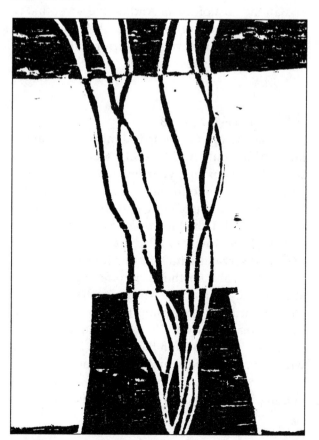

READING IV *Isaiah 54:5–14*

For your Maker is your husband,
    whose name is the LORD of hosts;
and the Holy One of Israel is your redeemer,
    who is called the God of the whole earth.
For the LORD has called you
    like a wife forsaken and grieved in spirit,
like a wife of youth when she is cast off,
    says your God.
For a brief moment I forsook you,
    But with great compassion I will gather you.
In overflowing wrath for a moment
    I hid my face from you,
but with everlasting love
    I will have compassion on you,
    says the LORD, your Redeemer.
For this is like the days of Noah to me:
    as I swore that the waters of Noah
    should no more go over the earth,
so I have sworn that I will not be angry with you
    and will not rebuke you.
For the mountains may depart
    and the hills be removed,
but my steadfast love shall not depart from you,
    and my covenant of peace shall not be removed,
    says the LORD, who has compassion on you.
"O afflicted one, storm-tossed and not comforted,
    behold, I will set your stones in antimony,
    and lay your foundations with sapphires.
I will make your pinnacles of agate,
    your gates of carbuncles,
    and all your wall of precious stones.
All your children shall be taught by the LORD,
    and great shall be the prosperity
    of your offspring.
In righteousness you shall be established;
    you shall be far from oppression,
    for you shall not fear;
    and from terror, for it shall not come near you.

READING V *Isaiah 55:1–11*

"Ho, every one who thirsts,
    come to the waters;
and whoever has no money,
    come, buy and eat!
Come, buy wine and milk
    without money and without price.
Why do you spend your money for that
    which is not bread,
    and your labor for that which does not satisfy?
Hearken diligently to me, and eat what is good,
    and delight yourselves in fatness.
Incline your ear, and come to me:
    hear, that your soul may live;
and I will make with you an everlasting covenant,
    my steadfast, sure love for David.
Behold, I made him a witness to the peoples,
    a leader and commander for the peoples.
Behold, you shall call nations that you know not,
    and nations that knew you not shall run to you,
because of the LORD your God,
    and of the Holy One of Israel,
    for the LORD had glorified you.
Seek the LORD while the LORD may be found,
    call upon God, while God is near;
let the wicked forsake their ways,
    and the unrighteous their thoughts;
let them return to the LORD, who will have mercy
    on them,
    and to our God, who will abundantly pardon.
For my thoughts are not your thoughts,
    neither are your ways my ways, says the LORD.
For as the heavens are higher than the earth,
    so are my ways higher than your ways
    and my thoughts than your thoughts.
For as the rain and the snow come down from
    heaven,
    and return not thither but water the earth,

making it bring forth and sprout,
  giving seed to the sower and bread to the eater,
so shall my word be that goes forth from my
    mouth;
  it shall not return to me empty,
but it shall accomplish that which I purpose,
  and prosper in the thing for which I sent it."

READING VI *Baruch 3:9–15, 32—4:4*

Hear the commandments of life, O Israel;
  give ear, and learn wisdom!
Why is it, O Israel, why is it that you are in the land
    of your enemies,
  that you are growing old in a foreign country,
that you are defiled with the dead,
  that you are counted among those in Hades?
You have forsaken the fountain of wisdom.
If you had walked in the way of God,
  you would be dwelling in peace for ever.
Learn where there is wisdom,
  where there is strength,
  where there is understanding,
that you may at the same time discern
  where there is length of days, and life,
  where there is light for the eyes, and peace.
Who has found the place of Wisdom?
  And who has entered her storehouses?
The one who knows all things knows her,
  and found her through understanding.
The one who prepared the earth for all time
  filled it with four-footed creatures;
the one who sends forth the light, and it goes,
  called it, and it harkened in fear;
the stars shone in their watches, and were glad;
  God called them, and they said, "Here we are!"
  They shone with gladness for the one
  who made them.

This is our God,
  with whom none other can be compared.
God found the whole way to knowledge,
  and gave her to Jacob, God's servant,
  and to Israel, the one whom God loved.
Afterward she appeared upon earth
  and lived among humankind.
She is the book of the commandments of God,
  and the law that endures for ever.
All who hold her fast will live,
  and those who forsake her will die.
Turn, O Jacob, and take her;
  walk toward the shining of her light.
Do not give your glory to another,
  or your advantages to an alien people.
Happy are we, O Israel,
  for we know that is pleasing to God.

READING VII *Ezekiel 36:16–28*

The word of the LORD came to me: "Son of man,
when the house of Israel dwelt in their own land,
they defiled it by their ways and their doings; their
conduct before me unclean. So I poured out my
wrath upon them for the blood which they had
shed in the land, for the idols with which they
defiled it. I scattered them among the nations, and
they were dispersed through the countries; in
accordance with their conduct and their deeds I
judged them. But when they came to the nations,
wherever they came, they profaned my holy name,
in that strangers said of them, 'These are the people
of the LORD, and yet they had to go out of God's
land.' But I had concern for my holy name, which
the house of Israel caused to be profaned among the
nations to which they came.

"Therefore say to the house of Israel, Thus says the LORD GOD: It is not for your sake, O house of Israel, that I am about to act, but for the sake of my holy name, which you have profaned among the nations to which you came. And I will vindicate the holiness of my great name, which has been profaned among the nations, and which you have profaned among them; and the nations will know that I am the LORD, says the LORD GOD, when through you I vindicate my holiness before their eyes. For I will take you from the nations, and gather you from all the countries, and bring you into your own land. I will sprinkle clean water upon you, and you shall be clean from all your uncleannesses, and from all your idols I will cleanse you. A new heart I will give you, and a new spirit I will put within you; and I will take out of your flesh the heart of stone and give you a heart of flesh. And I will put my spirit within you, and cause you to walk in my statutes and be careful to observe my ordinances. You shall dwell in the land which I gave to your ancestors; and you shall be my people, and I will be your God."

EPISTLE *Romans 6:3–11*

Do you not know that all of us who have been baptized into Christ Jesus were baptized into his death? We were buried therefore with Christ by baptism into death, so that as Christ was raised from the dead by the glory of the Father, we too might walk in newness of life.

For if we have been united with Christ in death, we shall certainly be united with Christ in resurrection. We know that our old self was crucified with Christ so that the sinful body might be destroyed, and we might no longer be enslaved to sin. For whoever has died is freed from sin. But if we have died with Christ, we believe that we shall also live with Christ. For we know that Christ being raised from the dead will never die again; death no longer has dominion over him. The death he died he died to sin, once for all, but the life he lives he lives to God. So you also must consider yourselves dead to sin and alive to God in Christ Jesus.

GOSPEL *Luke 24:1–12*

On the first day of the week, at early dawn, the women went to the tomb, taking the spices which they had prepared. And they found the stone rolled away from the tomb, but when they went in they did not find the body. While they were perplexed about this, behold, two men stood by them in dazzling apparel; and as the women were frightened and bowed their faces to the ground, the men said to them, "Why do you seek the living among the dead? Remember how he told you, while he was still in Galilee, that the Man of Heaven must be delivered into the hands of sinners, and be crucified, and on the third day rise." And the women remembered his words, and returning from the tomb they told all this to the eleven and to all the rest. Now it was Mary Magdalene and Joanna and Mary the mother of James and the other women with them who told this to the apostles; but these words seemed to the apostles an idle tale, and they did not believe them. But Peter rose and ran to the tomb; stooping and looking in, he saw the linen cloths by themselves; and he went home wondering what had happened.

READING I *Acts 10:34, 37–43*

Peter opened his mouth and said: "You know the word which God sent to Israel, preaching good news of peace by Jesus Christ (who is Lord of all), the word which was proclaimed throughout all Judea, beginning from Galilee after the baptism which John preached: how God anointed Jesus of Nazareth with the Holy Spirit and with power; how Jesus went about doing good and healing all that were oppressed by the devil, for God was with him. And we are witnesses to all that Jesus did both in the country of the Judeans and in Jerusalem. They put him to death by hanging him on a tree; but God raised Jesus on the third day and made him manifest; not to all the people but to us who were chosen by God as witnesses, who ate and drank with Jesus after he rose from the dead. And Jesus commanded us to preach to the people, and to testify that he is the one ordained by God to be judge of the living and the dead. To this Jesus all the prophets bear witness that every one who believes in him receives forgiveness of sins through his name."

READING II *Colossians 3:1–4*

If then you have been raised with Christ, seek the things that are above, where Christ is, seated at the right hand of God. Set your minds on things that are above, not on things that are on earth. For you have died, and your life is hid with Christ in God. When Christ who is our life appears, then you also will appear with him in glory.

[Alternate reading: 1 Corinthians 5:6–8.]

GOSPEL *John 20:1–9*

Now on the first day of the week Mary Magdalene came to the tomb early, while it was still dark, and saw that the stone had been taken away from the tomb. So she ran, and went to Simon Peter and the other disciple, the one whom Jesus loved, and said to them, "They have taken the Lord out of the tomb, and we do not know where they have laid him." Peter then came out with the other disciple, and they went toward the tomb. They both ran, but the other disciple outran Peter and reached the tomb first; and stooping to look in, he saw the linen cloths lying there, but did not go in. Then Simon Peter came, following him, and went into the tomb; he saw the linen cloths lying, and the napkin, which had been on Jesus' head, not lying with the linen cloths but rolled up in a place by itself. Then the other disciple, who reached the tomb first, also went in, and he saw and believed; for as yet they did not know the scripture, that Jesus must rise from the dead.

[Alternate reading for evening Mass: Luke 24:13–35.]

R E F L E C T I O N

Light and darkness are often-used symbols in John's gospel. So it is no coincidence that John has Mary Magdalene coming to the tomb "while it was still dark" (related to the noun *skotia*, meaning darkness, an atmosphere of obscurity). Yet Mary saw (*blepo*, actual sight, often contrasted with being blind), and what she saw caused her to run (*trecho*, to hasten, expressing both eagerness and urgency). Mary saw that the stone had been taken away, but she erroneously interpreted what she saw. Peter and the other disciple ran to the tomb, and the disciple saw (*blepo* again) the linen cloths without entering the tomb. Peter went in and saw the linens and the head covering. Then the other disciple went in, saw, and believed.

Clearly, there is an intentional progression. An initial sight pierces the obscurity just enough to let Mary know that things are not as they were; then there is an opening and a clearer view, an entering in, and a widening of the scope of vision. Finally, there is the sight that makes sense out of all the pieces, the sight that leads to belief.

This whole event, which begins in darkness, ushers in for John a series of seeings (Mary and the "gardener," the assembled disciples, Thomas) that will blossom into faith. These seeings are the culmination of the many signs and are the last of those recorded.

John's gospel is very clear about Jesus being sent from the Father and that the signs and wonders he effects are sparks to kindle the belief that Jesus is the Messiah, the Son of God. While we all will die, today's gospel proclaims that through believing in the living presence of Jesus the Christ, one receives life. But the gospel narrative is in no way a "proof" of the resurrection; rather, it is a testimony to the faith of the disciples that Jesus indeed lives.

■ **Read a parallel account of this event in Luke 24:1–11. What differences do you see? What similarities?**

■ **How do you think "Jesus lives"? Is the true life Jesus promised only to be found in the "afterlife"?**

PRACTICE OF FAITH

ALLELUIA. Rejoice, Christ is risen from the dead! Today we exalt in Christ's triumph and share in his life. It is time to bring out all that we put aside during Lent. Did you bury an Alleluia banner before Ash Wednesday? If you did, resurrect it with great celebration, song and flourish. If you did not bury one, make one today that can be at the center of your table throughout these days of Easter joy. The fast is over, prepare the feast! Gather with friends and family for a festive meal or picnic. If possible, include one of the former catechumens (now called neophytes, from the Greek word meaning "a young plant") or one of the candidates. Conclude the day with Evening Prayer, which can be found in this book, and be sure to include many sung Alleluias!

PRACTICE OF HOPE

JESUS ROSE FROM THE DEAD. One Easter morning, a friend shared with me a nightmare she had had the night before. In the dream she was on a stage. In one corner she was raped, then thrown to another corner and raped again. The violations happened repeatedly, and she woke up sobbing and shaking with terror.

But a feeling of deep reassurance enveloped her as she identified the message of the dream: She was experiencing the Stations of the Cross. The horror began to melt as she understood that Jesus too was a victim of her rape two years earlier. He had already borne her pain and carried it to the cross. Through the scars, resurrection was breaking through.

PRACTICE OF CHARITY

MARY MAGDALENE CAME TO THE TOMB EARLY. Mary Magdalene went to look for Jesus among the dead. She misunderstood what he had said before his death and did what we have a tendency to do in our own lives: look for the living among the dead. Despair, cynicism, anxiety and fear can keep us "among the tombs." But our God is longing to refresh us with divine life. How can we experience this? In part, by allowing others to wash our feet and by doing the same in return. This week as we celebrate Easter, walk among the living. Allow people to nourish you, and in turn nourish others with a life-giving spirit.

WEEKDAY READINGS Acts 2:14—4:21

EASTERTIME

Christ is risen! Christ is truly risen!

Give thanks, the Lord is good,
"God is lasting love!"
Now let Israel say,
"God is lasting love!"

I was pushed to falling,
but the Lord gave me help.
My strength, my song is the Lord,
who has become my savior.

I shall not die but live
to tell the Lord's great deeds.
The Lord punished me severely,
but did not let me die.

The stone the builders rejected
has become the cornerstone.
This is the work of the Lord,
how wonderful in our eyes.

This is the day the Lord made,
let us rejoice and be glad.
Lord, give us the victory!
Lord, grant us success!

Blest is the one who comes,
who comes in the name of the Lord.
We bless you from the Lord's house.
The Lord God is our light:
adorn the altar with branches.

—Psalm 118:1–2, 13–14, 17–18, 22–27

The heavens rumble alleluias,
earth dances to the tune
and the wail of the graves
itself becomes song.
All are singing with you, savior God,
at this wedding feast
for you have turned the world around,
inside out and upside down.
Now the homeless are at home
and the martyred embrace their assassins
and the rulers and bosses wonder
whose world this is after all.
After all, let us stand and sing
with the heavens and earth and the graves
and so proclaim that we live now only
in Christ who is Lord for ever and ever.

—Prayer of the Season

READING I *Acts 5:12–16*

Many signs and wonders were done among the people by the hands of the apostles. And they were all together in Solomon's Portico. None of the rest dared join the apostles, but the people held them in high honor. And more than ever believers were added to the Lord, multitudes both of men and women, so that they even carried out the sick into the streets, and laid them on beds and pallets, that as Peter came by at least his shadow might fall on some of them. The people also gathered from the towns around Jerusalem, bringing the sick and those afflicted with unclean spirits, and they were all healed.

READING II *Revelation 1:9–11, 12–13, 17–19*

I, John, your brother, who share with you in Jesus the tribulation and the dominion and the patient endurance, was on the island called Patmos on account of the word of God and the testimony of Jesus. I was in the Spirit on the Lord's day, and I heard behind me a loud voice like a trumpet saying, "Write what you see in a book, and send it to the seven churches."

Then I turned to see the voice that was speaking to me, and on turning I saw seven golden lampstands, and in the midst of the lampstands a figure like a human being, clothed with a long robe and with a golden belt round his breast.

When I saw this figure, I fell at his feet as though dead. But he laid his right hand on me, saying, "Fear not, I am the first and the last, and the living one; I died, and behold I am alive for evermore, and I have the keys of Death and Hades. Now write what you see, what is and what is to take place hereafter."

GOSPEL *John 20:19–31*

On the evening of that day, the first day of the week, the doors being shut where the disciples were, for fear of the Judeans, Jesus came and stood among them and said to them, "Peace be with you." Having said this, Jesus showed them his hands and his side. Then the disciples were glad when they saw the Lord. Jesus said to them again, "Peace be with you. As the Father has sent me, even so I send you." Having said this, Jesus breathed on them, and said to them, "Receive the Holy Spirit. If you forgive the sins of any, they are forgiven; if you retain the sins of any, they are retained."

Now Thomas, one of the twelve, called the Twin, was not with them when Jesus came. So the other disciples told Thomas, "We have seen the Lord." But he said to them, "Unless I see in his hands the print of the nails, and place my finger in the mark of the nails, and place my hand in his side, I will not believe."

Eight days later, Jesus' disciples were again in the house, and Thomas was with them. The doors were shut, but Jesus came and stood among them, and said, "Peace be with you." Then Jesus said to Thomas, "Put your finger here, and see my hands; and put out your hand, and place it in my side; do not be faithless, but believing." Thomas answered Jesus, "My Lord and my God!" Jesus said to him, "Have you believed because you have seen me? Blessed are those who have not seen and yet believe."

Now Jesus did many other signs in the presence of the disciples, which are not written in this book; but these are written that you may believe that Jesus is the Christ, the Son of God, and that believing you may have life in his name.

fear + doubt
forgiveness
seeing

R E F L E C T I O N

John's resurrection narratives focus on the unity of the resurrection, the ascension, and the coming of the Spirit. Today's gospel tells of two post-resurrection appearances. The first involves the giving of the Spirit and the second is of the strengthening of Thomas' faith. The final section (verses 30–31) forms the conclusion to John's gospel and is a statement of his purpose in writing it.

In the first segment, John highlights the contrast between the fear of the disciples gathered behind closed doors as evening sets in and their joy when Jesus stands in their midst. The core of this section is the sending of the disciples. John distinguishes, however, between the way the Father has sent Jesus (*apostello*, which emphasizes the source of Jesus' authority in the Father) and the way Jesus sends his disciples (*pempo*, which focuses on the action of sending). The Holy Spirit is then given to the disciples to carry on the saving work of Jesus. This sending, and its connection to forgiveness (*aphiemi*, to let go, release) and retention, are gifts entrusted *to the community* of disciples. Throughout this passage, it is a group of disciples that is present when Jesus appears. The community of Jesus' disciples is to bear witness to the centrality of forgiveness.

The second portion has to do with Thomas, "one of the Twelve," and illustrates the difference between seeing as an eyewitness and seeing as recognition and understanding. The same verb, *horao*, is used for both kinds of seeing. Not all can be eyewitnesses to Jesus' signs, like the first disciples. But no less blessed are those who believe in Jesus because they recognize (see) the signs recorded in the gospels.

■ **Read Matthew 18:15–20 and compare it with John's account here of forgiveness of sin within the community. Matthew speaks of the process of forgiveness, and the text is closely related to this gospel, which names forgiveness as an Easter gift to the community of the disciples.**

■ **Is mutual forgiveness an important element within your family and within your parish community? How is it expressed in each group?**

■ **Read Acts 5:12–32 (a longer version of our first reading), which relates (in v. 31) to the gospel account and the importance of the forgiveness of sins in Jesus' mission. Do you know of any families or communities that are torn apart by long-standing grudges? How forgiving are you of those who have hurt you?**

PRACTICE OF FAITH

SAINT OF PEACE. On Saturday, we will celebrate the feast of a great saint who worked for peace within the church, Catherine of Siena. Catherine's deeply mystical relationship with Jesus began in her childhood after a vision at the age of six. Catherine's holiness and teaching became so renowned that many noted theologians traveled to Siena to attempt to prove her a fake. However, by the time they left, Catherine had become their teacher! Catherine is remembered in history for her successful efforts to have Pope Gregory XI move from Avignon in France back to Rome. She left records of her mystical experiences in a volume called the *Dialogue*. Catherine is one of only two women who have been declared Doctors of the church.

PRACTICE OF HOPE

PEACE BE WITH YOU. In Transylvania County, North Carolina, a man threatened a woman's life because he believed she was trying to turn his daughter against him. A warrant for his arrest was issued. Ordinarily this case would have gone to an already overloaded court system, which would proclaim a "winner" and a "loser" and likely intensify the bitter feelings and escalate the conflict.

But since October 1989, such cases have often wound up at the Transylvania Dispute Settlement Center, where trained volunteer mediators help conflicting parties talk through their concerns at no financial cost to them. In this case, after two and a half hours of conversation, apologies were made by both parties, the warrant was dropped, and an agreement was reached about settling future problems. The settlement center, one of 18 in the state, is part of a growing nationwide movement.

PRACTICE OF CHARITY

THEY WERE ALL HEALED. *Healing* does not always mean the same thing as physical *curing*. Many times, healing takes place when a person who is ill or disabled is welcomed into the community as a brother or sister. Jesus knew this. He not only physically cured people, he also healed people; he brought them back into the community. St. Coletta's of Illinois is concerned with healing. St. Coletta's enables people with developmental disabilities to reach their full potential with dignity. Through a job training center, a residential program and two children's centers, St. Coletta's of Illinois is making it possible for persons with disabilities to have brighter futures in our society. To receive more information, to volunteer or to make a donation, contact: St. Coletta's of Illinois, 123rd and Wolf Road, Palos Park IL 60464; 708-448-6520.

WEEKDAY READINGS Acts 4:23–31; 1 Peter 5:5–14; (We–Sa) Acts 5:17—6:7

READING I *Acts 5:27–32, 40–41*

The high priest questioned the apostles, saying, "We strictly charged you not to teach in this name, yet here you have filled Jerusalem with your teaching and you intend to bring this man's blood upon us." But Peter and the apostles answered, "It is God rather than human beings whom we must obey. The God of our forebears raised Jesus whom you killed by hanging him on a tree. God exalted this Jesus at the right hand of Power as Leader and Savior, to give repentance to Israel and forgiveness of sins. And we are witnesses to these things, and so is the Holy Spirit who has been given to those who obey God."

The officers beat the apostles and charged them not to speak in the name of Jesus, and let them go. Then the apostles left the presence of the council, rejoicing that they were counted worthy to suffer dishonor for the name.

READING II *Revelation 5:11–14*

I looked, and I heard around the throne and the living creatures and the elders the voice of many angels, numbering myriads of myriads and thousands of thousands, saying with a loud voice, "Worthy is the Lamb who was slain, to receive power and wealth and wisdom and might and honor and glory and blessing!" And I heard every creature in heaven and on earth and under the earth and in the sea, and all therein, saying, "To the one who sits upon the throne and to the Lamb be blessing and honor and glory and might for ever and ever!" And the four living creatures said, "Amen!" and the elders fell down and worshiped.

GOSPEL *John 21:1–14*

Jesus revealed himself again to the disciples by the Sea of Tiberias in this way. Simon Peter, Thomas called the Twin, Nathanael of Cana in Galilee, the sons of Zebedee, and two others of Jesus' disciples were together. Simon Peter said to them, "I am going fishing." They said to him, "We will go with you." They went out and got into the boat; but that night they caught nothing.

Just as day was breaking, Jesus stood on the beach; yet the disciples did not know that it was Jesus. Jesus said to them, "Children, have you any fish?" They answered him, "No." Jesus said to them, "Cast the net on the right side of the boat, and you will find some." So they cast it, and now they were not able to haul it in, for the quantity of fish. That disciple whom Jesus loved said to Peter, "It is the Lord!" When Simon Peter heard that it was the Lord, he put on his clothes, for he was stripped for work, and sprang into the sea. But the other disciples came in the boat, dragging the net full of fish, for they were not far from the land, but about a hundred yards off.

When they got out on land, they saw a charcoal fire there, with fish lying on it, and bread. Jesus said to them, "Bring some of the fish that you have just caught." So Simon Peter went aboard and hauled the net ashore, full of large fish, a hundred and fifty-three of them; and although there were so many, the net was not torn. Jesus said to them, "Come and have breakfast." Now none of the disciples dared ask him, "Who are you?" They knew it was the Lord. Jesus came and took the bread and gave it to them, and so with the fish. This was now the third time that Jesus was revealed to the disciples after having been raised from the dead.

[Complete reading: John 21:1–19]

forgiveness

R E F L E C T I O N

All of John 21 is an addition to the Gospel of John that probably originated in a later Johannine community. It seems to have been an editor's attempt to reconcile Johannine communities with other Christian churches that gave Peter a leading role. The narrative itself is actually a tapestry of disparate elements, woven together around Peter as the unifying thread.

The author/editor has captured the Johannine symbolism of contrasting night (when the disciples fished without a catch) and daybreak (with its abundant haul and the presence of Jesus). The text refers to this as the third time Jesus revealed himself after having been raised from the dead. The miraculous catch of fish is also a reminder of another miracle by the sea of Tiberias (see Matthew 14:13 – 21; Mark 6:32 – 44; Luke 9:10 – 17; John 6:1 – 15); the breakfast reflects the practice of the ritual meal of the Christian communities.

Of particular significance in this sign, however, is the central role given to Peter. He initiates the fishing trip, he impetuously leaps into the water, and it is he who hauls the net ashore. Finally, in verses 15 – 19, Peter and Jesus engage in the dialogue intended by the author to highlight the key role of Peter within many Christian communities.

The dominant theme in the question and answer about Peter's love is that forgiveness is the cornerstone of the Christian faith. Even denial is forgiven if it is followed by repentance, a deep inner confession of love and the readiness to stretch out one's hands to be carried where one would prefer not to go. This first portion of the epilogue reflects the conviction of the late first century Christian communities that Jesus lives and works wonders in and through these communities. It reflects the faith that Jesus lives to provide food and forgiveness and to prepare those who believe for the hardships to come.

■ **Peter, graced as he was, had denied knowing Jesus. Yet even this is forgiven. Reflect on the fact that the ability to forgive is a gift we must ask for in prayer.**

■ **When others speak of retaliation or revenge, how can you express your faith in the importance of healing and forgiveness?**

■ **Is it by chance that the account of the forgiveness of Peter is placed alongside the story of the meal prepared by Jesus? How does this narrative relate to our shared communion?**

PRACTICE OF FAITH

WORTHY IS THE LAMB. There are many ancient homilies and poems that exalt Jesus as the Lamb of God. Here is part of a second century homily on Easter written by Melito of Sardis:

Born as Son, led like a lamb.
Sacrificed like a sheep, buried as a man
he rises from the dead as God,
being by nature both God and man.
He is all things: when he judges, he is law;
when he teaches, Word; when he saves, grace;
when he begets, father; when he is begotten, son;
when he suffers, lamb; when he is buried, man;
when he rises, God. Such is Jesus Christ!
To him be glory forever! Amen.

PRACTICE OF HOPE

WE MUST OBEY GOD. In the summer of 1993, Pastors for Peace sponsored a caravan taking food, medicine and other supplies to Cuba. The caravan was in direct violation of the U.S. embargo against that country, but Pastors for Peace believed the embargo created immense suffering for the Cuban people.

Eighty-nine of the vehicles in the caravan were allowed into Mexico. But the last one, a school bus driven by Pastors for Peace founder Rev. Lucius Walker, was stopped at the border by U.S. Customs agents. He and his 13 passengers held a hunger strike, which lasted 23 days. Supporters in 40 cities and four countries held demonstrations to demand the release of the bus. Eventually, the U.S. Treasury Department declared the supplies on the bus to be humanitarian aid rather than illegal export, and the effort went forward.

PRACTICE OF CHARITY

COME AND HAVE BREAKFAST. Think about your schedule this week. Do you find yourself with little or no time because of your commitments? Do you wonder if it will be Thanksgiving before the family will sit down together for a non-microwaved meal? Jesus gave a simple invitation to the disciples: Come and share a meal together. What a wonderful practice of charity! Imagine your family setting aside an evening a week to share a meal—no meetings, no work, no soccer practice, no television. Just a time for family; or, if you live alone, a time for friends to gather and share life. Take the calendar and set the date. Make it a sacred time.

WEEKDAY READINGS **Acts 6:8 – 15; 7:51 — 8:1; 1 Corinthians 15:1 – 8; (Th – Sa) Acts 8:26 — 9:42**

READING I *Acts 13:14, 43–52*

Paul and his company passed on from Perga and came to Antioch of Pisidia. And on the sabbath day they went into the synagogue and sat down.

And when the meeting of the synagogue broke up, many Jewish people and devout converts to Judaism followed Paul and Barnabas, who spoke to them and urged them to continue in the grace of God.

The next sabbath almost the whole city gathered together to hear the word of God. But when the Jewish people saw the multitudes, they were filled with jealousy, and contradicted what was spoken by Paul, and reviled him. And Paul and Barnabas spoke out boldly, saying, "It was necessary that the word of God should be spoken first to you. Since you thrust it from you, and judge yourselves unworthy of eternal life, behold, we turn to the Gentiles. For so the Lord has commanded us, saying,

'I have set you to be a light for the Gentiles,
that you may bring salvation
to the uttermost parts of the earth.' "

And when the Gentiles heard this, they were glad and glorified the word of God; and as many as were appointed to eternal life believed. And the word of the Lord spread throughout all the region. But some of the Jewish people incited the devout women of high standing and the leading men of the city, and stirred up persecution against Paul and Barnabas, and drove them out of their district. But Paul and Barnabas shook off the dust from their feet against them, and went to Iconium. And the disciples were filled with joy and with the Holy Spirit.

READING II *Revelation 7:9, 14–17*

I looked, and behold, [I saw] a great multitude which no one could number, from every nation, from all tribes and peoples and tongues, standing before the throne and before the Lamb, clothed in white robes, with palm branches in their hands.

Then one of the elders said to me, "These are they who have come out of the great tribulation; they have washed their robes and made them white in the blood of the Lamb.

"Therefore are they before the throne of God,
worshiping day and night within the temple;
and the one who sits upon the throne
will overshadow them.
They shall hunger no more, neither thirst any more;
the sun shall not strike them,
nor any scorching heat.
For the Lamb in the midst of the throne
will be their shepherd,
and will guide them to springs of living water;
and God will wipe away every tear from
their eyes."

GOSPEL *John 10:27–30*

[At that time Jesus said,] "My sheep hear my voice, and I know them, and they follow me; and I give them eternal life, and they shall never perish, and no one shall snatch them out of my hand. My Father, who has given them to me, is greater than all, and no one is able to snatch them out of the Father's hand. I and the Father are one."

faith as gift

REFLECTION

This short reading from John's gospel must be read within its larger context. Prior to this reading, opposition to Jesus had been mounting, resulting in attempts to trap him: The woman taken in adultery was used as a ploy to provoke Jesus into words that would contradict the Law of Moses (8:2–11); Jesus had recently cured a man born blind (9:1–41); and opposition to Jesus erupted in the portico of Solomon when the Judeans challenged Jesus to state openly who he really was, and Jesus replied that his actions speak for him (10:22–26). The present chapter began with the metaphors of shepherd, sheep and gate. The brief passage given us today is at once a summing up of the shepherd metaphor and a clear repetition of Jesus' claim to be one with the Father.

Only those who are already followers (sheep) are capable of recognizing in Jesus' works the witness to who he is. Belonging is a condition for being able to hear; belonging is a prerequisite for belief. The sheep metaphor has nothing to do with the personality traits of sheep; it is the relationship between shepherd and sheep (they belong together), and among sheep as a flock (community), that is hidden in this image.

This passage exposes one of the deepest mysteries of the human spirit. Faith, the ability to hear and to follow a call, is a gift: It is a gift to Jesus and a gift to the followers of Jesus. Due to his claim of being one with the Father, Jesus would once again face the threat of stoning (10:31–39). Why are some capable of the hearing that leads to faith? Why are some capable of recognizing the Father in the works of Jesus? The only answer presented is that faith is a gift. But why is it given to some and not to others? This gospel passage has no answer to that troubling question.

■ Read Acts 13:15–33, which repeats the observation that mere membership in a faith community does not guarantee either faith or the ability to recognize the one sent by God. In what ways are you content as a faithful churchgoer? In what areas of your life are you ready to meet the challenges of new insights and different outlooks as possible gifts and signs of salvation?

■ If your ideas and ways of being a Christian and a disciple are just as they were some years ago, is this a sign of stability or stagnation? How can you discern this?

■ Luke's favored image for discipleship is that of a journey. Does that image make sense for you? What images of discipleship do you have?

PRACTICE OF FAITH

MARY AND ALL MOTHERS. By long tradition, May has been a month to honor Mary. Many prepare a special flower-decorated shrine to honor Mary in their homes. Next Sunday, in addition to the honor we offer Mary, we honor all mothers. Here is a prayer from *Catholic Household Blessings and Prayers* to pray with and for your mother next Sunday:

Loving God,
as a mother gives life and nourishment
   to her children,
so you watch over your church.
Bless our mother.
Let the example of her faith and love shine forth.
Grant that we, her family,
may honor her always
with a spirit of profound respect.
Grant this through Christ our Lord. Amen.

PRACTICE OF HOPE

I GIVE THEM ETERNAL LIFE. A 32-year-old man was dying of AIDS. Disfigured and almost blind, he scanned the room every time he awoke to see if he was alone. He always smiled when he saw friends keeping vigil with him. One of them asked, "What do you think heaven is like?" He replied, "It's either wonderful, or nothing at all."

The friends surrounding his bed were quiet, taken aback. Then he smiled again and said, "My friend George died two years ago. He came to see me today. And he said it's very wonderful.... Yes, I believe it is wonderful."

PRACTICE OF CHARITY

THEY SHALL HUNGER NO MORE. We live in a world where the vast majority of people hunger, not just for food, but for employment, health, justice, education, dignity and peace. This reality is so overwhelming that it seems easier to just pull the shade down on the outside world, hoping it goes away. However, doing so would make us part of the problem; when people stand silently behind their walls, suffering continues to grow. This is not what Easter calls us to do. Catholic Relief Services works to spread the hopeful message of Easter. Its mission is to alleviate suffering and provide hope and compassionate assistance throughout the world. The wonderful component of this is that you know your contribution reaches those in need; over 94% of your contribution goes directly to CRS programs. To make a gift of hope, write: Catholic Relief Services, PO Box 17090, Baltimore MD 21298-9664. Or call 410-625-2220.

WEEKDAY READINGS **Acts, chapters 11–13**

READING I *Acts 14:21–27*

Paul and Barnabas returned to Lystra and to Iconium and to Antioch, strengthening the souls of the disciples, exhorting them to continue in the faith, and saying that through many tribulations we must enter the dominion of God. And when they had appointed elders for them in every church, with prayer and fasting they committed them to the Lord in whom they believed.

Then they passed through Pisidia, and came to Pamphylia. And when they had spoken the word in Perga, they went down to Attalia; and from there they sailed to Antioch, where they had been commended to the grace of God for the work which they had fulfilled. And when they arrived, they gathered the church together and declared all that God had done with them, and how God had opened a door of faith to the Gentiles.

READING II *Revelation 21:1–5*

Then I saw a new heaven and a new earth; for the first heaven and the first earth had passed away, and the sea was no more. And I saw the holy city, new Jerusalem, coming down out of heaven from God, prepared as a bride adorned for her husband; and I heard a loud voice from the throne saying, "Behold, the dwelling of God is with humankind. God will dwell with them, and they shall be God's people, and that very God will be with them and will wipe away every tear from their eyes, and death shall be no more, neither shall there be mourning nor crying nor pain any more, for the former things have passed away."

And the one who sat upon the throne said, "Behold, I make all things new."

GOSPEL *John 13:31–35*

When Judas had gone out, Jesus said, "Now is the Man of Heaven glorified, in whom God is glorified; if in the Man of Heaven God is glorified, God will also glorify him in God's very self, and that at once. Little children, yet a little while I am with you. A new commandment I give to you, that you love one another; even as I have loved you, that you also love one another. By this every one will know that you are my disciples, if you have love for one another."

love one another

REFLECTION

John's is the only gospel that does not record the ritual blessing of the cup and sharing of the bread at the Last Supper. Instead, it tells of a ritual washing of feet, the paradigm for the attitude that the disciples would be called on to express in action. Jesus addresses his disciples in words that are used only here in the gospels: "little children" (*teknia*, you who are part of me, close to me). The betrayal by one of his disciples, one of his *teknia*, ignited the searing coals of sadness and dread that would be heaped on Jesus during the long hours of his exodus. John conveys both this sense of dread as well as the determination of Jesus to walk into that hour of darkness.

It is important to keep in mind all of the events that preceded those in today's gospel. It is also important to review them in order to understand the significance of the new commandment that Jesus presents. Having experienced the growing opposition of the religious leaders and having experienced the bitterness of being betrayed, Jesus insists on the necessity of mutual love. This reciprocal love will be the mark by which disciples will be known, the canon by which they will be measured. This *agape*, in its classical Greek origins, denotes an active, unselfish love. As the hour of testing approaches, Jesus leaves the clearest and yet most difficult commandment with the community of his disciples: the law of *agape*.

■ We have no custom of footwashing in our culture. Can you think of a contemporary form of service that would capture the depth of the attitude Jesus teaches here? In your family, community or workplace, what are the ways in which you see this kind of service in action?

■ John uses this narrative as an alternate to the accounts of the Last Supper in the synoptics. How do you experience this connection between the eucharist and service in your life? How does your parish, as a community, make this connection?

PRACTICE OF FAITH SAN ISIDRO. Tomorrow, Catholics throughout the Southwest will keep the feast of a beloved saint, San Isidro, patron of farmers and all who work the land. Isidro was born in Madrid and worked as a hired laborer on an estate outside the city. Though he was impoverished himself, he and his wife, Santa Maria de la Cabeza, shared generously with others in greater need. Many miracles have been attributed to him, both during his life and since his death on May 15, 1130. In honor of San Isidro, bless your garden this week and pray for those who, like Isidro, labor to bring forth food from the earth.

PRACTICE OF HOPE LOVE ONE ANOTHER. Rev. Fred Craddock tells the story of an 11-year-old boy who underwent chemotherapy treatment for cancer. When the time came for him to return to school, he and his parents experimented with wigs, hats and bandanas to try to conceal his hair loss. They finally settled on a baseball cap, but the boy still feared the taunts he might receive for looking "different." Mustering up his courage, he went to school wearing his cap — only to discover that all of his friends had shaved their heads.

PRACTICE OF CHARITY THEY GATHERED THE CHURCH TOGETHER. Most of us have some definition of church that we most frequently rely on. To some it is the building on the corner, to others it is their local faith community, and to a few it is whoever is a member of the Body of Christ. To be truly catholic in our understanding of church, we must include not only our local community gathered around the bishop but also our brothers and sisters all over the world. There must be a sense of being in communion with the local churches throughout the world. The Catholic Near East Welfare Association was established to assist the pastoral work of the Eastern Catholic Churches and to bring humanitarian aid to those in need in 28 regions, including India, northeast Africa and eastern Europe. To help in this work of compassion, write or call: Catholic Near East Welfare Association, 1011 First Avenue, New York NY 10022-4195; 212-826-1480.

WEEKDAY READINGS **Acts 14:5 — 16:10**

99

READING I *Acts 15:1–2, 22–29*

Some people having come down from Judea were teaching the community, "Unless you are circumcised according to the custom of Moses, you cannot be saved." And when Paul and Barnabas had no small dissension and debate with them, Paul and Barnabas and some of the others were appointed to go up to Jerusalem to the apostles and the elders about this question.

Then it seemed good to the apostles and the elders, with the whole church, to choose men from among them and send them to Antioch with Paul and Barnabas. They sent Judas called Barsabbas, and Silas, leading men within the community, with the following letter: "The community of the apostles and the elders, to the community among the Gentiles in Antioch and Syria and Cilicia, greeting. Since we have heard that some persons from us have troubled you with words, unsettling your minds, although we gave them no instructions, it has seemed good to us, having come to one accord, to choose men and send them to you with our beloved Barnabas and Paul, who both have risked their lives for the sake of our Lord Jesus Christ. We have therefore sent Judas and Silas, who themselves will tell you the same things by word of mouth. For it has seemed good to the Holy Spirit and to us to lay upon you no greater burden than these necessary things: that you abstain from what has been sacrificed to idols and from blood and from what is strangled and from unchastity. If you keep yourselves from these, you will do well. Farewell."

READING II *Revelation 21:10–14, 22–23*

In the Spirit the angel carried me away to a great, high mountain, and showed me the holy city Jerusalem coming down out of heaven from God, having the glory of God, its radiance like a most rare jewel, like a jasper, clear as crystal. It had a great, high wall, with twelve gates, and at the gates twelve angels, and on the gates the names of the twelve tribes of the children of Israel were inscribed; on the east three gates, on the north three gates, on the south three gates, and on the west three gates. And the wall of the city had twelve foundations, and on them the twelve names of the twelve apostles of the Lamb.

And I saw no temple in the city, for its temple is the Lord God the Almighty and the Lamb. And the city has no need of sun or moon to shine upon it, for the glory of God is its light, and its lamp is the Lamb.

GOSPEL *John 14:23–29*

Jesus said, "They who love me will keep my word, and my Father will love them, and we will come to them and make our home with them. They who do not love me do not keep my words; and the word which you hear is not mine but the Father's who sent me.

"These things I have spoken to you, while I am still with you. But the Counselor, the Holy Spirit, whom the Father will send in my name, will teach you all things, and bring to your remembrance all that I have said to you. Peace I leave with you; my peace I give to you; not as the world gives do I give to you. Let not your hearts be troubled, neither let them be afraid. You heard me say to you, 'I go away, and I will come to you.' If you loved me, you would have rejoiced, because I go to the Father; for the Father is greater than I. And now I have told you before it takes place, so that when it does take place, you may believe."

Thursday, May 25, 1995 (U.S.A.)
Sunday, May 28, 1995 (CANADA)

THE ASCENSION OF THE LORD

Acts 1:1–11 *Why stand staring at the skies?*

Ephesians 1:17–23 *The fullness of Christ has filled the universe.*

Luke 24:46–53 *You are witnesses of all this.*

R E F L E C T I O N

This passage from John's gospel, a prelude to the Ascension, is taken from the last discourse of Jesus as he prepared his disciples for the trauma of his departure. The reading may be divided into two sections.

The first section explains the connection between loving Jesus and keeping his word. But it is not just Jesus' word; it is the word given to him by the Father. Reference to the Father and Jesus abiding with those who obey is an example of John's "realized eschatology": The day of salvation, the end time, is already here (realized). Salvation is to be found in this world, at this hour, among those who hear the word and follow where it leads.

The second section focuses on the role of the Spirit. As an advocate, the Spirit will teach and remind the disciples of all they need to know. The advocate brings no new teaching, nor does the advocate create fantasies of what has never happened; the role of the Spirit is to bring to light the teachings of Jesus that have not yet been understood. The role of the Spirit is to prod recall, to provoke a sleeping memory.

Another role of the Spirit is that of public defender, counselor to Christians who are fearful and troubled in the face of opposition. The image given in this passage is of a group of disciples facing the same committed opposition that confronted Jesus. They will not be alone to face this opposition but will be defended, strengthened and made peaceful by the Spirit sent by the Father in Jesus' name.

■ **Do you find the images of a dove, fire and wind useful in helping you perceive the Spirit as a personal, dynamic presence? What are your personal images of the Spirit? What draws you to these images? In what ways do you experience the action of the Spirit in your life?**

■ **A careful reading of the texts will reveal that the Spirit is given to *the community*. In what direction have you experienced the Spirit moving within your community? How has this been done?**

PRACTICE OF FAITH

HOLY SPIRIT. The church has always acknowledged that its guide is the Holy Spirit. The account from Acts recounts that first gathering of the leaders of the church to collectively discern what seemed "good to the Holy Spirit and to us." Since then, there have been dozens of councils to determine important church matters. The last council, held in the Vatican, was concluded thirty years ago this year. As a result of Vatican II, there have been many changes in the way we pray and think of ourselves in relation to others. In preparation for the feast of Pentecost, which is coming in two weeks, and in honor of the anniversary of the close of this important council, find a copy of its documents and read or reread one of its four constitutions: the *Dogmatic Constitution on the Church*, the *Constitution on the Sacred Liturgy*, the *Dogmatic Constitution on Divine Revelation* or the *Pastoral Constitution on the Church in the Modern World*.

PRACTICE OF HOPE

PEACE I GIVE TO YOU. Twenty women and myself spent the weekend together, sharing the joys and sorrows that came to us as we reflected on the stories of biblical women — those who were defined as property, used as pawns in the strategies of men or marginalized for their gender, as well as those who courageously broke free of limitations and claimed freedom. We ended our weekend by building an altar to these women and to others we knew. By turn, we took stones and piled them together as we named saints, heroes, and survivors of violence and abuse. We brought them all into our presence and offered them up for prayer. Tears flowed freely as we claimed both the devastation and strength of our heritage. And in the end, we found peace in embracing both sides of truth.

PRACTICE OF CHARITY

SOME PERSONS FROM US HAVE TROUBLED YOU WITH WORDS. From time to time we can fall into the bad habit of talking unkindly about others. We have all experienced the pain that this causes. We know how deeply it hurts, and yet we seem to do it all too often. Think of someone who has been wounded by your words and make the effort to contact him or her. Reach out in compassion; listen to them; seek forgiveness from them. Work to heal the wound by letting them know that you are sorry.

WEEKDAY READINGS (Mo–We) Acts 16:11 — 18:1; (Th) The Ascension of the Lord; (Fr–Sa) Acts, chapter 18

MAY 28, 1995 Seventh Sunday of Easter

In Canada, May 28, 1995 is the Solemnity of the Ascension of the Lord. See page 100 for the scripture citations of the feast.

READING I *Acts 7:55–60*

Stephen, full of the Holy Spirit, gazed into heaven and saw the glory of God, and Jesus standing at the right hand of God; and he said, "Behold, I see the heavens opened, and the Man of Heaven standing at the right hand of God." But they cried out with a loud voice and stopped their ears and rushed together upon him. And they cast Stephen out of the city and stoned him; and the witnesses laid down their garments at the feet of a youth named Saul. And as they were stoning Stephen, he prayed, "Lord Jesus, receive my spirit." And he knelt down and cried with a loud voice, "Lord, do not hold this sin against them." And when he had said this, he fell asleep.

READING II *Revelation 22:12–14, 16–17, 20*

"Behold, I am coming soon, bringing my recompense, to repay all for what they have done. I am the Alpha and the Omega, the first and the last, the beginning and the end.

"Blessed are those who wash their robes, that they may have the right to the tree of life and that they may enter the city by the gates.

"I Jesus have sent my angel to you with this testimony for the churches. I am the root and the offspring of David, the bright morning star."

The Spirit and the Bride say, "Come." And let the hearer say, "Come." And let the thirsty come, let the one who desires take the water of life without price.

The one who testifies to these things says, "Surely I am coming soon." Amen. Come, Lord Jesus!

GOSPEL *John 17:20–26*

[At that time Jesus said,] "I do not pray for these only, but also for those who believe in me through their word, that they may all be one; even as you, Father, are in me, and I in you, that they also may be in us, so that the world may believe that you have sent me. The glory which you have given me I have given to them, that they may be one even as we are one, I in them and you in me, that they may become perfectly one, so that the world may know that you have sent me and have loved them even as you have loved me. Father, I desire that they also, whom you have given me, may be with me where I am, to behold my glory which you have given me in your love for me before the foundation of the world. O righteous Father, the world has not known you, but I have known you; and these know that you have sent me. I made known to them your name, and I will make it known, that the love with which you have loved me may be in them, and I in them."

Wednesday, May 31, 1995

THE VISIT OF THE VIRGIN MARY TO ELIZABETH

Zephaniah 3:14–18 *The Lord is in your midst.*
or
Romans 12:9–16 *Cling to what is good.*

Luke 1:39–56 *Blessed is the fruit of your womb.*

The life of a disciple is always one of a journey. And hastening to share the good news with others is our springtime joy.

Saturday night through Sunday dawn, June 3 – 4, 1995

PENTECOST VIGIL

Genesis 11:1–19 *At Babel the Lord confused their speech.*

Exodus 19:3–8, 16–20 *Fire and wind descended on Sinai.*

Ezekiel 37:1–14 *O spirit, breathe on the dead!*

Joel 3:1–5 *On the Day of the Lord I will impart my own spirit.*

Romans 8:22–27 *We have the Spirit as firstfruits.*

John 7:37–39 *Let the thirsty come to drink of living waters.*

We end Eastertime the way we began it—with a nighttime vigil, poring over the scriptures. We keep watch on Mount Sinai, where we meet God face to face, where we receive the life-giving Spirit. Our paschal journey, begun so long ago in ashes, is finished in fire.

REFLECTION

Today's gospel is part of what is sometimes referred to as Jesus' high priestly prayer (John 17:1–26). The first section (verses 1–5) is Jesus' prayer for strength as his hour approaches; the second (verses 6–19) is a prayer that the disciples be faithful in this world; the third section, today's gospel reading, is Jesus' prayer for unity.

The concept of Christian unity has its foundation in the oneness, the uniqueness, of God. As the Father and Jesus are united, so is the community of disciples to be united in God. The dispersion described in the story of the tower of Babel (Genesis 11:1–9) will soon see its reversal through the pentecostal outpouring of the Holy Spirit. In the Babel story, God caused the people to be separated by diverse languages. In the Pentecost event, the Spirit caused those of diverse nations and languages to be able to understand each other. This was the miracle of unity that gave witness to the presence of God in Jesus; this was the testimony that God sent Jesus to gather together all the dispersed peoples of the human race.

The unity of the human race was obscured by sin and by the frantic building of monuments to individual achievement. Jesus, present in the human communities of disciples through the power of the Spirit, is the unifying center of all human diversity. The witness of communities that try to live in love is the only believable sign for the world of the message and authority of Jesus. This love (here *agape,* the love of preference, of choice) is not the same as vibrant, spontaneous love (*eros*). Nor is it the warm love of friendship and family love (*philia*). The *agape* for which Jesus prays may have the spontaneity of *eros* and the warmth of *philia*, but it is above all a choice, a preference, a remembering that all are one in a common humanity. The world will have an ever more credible testimony to the presence of Jesus when the communities of his disciples practice inclusivity as a sign of Jesus' love for us in our humanity.

■ **Read Romans 1—6, focusing on chapter 6 and on what Paul has to say about the unity of the human race. Do you live more from a sense of individual effort and responsibility or more from a sense of solidarity with others?**

■ **How do you understand Jesus' commandment to love others? What role do your feelings toward someone play in your efforts to love as Jesus taught? How do you move beyond your feelings to a deeply-rooted attitude of love and respect?**

PRACTICE OF FAITH

COME, LORD JESUS. We know that Jesus is the Word made flesh, and that in Jesus, God has visited us. But how often do we think of how we embody the presence of Christ for others? For those who are alone or isolated, quite often a visit from someone is the very touch of God's hand in their lives. This week, we remember Mary's visit to her pregnant cousin, Elizabeth. Make some time to visit someone who may need to see the presence of God enfleshed in a human being, someone who may be praying for the Lord to come to them. Recognize the presence of God within you as well as within the other person. Give thanks to God that the Lord has come.

PRACTICE OF HOPE

THAT THEY MAY BE ONE. In August 1989, the Ku Klux Klan scheduled a march in Brevard, North Carolina. Some local residents wanted to stop it but knew that the right to assembly was guaranteed by the Constitution. So they held their own gathering at the same hour. Fourteen of them—seven black and seven white—met at a local church.

The fellowship that took place was so rich that one of them asked, "When will we get together again?" Fay Walker said, "How about tomorrow night?" The group has been meeting once a month ever since. An ad they ran in a local paper opposing the hate and violence of the Klan garnered 1,400 signatures. Larry Fortenberry, a black resident, said, "You could never have convinced me that that many people in Brevard opposed the Klan. I feel like a have a new community."

PRACTICE OF CHARITY

I MADE KNOWN TO THEM YOUR NAME. Sometimes we hear that we are to defend the faith that has been passed on to us. Defending the faith is about sharing and giving witness to those who do not know Jesus. The Glenmary Home Missioners are dedicated to serving the spiritual and material needs of the regions of Appalachia and the South where the majority do not belong to any organized religion. Through their ministry of witnessing to the gospel, many have come to know the Lord. In 1994, they operated more than 80 missions in 12 states. If you would like to know more about their ministry, write or call: Glenmary Home Missioners, PO Box 465618, Cincinnati OH 45246-5618; 513-874-8900.

WEEKDAY READINGS Acts 19:1–8; 20:17–27; (We) The Visit of the Virgin Mary to Elizabeth; Acts 22:30—23:11; 25:13–21; 28:16–31

READING I *Acts 2:1–11*

When the day of Pentecost had come, the company was all together in one place. And suddenly a sound came from heaven like the rush of a mighty wind, and it filled all the house where they were sitting. And there appeared to them tongues as of fire, distributed and resting on each one of them. And they were all filled with the Holy Spirit and began to speak in other tongues, as the Spirit gave them utterance.

Now there were dwelling in Jerusalem Jewish people, devout people from every nation under heaven. And at this sound the multitude came together, and they were bewildered, because all heard them speaking in their own language. And they were amazed and wondered, saying, "Are not all these who are speaking Galileans? And how is it that we hear, all of us in our own native language? Parthians and Medes and Elamites and residents of Mesopotamia, Judea, and Cappadocia, Pontus and Asia, Phrygia and Pamphylia, Egypt and the parts of Libya belonging to Cyrene, and visitors from Rome, both Jewish born and proselytes, Cretans and Arabians, we hear them telling in our own tongues the mighty works of God."

READING II *1 Corinthians 12:3–7, 12–13*

No one can say "Jesus is Lord" except by the Holy Spirit.

Now there are varieties of gifts, but the same Spirit; and there are varieties of service, but the same Lord; and there are varieties of working, but it is the same God who inspires them all in every one. To each is given the manifestation of the Spirit for the common good.

For just as the body is one and has many parts, and all the parts of the body, though many, are one body, so it is with Christ. For by one Spirit we were all baptized into one body—Jews or Greeks, slaves or free—and all were made to drink of one Spirit.

GOSPEL *John 20:19–23*

On the evening of that day, the first day of the week, the doors being shut where the disciples were, for fear of the Judeans, Jesus came and stood among them and said to them, "Peace be with you." Having said this, Jesus showed them his hands and his side. Then the disciples were glad when they saw the Lord. Jesus said to them again, "Peace be with you. As the Father has sent me, even so I send you." Having said this, Jesus breathed on them, and said to them, "Receive the Holy Spirit. If you forgive the sins of any, they are forgiven; if you retain the sins of any, they are retained."

REFLECTION

The first reading presents Luke's account of the Pentecost event. The theme is that of a gathering together. It is an image of that unity for which Jesus prayed in John's gospel last Sunday.

The account begins with the words, "When the day of Pentecost had come." The Greek verb *symplerousthai* means the days "had been completed, come to a head in their fullness." The disciples had gathered and the multitude had come together, and *together* they were bewildered, amazed and wondering. Luke's narrative is clearly illustrating the reversal of the Babel narrative (see Genesis 11:1–9); in the power of the Spirit, language barriers were broken down, enabling all to hear with understanding.

In the vivid description of the event, Luke communicates a sense of drama and urgency. The disciples were all together when suddenly a sound (*echos* in verse 2, which becomes *phone*, a roar, in verse 6) as of a violent wind filled the house; then they were filled with the Holy Spirit. Luke continues by saying that while it was the noise that brought the multitude together, it was the "babble" of the Spirit-filled Galileans that reached the attentive ears of the crowd and was the clear message of the mighty works of God.

This narration, and all of Acts 2, bears witness to the fact that the band of disciples would carry on the work of Jesus. Like Jesus, they would be greeted with the enthusiasm of some and the opposition of others.

■ **Read all of Acts 2 as you would read a story that grabs you. It may help you learn something of the spirit of the early Christian communities.**

PRACTICE OF FAITH

BREATH OF GOD. The Hebrew word that we translate as "spirit" is *ruhah*. This word also means breath or wind. Today we celebrate the Holy Spirit breathing on the followers of Christ, inspiring them and forming them as church. Go out today and feel the wind, the breath of God that continues to create the world and inspire the church. Recall, and even record, the ways the spirit has breathed life into you and through you into others. Pray for the neophytes who are a breath of fresh life in your parish. If your parish has prepared Evening Prayer to close the Easter season, make plans to attend. Or, gather with family and friends in the evening twilight, with candles lit to praise and thank our God, the giver of life, light and breath.

PRACTICE OF HOPE

ONE IN THE SPIRIT. Flora Smith is 86 years old. Her grandfather was a slave. She was arrested 30 years ago for praying on the steps of City Hall in Birmingham, Alabama, during the height of the civil rights movement. It was the day before Mother's Day, 1963. She woke up and told herself, "I'm going to go to jail today, and be somebody's mother tomorrow."

When the Baptist Peace Fellowship of North America worshiped with members of Birmingham's Sixteenth Street Baptist Church in 1993, she was the first person on her feet when the congregation began singing "We Shall Overcome." Arms crossed and hands clasped around the sanctuary. When I asked Flora Smith if, in 1963, she ever thought that blacks and whites would be sitting in that church together singing freedom songs, tears welled in her eyes as she said, "Praise the good Lord, I never thought I'd see this day."

PRACTICE OF CHARITY

OUR OWN NATIVE LANGUAGE. Observing a child learning to form sounds and syllables, one cannot help but marvel at the acquisition of language. It is a wonderful gift to be able to verbally communicate feelings and thoughts. However, too frequently in our daily lives we pass up opportunities to engage in the art of conversation. We have become so accustomed to rapid change and instant information that the time needed to develop thoughts and share stories is often lost. A simple suggestion to help recapture the gift of communication: Set aside an evening a week this summer to spend with family or friends. Make sure you are away from distractions like TV. Enjoy the rhythm and richness of language. Hopefully, this will deepen your appreciation of being both able to communicate and able to establish life-long friendships.

WEEKDAY READINGS **Tobit, entire book**

SUMMER ORDINARY TIME

You crown the year with riches.
All you touch is fertile.

Praise is yours, God in Zion.
Now is the moment
to keep our vow.

You soak the furrows
and level the ridges.
With softening rain
you bless the land with growth.

You crown the year with riches.
All you touch comes alive:
untilled lands yield crops,
hills are dressed in joy,

flocks clothe the pastures,
valleys wrap themselves in grain.
They all shout for joy
and break into song.

—Psalm 65: 2, 11 – 14

God who called each day's creation good,
all we have for our food
and shelter and clothing
are the crust and air, the light and water
    of this planet.
Give us care like yours for this earth:
to share its bounty
with generations to come
and with all alike in this generation,
to savor its beauty and respect its power,
to heal what greed and war and foolishness
have done to your earth and to us.
Bring us finally to give thanks,
always and everywhere.

— Prayer of the Season

READING I *Proverbs 8:22–31*

[Wisdom speaks:] At the beginning of the LORD's
     work I was created,
   the first of the LORD's acts of old.
Ages ago the LORD set me up,
   at the first, before the beginning of the earth.
When there were no depths I was brought forth,
   when there were no springs abounding
     with water.
Before the mountains had been shaped,
   before the hills, I was brought forth;
before the LORD had made the earth with its fields,
   or the first of the dust of the world.
I was there when the LORD established the heavens,
   and drew a circle on the face of the deep,
and made firm the skies above,
   and established the fountains of the deep,
and assigned to the sea its limit,
   so that the waters might not transgress
     the LORD's command,
when the foundations of the earth were marked
     out,
   then I was beside the LORD, like a skilled worker;
and I was daily the LORD's delight,
   rejoicing always before the LORD,
rejoicing in the LORD's inhabited world
   and delighting in the human race.

READING II *Romans 5:1–5*

Therefore, since we are justified by faith, we have
peace with God through our Lord Jesus Christ,
through whom we have obtained access to this
grace in which we stand, and we rejoice in our hope
of sharing the glory of God. More than that, we
rejoice in our sufferings, knowing that suffering
produces endurance, and endurance produces
character, and character produces hope, and hope
does not disappoint us, because God's love has
been poured into our hearts through the Holy Spirit
which has been given to us.

GOSPEL *John 16:12–15*

[At that time Jesus said,] "I have yet many things
to say to you, but you cannot bear them now. When
the Spirit of truth comes, you will be guided into all
the truth; for the Spirit of truth will not speak out of
the Spirit's own authority, for the Spirit of truth will
speak whatever the Spirit hears, and will declare
to you the things that are to come. The Spirit will
glorify me, taking what is mine and declaring it to
you. All that the Father has is mine; therefore I said
that the Spirit will take what is mine and declare it
to you."

R E F L E C T I O N

On this feast dedicated to the Holy Trinity, the passage taken from John's gospel speaks of the unity and uniqueness of God. Frequently in John 16, Jesus refers to his being one with the Father (16:3, 5, 10, 23, 25-28, 32).

The focus of this brief reading, however, is the Spirit. The Greek *pneuma* connotes power and has been the most frequently used translation of the Hebrew word for spirit, *ru(a)h* (breath, wind). The association of *pneuma* with the power of God is especially clear in the Acts of the Apostles. Jesus had not finished all he wanted to say, because the disciples were not able to take it in. But here, the one to be sent is called the Spirit of truth, the guide into the fullness of truth.

The Greek word for truth, *aletheia*, was also associated in Hellenistic usage with power. In translating the Hebrew Bible, the word was used to convey the idea of truth as something solid and trustworthy. The use of *aletheia* focuses on the transparency of truth — its authenticity — as opposed to mere appearances; the Spirit sent to the disciples would enable them to discern authentic truth from pseudo-truths.

The word used for guide *(hodegeo)* connotes teaching but especially connotes leading, or showing the way (*hodos*, road, manner of life). The Father sent Jesus to be the way, the truth and the life in the flesh, within a particular culture, among those of one religious tradition, at a moment in time. The Spirit of truth is sent as the unseen enabler and hidden power to show the way for the Christian communities of many cultures throughout many moments in time.

■ **What does "truth" mean to you? How do you recognize truth from untruth? What criteria do you use?**

■ **Describe some ways that you attempt to live by the truth. What choices does living by the truth force you to make?**

PRACTICE OF FAITH

FATHERS. Next Sunday is Father's Day. This week pray for your father, your grandfather and all who fostered your growth in wholeness and holiness. Here is a prayer from *Catholic Household Blessings and Prayers* that you can use.

God our Father,
in your wisdom and love you made all things.
Bless our father.
Let the example of his faith and love shine forth.
Grant that we, his family,
may honor him always
with a spirit of profound respect.
Grant this through Christ our Lord. Amen.

PRACTICE OF HOPE

SUFFERING PRODUCES ENDURANCE. It was a time when the Soviet secret police kept a close watch on citizens' activities. But they chose to ignore an old woman who was badly crippled with multiple sclerosis. How much of a threat could she be?

Little did they know that every morning the woman's husband propped her up in front of a typewriter. With her gnarled index finger, she painstakingly translated parts of the Bible and devotional books into the language of her people, a page or two a day. While she typed, she prayed for those who would read the words. This was her service to a loving God.

PRACTICE OF CHARITY

DELIGHTING IN THE HUMAN RACE. There are many ways to take delight in the human race: observe athletes in motion; take in a summer theater performance; watch and listen to children at play; visit an art gallery; spend time with a good friend.... All of God's people are to be delighted in. Make it a point this week to look for the good in everyone you encounter and to take delight in them.

WEEKDAY READINGS *2 Corinthians, chapters 1 — 5*

READING I *Genesis 14:18–20*

Melchizedek king of Salem brought out bread and wine; he was priest of God Most High. And Melchizedek blessed Abram and said,

> "Blessed be Abram by God Most High,
> maker of heaven and earth;
> and blessed be God Most High,
> who has delivered your enemies into your hand!"

READING II *1 Corinthians 11:23–26*

For I received from the Lord what I also delivered to you, that the Lord Jesus on the night when he was betrayed took bread, and having given thanks, broke it, and said, "This is my body which is for you. Do this in remembrance of me." In the same way also the cup, after supper, saying, "This cup is the new covenant in my blood. Do this, as often as you drink it, in remembrance of me." For as often as you eat this bread and drink the cup, you proclaim the Lord's death until he comes.

GOSPEL *Luke 9:11–17*

Jesus welcomed the crowds and spoke to them of the dominion of God, and cured those who had need of healing. Now the day began to wear away; and the twelve came and said to Jesus, "Send the crowd away, to go into the villages and country round about, to lodge and get provisions; for we are here in a lonely place." But Jesus said to them, "You give them something to eat." They said, "We have no more than five loaves and two fish—unless we are to go and buy food for all these people." For there were about five thousand men. And Jesus said to his disciples, "Make them sit down in companies, about fifty each." And they did so, and made them all sit down. And taking the five loaves and the two fish Jesus looked up to heaven, and blessed and broke them, and gave them to the disciples to set before the crowd. And all ate and were satisfied. And they took up what was left over, twelve baskets of broken pieces.

Friday, June 23, 1995

THE SACRED HEART OF JESUS

Ezekiel 34:11–16 *I will pasture my sheep and give them rest*

Romans 5:5–11 *The love of God is in our hearts*

Luke 15:3–7 *Rejoice with me! I have found my lost sheep*

Today is an echo of Good Friday, a reminder that every Friday is kept with renewed efforts to understand and to share the compassion of God. If Christ lives in our hearts, we bear the love of God in our own bodies.

Saturday, June 24, 1995

THE BIRTH OF JOHN THE BAPTIST

VIGIL

Jeremiah 1:4–10 *Before I formed you in the womb, I knew you.*

1 Peter 1:8–12 *Rejoice with inexpressible joy.*

Luke 1:5–17 *Many will rejoice at John's birth.*

DAY

Isaiah 49:1–6 *From my mother's womb I am given my name.*

Acts 13:22–26 *John's message is for all children of Abraham.*

Luke 1:57–66, 80 *What will the child be?*

John said, I must decrease if Christ is to increase. Today the daytime begins to decrease. It is the midsummer nativity. John is born to be the best man of the Bridegroom, the lamp of the Light and the voice of the Word. Rejoice in John's birth!

REFLECTION

In today's gospel, it seems that Jesus is teaching two lessons. First, Jesus welcomes the crowd (*ochlos,* throng, common people), though "the Twelve" wanted to send them away. Luke's considered use of "the Twelve" to indicate a special group of disciples is a reflection of the significance of that number in the traditions of Jesus' people; in particular, it recalls the twelve tribes of Israel. By using this term, Luke indicates that being chosen to serve in a particular way is not an excuse for distancing oneself from the crowd, the common people; on the contrary, the Twelve, like Jesus, should be welcoming.

The second point Jesus seems to be making here is that the disciples are to share whatever they have. In the sharing there will be more than enough for everyone. Logic and human reason say, "We have no more than five loaves and two fish." But Jesus asks that these meager provisions be stretched to their limits. The reality of being one people, inheritors of the promises made to the twelve tribes of Israel, is a reality capable of transforming not only the spiritual realm but social and economic life as well. Luke, of all the evangelists, was most emphatic: Salvation reaches into the practical realities of human life.

The feast of the Body and Blood of Christ reminds us of the presence of Jesus in the eucharistic celebration. It also reminds us that we are the body and blood of Christ, present within—and not apart from—the *ochlos* of the human race. Luke's account of this miracle places particular emphasis on Jesus' welcoming and healing presence in contrast to the inclination of the Twelve to send the others away so that they could eat in peace what they had brought for themselves. Luke and the other evangelists considered this miracle and its meaning so important that none of them failed to include it in his gospel.

■ **Read about the miracle of the feeding of the crowd in Matthew (14:13–21), Mark (6:30–44) and John (6:1–14). Do the slight differences in the accounts surprise you? How do these differences enrich your understanding? How are they a source of conflict for you?**

■ **Recall from your own life those times of sharing that made a difference to you or to others.**

PRACTICE OF FAITH

MANY BLESSINGS. In addition to honoring our fathers today, we celebrate the feast of the Body and Blood of Christ. The heart of the eucharist is memorial and thanksgiving. Remember your father and our God, who sent the Son that we might have life. Remember and give thanks through blessing your father and the food that you share this day. Resolve to make blessing and thanksgiving a part of your daily mealtime, even when you are alone. Find ways to share meals with others as often as possible and to have at least one important festive meal a week. Bake or buy a loaf of bread today that can be broken and shared by all and, if possible, serve it with fruited sangria (a red wine and fruit juice beverage whose name comes from the Latin word *sanguis,* meaning blood).

PRACTICE OF HOPE

ALL ATE AND WERE SATISFIED. The small town of Ocotal in northern Nicaragua was under alert. Our Witness for Peace delegation spent the night in the Baptist church, which we shared with refugees who had fled their scattered mountain homes during contra attacks. Gunshots in the distance punctuated the night.

We awoke before dawn. The refugee women had arisen even earlier. Firewood was already stacked in their dome-shaped clay oven, and they were slapping out tortillas. They had fled with their children and little more than the clothes on their backs, but they invited us to partake in their meager breakfast. Our communion of tortillas and coffee at daybreak was a sacrament of generosity and hope.

PRACTICE OF CHARITY

YOU GIVE THEM SOMETHING TO EAT. No passing the buck on this one. The directive is quite clear. So what can you do? Here are a couple suggestions. Call your local food pantry and find out what they need. Then invite some friends to go to the grocery store with you to purchase the needed items. A second option, for those who live in larger cities, is to help out at a soup kitchen. Call first, and then gather some people to go with you. Some communities have programs that collect prepared, unserved food from restaurants at the end of the day and deliver it to shelters or soup kitchens. Learn more about your community's programs and make helping them a priority.

WEEKDAY READINGS 2 Corinthians 6:1–10; 8:1–9; 9:6–11; 11:1–11; (Fr) The Sacred Heart of Jesus; (Sa) The Birth of John the Baptist

READING I *Zechariah 12:10–11*

"And I will pour out on the house of David and the inhabitants of Jerusalem a spirit of compassion and supplication, so that, looking on me, on the one whom they have pierced, they shall mourn, as one mourns for an only child, and weep bitterly, as one weeps over a first-born. On that day the mourning in Jerusalem will be as great as the mourning for Hadadrimmon in the plain of Megiddo.

READING II *Galatians 3:26–29*

For in Christ Jesus you are all children of God, through faith. For as many of you as were baptized into Christ have put on Christ. There is neither Jew nor Greek, there is neither slave or free, there is neither male nor female; for you are all one in Christ Jesus. And if you are Christ's, then you are Abraham's offspring, heirs according to promise.

GOSPEL *Luke 9:18–24*

Now it happened that as Jesus was praying alone the disciples were with him; and he asked them, "Who do the people say that I am?" And they answered, "John the Baptist; but others say, Elijah; and others, that one of the old prophets has risen." And Jesus said to them, "But who do you say that I am?" And Peter answered, "The Christ of God." But Jesus charged and commanded them to tell no one, saying, "The Man of Heaven must suffer many things, and be rejected by the elders and chief priests and scribes, and be killed, and on the third day be raised."

And Jesus said to all, "Those who would come after me, let them deny themselves and take up their cross daily and follow me. For those who would save their life will lost it; and those who lose their life for my sake, they will save it."

Thursday, June 29, 1995

PETER AND PAUL

VIGIL

Acts 3:1–10 *Peter cried, "Look at us!"*

Galatians 1:11–20 *God chose to reveal Christ to me.*

John 21:15–19 *Simon Peter, do you love me?*

DAY

Acts 12:1–11 *The chains dropped from Peter's wrists.*

2 Timothy 4:6–8, 17–18 *I have kept the faith.*

Matthew 16:13–19 *I entrust to you the keys of the kingdom.*

This season is the beginning of the grain harvest. So today we keep a festival in honor of the two apostles who began the harvest of God's reign. They preached from Jerusalem to Rome, keeping the Easter commandment to bring good news to the ends of the earth.

REFLECTION

The passage selected for today's gospel reading follows immediately after the miraculous feeding of the five thousand. As is usual in Luke, before a particularly significant moment Jesus withdraws in prayer. He is alone in prayer, even in the company of his disciples. Last week's gospel emphasized the welcoming attitude the disciples should have toward the *ochlos,* the crowd. Here, Jesus points to the difference between what "people" *(ochloi)* have to say and what a disciple has to say. The division that Jesus has come to bring (see Luke 12:51) is between people with varying opinions and the disciples, who acknowledge Jesus as one sent from God.

The disciples, however, are warned not to talk about their faith conviction until after Jesus has undergone all that he must suffer. The word used by Luke for "must" is *dei,* which is much stronger than its English equivalent. *Dei* means "it must be," and among New Testament writers, it is used most frequently by Luke. It is the expression of God's plan, and so for Jesus it is a way of life; the suffering and rejection he is to undergo are included in the *dei* of God. We have frequently seen the opposition that Jesus encountered, especially from those who might have been expected to support him, the religious leaders. Today's reading presents the first of three "predictions" in Luke of Jesus' suffering and death (see also 9:43–45 and 18:31–34).

Jesus' final words in this passage are that the suffering and rejection awaiting him will also await all those who wish to follow him. The image is that of a journey, a way of life focused on bearing the burden — the cross — day after day. The paradox that concludes this teaching on discipleship is that the effort to hold onto one's self *(psyche)* results in loss; only those who let go of this preoccupation out of deep conviction and commitment will find and save themselves.

■ **Can you recall an incident in your life in which letting go — "losing" — became an occasion for "saving," for discovering some new dimension in your life?**

■ **We all want to belong, to be part of the group. Yet sometimes, we must take an unpopular stand. Can you think of an experience in your life, or in the life of someone you know, when this happened? What was the result?**

PRACTICE OF CHARITY

THE CROSS: A SIGN OF FAITH. Many of us were infants when we were first marked with the cross, the sign of our faith. Often we take that sign for granted, hurriedly blessing ourselves as we enter the church building or begin our prayers. For catechumens — those preparing for baptism, confirmation and eucharist — being marked with the sign of the cross is an important ritual moment. Perhaps you have been present at your parish celebration of the rite of entrance into the catechumenate, when those who have formally asked to be prepared for initiation are solemnly signed on their forehead, eyes, ears, lips, heart, hands, shoulders and even on their feet. We blanket these new "apprentice" members of our community with the cross of Christ, the sign of salvation and faith. Find out more about the Rite of Christian Initiation of Adults in your own parish and how you can support those seeking to follow Christ.

PRACTICE OF HOPE

A SPIRIT OF COMPASSION. For two weeks in June 1993, members of Murder Victims Families for Reconciliation took a Journey of Hope throughout Indiana. Through rallies, educational events and meetings with local officials, participants reached out to spread their message that capital punishment should be abolished.

The message carries particular weight coming from MVFR members, all of whom have lost loved ones to violent crime. Founder Marie Dean, whose mother-in-law was murdered, says, "Through our own painful experience, we have learned that vengeance is not the answer." The group offers support to those seeking to forgive as a means of healing their grief.

PRACTICE OF CHARITY

ALL ARE ONE IN CHRIST JESUS. One of the joys of our tradition is that we are committed to speaking out against injustice. This commitment, lucidly presented in the social teachings of our church, is based on our belief that the gospel calls us to be there for others. Witness for Peace, a national faith-based organization, lends its voice to the unempowered people of Central America — those who have become forgotten on the world's agenda. For the past 12 years, Witness for Peace has provided a non-violent presence in Guatemala and Nicaragua and has worked to ensure the safety of peasants whose only crime is that they have no political voice. If you would like to become a partner with WFP in this important work, write or call: Witness for Peace, 2201 P Street NW, Room 109, Washington DC 20037; 202-797-1160.

WEEKDAY READINGS (Mo–We, Fr–Sa) Genesis 12:1–18:15; (Th) Peter and Paul

READING I *1 Kings 19:16, 19–21*

The LORD said to Elijah, "Elisha the son of Shaphat of Abel-meholah you shall anoint to be prophet in your place."

So Elijah departed from there, and found Elisha the son of Shaphat, who was plowing, with twelve yoke of oxen before him, and he was with the twelfth. Elijah passed by him and cast his mantle upon him. And Elisha left the oxen, and ran after Elijah, and said, "Let me kiss my father and my mother, and then I will follow you." And Elijah said to him, "Go back again; for what have I done to you?" And Elisha returned from following Elijah, and took the yoke of oxen, and slew them, and boiled their flesh with the yokes of the oxen, and gave it to the people, and they ate. Then Elisha arose and went after Elijah, and ministered to him.

READING II *Galatians 5:1, 13–18*

For freedom Christ has set us free; stand fast therefore, and do not submit again to a yoke of slavery.

For you were called to freedom, my dear people; only do not use your freedom as an opportunity for the flesh, but through love be servants of one another. For the whole law is fulfilled in one word, "You shall love your neighbor as yourself." But if you bite and devour one another take heed that you are not consumed by one another.

But I say, walk by the Spirit, and do not gratify the desires of the flesh. For the desires of the flesh are against the Spirit, and the desires of the Spirit are against the flesh; for these are opposed to each other, to prevent you from doing what you would. But if you are led by the Spirit you are not under the law.

GOSPEL *Luke 9:51–62*

When the days drew near for Jesus to be received up, he set his face to go to Jerusalem. And he sent messengers ahead of him, who went and entered a village of the Samaritans, to make ready for him; but the people would not receive him, because his face was set toward Jerusalem. And when his disciples James and John saw it, they said, "Lord, do you want us to bid fire come down from heaven and consume them?" But Jesus turned and rebuked them. And they went on to another village.

As they were going along the road, a man said to Jesus, "I will follow you wherever you go." And Jesus said to the man, "Foxes have holes, and birds of the air have nests; but the Man of Heaven has nowhere to lay his head." To another Jesus said, "Follow me." But he said, "Lord, let me first go and bury my father." But Jesus said to him, "Leave the dead to bury their own dead; but as for you, go and proclaim the dominion of God." Another said, "I will follow you, Lord; but let me first say farewell to those at my home." Jesus answered, "No one who puts a hand to the plow and looks back is fit for the dominion of God."

REFLECTION

During these Sundays in Ordinary Time, the focus is on discipleship. The gospel today speaks of the steadfast commitment that is essential to the denial of self, which Jesus spoke of in last Sunday's gospel. The reading from Galatians characterizes this commitment as a standing fast in freedom, refusing to submit again to the yoke of slavery.

The language used by Luke in this gospel passage is especially significant: Jesus set his face to go up to Jerusalem. The rejection by Samaritan villagers did not arouse the anger of Jesus, nor did it deter him; it was to be expected. Luke also uses language that conveys a sense of movement, and adds the detail of "going along the road" (*hodos*, also with the meaning of a way of life). In Luke/Acts the symbolism of road and journey recurs often.

On the way, Jesus encounters three people, all potential disciples. To the first, he states clearly (no false promises here) that a certain homelessness, rootlessness and readiness to be on the move is part of discipleship. Jesus then invites the second person, who asks leave to fulfill a legitimate family obligation. Jesus' response about leaving the dead to bury their own seems to have a double meaning: In the early Christian communities, the baptized were considered the living while the unbaptized were considered dead. The stress here is the primacy of proclaiming the good news.

Finally, a third person approaches with the promise to follow Jesus after saying good-bye to those at home. Jesus' reply is that the call to discipleship cannot always survive the busyness of all the arrangements for family and possessions.

The final verse sums up Jesus' teaching on discipleship and contrasts it with the more lenient attitude of Elijah (first reading, 1 Kings 19:21). The domestic metaphor of the plow, and the resolute action of putting a hand to it and keeping one's eyes on the land to be furrowed, sketches a portrait of the disciple. Looking back is distracting; looking behind serves no purpose. The attitude and disposition of a disciple, like that of Jesus, is to set out at once with determination and with the hand and eye stretched forward, toward the open field.

■ **Read Paul's description of his attitude as a disciple in Philippians 3:4–16.**

PRACTICE OF FAITH

INDEPENDENCE DAY. Pray this week that our nation will truly be a place of liberty and justice for all. Use this prayer from *Catholic Household Blessings and Prayers*:

God, source of all freedom,
this day is bright with the memory
of those who declared that life and liberty
are your gift to every human being.
Help us to continue a good work begun long ago.
Make our vision clear and our will strong:
that only in human solidarity will we find liberty,
and justice only in the honor that belongs
to every life on earth.
Turn our hearts toward the family of nations:
to understand the ways of others,
to offer friendship,
and to find safety only in the common good of all.
We ask this through Christ our Lord. Amen.

PRACTICE OF HOPE

CALLED TO HUMAN SOLIDARITY. While many U.S. citizens celebrated the 500th anniversary of Columbus' "discovery" of America in 1992, many Native Americans used the milestone to remind the nation that they were already here when the lost explorer arrived. Alternative events to the official celebrations brought together native peoples from every continent in a powerful sharing about such issues as land rights, honoring of treaties and environmental justice. The voice of Lilla Watson, an aboriginal woman from Australia, issues an invitation to the rest of us: "If you have come to help me, you are wasting your time. But if you have come because your liberation is bound up with mine, then let us walk together."

PRACTICE OF CHARITY

CALLED TO FREEDOM. In the work of charity, freedom usually means freedom from poverty, oppression, disease and injustice. However, it can also mean freedom from an attachment to things. The quest for acquiring the latest fashions or gadgets can become a type of enslavement. In this context, freedom comes when we commit ourselves to living more simply. In finding ways to consume less, we are freeing ourselves from things. We are doing simple justice. Amy Dacyczyn's book, *The Tightwad Gazette* (Villard Books, 1993), offers many tips for living simply. She also offers a newsletter for $12 a year. Contact: The Tightwad Gazette, RR 1, Box 3570, Leeds ME 04263-9710.

WEEKDAY READINGS Ephesians 2:19–22; (Tu–Sa) Genesis 19:15—27:29

READING I *Isaiah 66:10–14*

[Thus says the LORD:] "Rejoice with Jerusalem, and
   be glad for the city,
  all you who love her;
rejoice with Jerusalem in joy,
  all you who mourn over her;
that you may suck and be satisfied
  with her consoling breasts;
that you may drink deeply with delight
  from the abundance of her glory."
For thus says the LORD:
"Behold, I will extend prosperity to Jerusalem
  like a river,
  and the wealth of the nations
  like an overflowing stream;
and you shall suck, you shall be carried upon
  her hip,
  and dandled upon her knees.
As a child is comforted by its mother,
  so I will comfort you;
  you shall be comforted in Jerusalem.
You shall see, and your heart shall rejoice;
  your bones shall flourish like the grass;
and it shall be known that the hand of the LORD
  is with the servants of the LORD."

READING II *Galatians 6:14–18*

Far be it from me to glory except in the cross of our
Lord Jesus Christ, by which the world has been crucified to me, and I to the world. For neither circum-
cision counts for anything, nor uncircumcision, but
a new creation. Peace and mercy be upon all who
walk by this rule, upon the Israel of God.

Henceforth let no one trouble me; for I bear on
my body the marks of Jesus.

The grace of our Lord Jesus Christ be with your
spirit, my dear people. Amen.

GOSPEL *Luke 10:1–12, 17–20*

The Lord appointed seventy others, and sent them
on ahead of him, two by two, into every town and
place where he was about to come. And Jesus said
to them, "The harvest is plentiful, but the laborers
are few; pray therefore the Lord of the harvest to
send out laborers for the harvesting. Go your way;
behold, I send you out as lambs in the midst of
wolves. Carry no purse, no bag, no sandals; and
salute no one on the road. Whatever house you
enter, first say, 'Peace be to this house!' And if there
should be people of peace there, your peace shall
rest upon them; but if not, it shall return to you.
And remain in the same house, eating and drinking
what they provide, for laborers deserve their wages;
do not go from house to house. Whenever you enter
a town and they receive you, eat what is set before
you; heal the sick in it and say to them, 'The dominion of God has come near to you.' But whenever
you enter a town and they do not receive you, go
into its streets and say, 'Even the dust of your town
that clings to our feet, we wipe off against you; nevertheless know this, that the dominion of God has
come near.' I tell you, it shall be more tolerable on
that day for Sodom than for that town."

The seventy returned with joy, saying, "Lord,
even the demons are subject to us in your name!"
And Jesus said to them, "I saw Satan fall like light-
ning from heaven. Behold, I have given you authority to tread upon serpents and scorpions, and over
all the power of the enemy; and nothing shall hurt
you. Nevertheless do not rejoice in this, that the
spirits are subject to you; but rejoice that your
names are written in heaven."

REFLECTION

Today's gospel continues the description of discipleship as outlined by Luke. Three elements emerge from a reading of this account of the sending out of the large group of disciples.

The first is that of a commission. The verb *anadeiknymi* was used classically in the political sphere and was related to an official action. Luke also uses the verb *apostello,* which signifies a sending out, a commission to go forth. The idea of a mission coming from the Father, to Jesus, and then to the disciples, is strengthened when Jesus states that hearing or rejecting the disciple is the same as hearing or rejecting himself as well as the one who sent him.

The movement involved in sending is intensified when Luke uses the verb *ekballo* (thrust forth) to describe the action of the Lord of the harvest sending laborers into the fields. And this is the second element that emerges — that of work and workers. Discipleship demands energetic action. Disciples are workers and so should not be burdened with excess baggage. Nor should they prolong the customary greeting; they have work to do. Because they are on the road bearing the message of peace, they earn the food they are given yet do not present themselves for free meals at every house in the neighborhood. And, like Jesus, they too can expect opposition and rejection.

The third element in this description of a disciple is that of joy. The seventy (or seventy-two, according to some manuscripts) returned with joy, surprised that they could even cast out demons. Jesus' response to them contains a statement that makes clear the absolute, unique power of the one God: While there exist forces of evil that can wreak havoc, such forces are no match for the capability, the power, of the One God in Jesus and in his disciples. Jesus affirms the disciples' joy but reminds them that the source of that happiness is not to be found in power but in the fact that they are followers of Jesus.

■ **Reflect on today's first reading, focusing especially on what it has to say about joy. Is being a Christian a source of deep joy for you? If so, in what way? If not, why do you think this is so?**

■ **Can you recall any incident in your life, or in the life of someone you have read about, that shows a willingness to let go of something good in order to answer the call of discipleship?**

PRACTICE OF FAITH

SERVANT OF THE LORD. This week we celebrate the feast of Blessed Kateri Tekakwitha, daughter of a Christian Algonquin woman and a non-Christian Mohawk chief. Blessed Kateri is an example of one who found joy in Christ even in the midst of suffering. When she was still a small child, all of Kateri's family died of smallpox. The disease left her disfigured, nearly blind and with a limp. She was left in the care of a Christian friend and was eventually baptized. Even with all her physical ailments and the persecution of others in the tribe, Kateri kept her faith, hope and joy. Eventually she found her way to a Christian settlement in Canada where she taught children and served the sick and the elderly. She died in 1680 at the age of 23. Native American Catholics hold the annual National Tekakwitha Conference to strengthen the connection between their native heritage and the tradition of the church.

PRACTICE OF HOPE

YOU SHALL BE COMFORTED. In 1986, 365 children — one a day — were shot in Detroit, 43 fatally. One of the fatalities was Derick Barfield, an athlete who wanted to be a minister. His mother, Clementine Barfield, turned her grief into a force for change. She and several other mothers founded SOSAD (Save Our Sons and Daughters).

SOSAD members march in the streets against violence, picket at drug houses and run a variety of programs designed to encourage their children and build self-esteem. Clementine Barfield says, "Derick would have done a fantastic job as a minister. But even now I feel as though Derick is ministering; he's doing it through me."

PRACTICE OF CHARITY

THE LABORERS ARE FEW. Needed: Teachers for the parish school of religion. Needed: People to help with cleaning the church on Saturdays. Needed: Workers to do odd jobs at the parish school once a month. Needed: People to work the parish spaghetti supper. In order for our parishes to run smoothly, many varied tasks need attention. The cry for help is written in our parish bulletins week after week. Many times only a few people respond. A parish community grows because the members are willing to be just that: a parish family. So next time the summons for aid goes out, consider responding. Your talents will certainly be of help, and you will begin to feel even more a part of the family.

WEEKDAY READINGS *Genesis, 28: 10–22; 32:23–33; 41:55—42:24; 44:18—45: 5; 46:1–7, 28–30; 49:29—50:26*

READING I *Deuteronomy 30:10–14*

[Moses said,] "The LORD will again take delight in prospering you, delighting in you as in your forebears, if you obey the voice of the LORD your God, to keep the commandments and the statutes of the LORD which are written in this book of the law, if you turn to the LORD your God with all your heart and with all your soul.

"For this commandment which I command you this day is not too hard for you, neither is it far off. It is not in heaven, that you should say, 'Who will go up for us to heaven, and bring it to us, that we may hear it and do it?' Neither is it beyond the sea, that you should say, 'Who will go over the sea for us, and bring it to us, that we may hear it and do it?' But the word is very near you; it is in your mouth and in your heart, so that you can do it."

READING II *Colossians 1:15–20*

Christ is the image of the invisible God, the firstborn of all creation; for in Christ all things were created, in heaven and on earth, visible and invisible, whether thrones or dominions or principalities or authorities — all things were created through him and for him. Christ is before all things, and in him all things hold together. Christ is the head of the body, the church; Christ is the beginning, the firstborn from the dead, that in everything he might be preeminent. For in Christ all the fullness of God was pleased to dwell, and through Christ to reconcile to God all things, whether on earth or in heaven, making peace by the blood of his cross.

GOSPEL *Luke 10:25–37*

Behold, a lawyer stood up to put Jesus to the test, saying, "Teacher, what shall I do to inherit eternal life?" Jesus said to him, "What is written in the law? How do you read it?" And the lawyer answered, "You shall love the Lord your God with all your heart, and with all your soul, and with all your strength, and with all your mind; and your neighbor as yourself." And Jesus said to him, "You have answered right; do this, and you will live."

But the lawyer, desiring to justify himself, said to Jesus, "And who is my neighbor?" Jesus replied, "A man was going down from Jerusalem to Jericho, and he fell among robbers, who stripped him and beat him, and departed, leaving him half dead. Now by chance a priest was going down that road; and seeing the man, he passed by on the other side. So likewise a Levite, when he came to the place and saw him, passed by on the other side. But a Samaritan, as he journeyed, came to where the man was; and seeing him, the Samaritan had compassion, and went to him and bound up his wounds, pouring on oil and wine; then he set him on his own beast and brought him to an inn, and took care of him. And the next day the Samaritan took out two denarii and gave them to the innkeeper, saying, 'Take care of him; and whatever more you spend, I will repay you when I come back.' Which of these three, do you think, proved neighbor to the man who fell among the robbers?" The lawyer said, "The one who showed mercy on him." And Jesus said to him, "Go and do likewise."

Saturday, July 22, 1995

MARY MAGDALENE

Song of Songs 3:1–4 *I found him whom my heart loves.*
or
2 Corinthians 5:14–17 *Anyone in Christ is a new creation.*

John 20:1–2, 11–18 *I have seen the Lord!*

The church's memory is fuzzy: Exactly who is Mary Magdalene? Some confuse her with other women in scripture; some think her portrayal in the gospels is a composite of a number of faithful disciples. One thing is clear: This loving woman of the Fourth Gospel was faithful to Jesus to his death and was the first messenger of his resurrection. She went to the tomb weeping, carrying myrhh. She left the tomb rejoicing, carrying good news.

R E F L E C T I O N

Today we hear Luke's moving parable of the Good Samaritan. Jesus had just praised God for the gift of discipleship when a lawyer, one of "the wise and intelligent," stood up to test him. Jesus refers the man to the law, asking two questions: what is *written,* and, how do you *read* it? Jesus, speaking from within his religious tradition, recognized that what is written is capable of a variety of interpretations. The lawyer's response reveals a clear understanding of the core teaching of the law. So Jesus replies to the lawyer's initial question as to what he should do by telling him to do what the law says.

The lawyer would not give up, however, and asked Jesus a further question. So there follows the parable of the man who was attacked by robbers. Luke mentions a priest, a Levite and a journeying Samaritan going down the road. The priest and the Levite—both religious leaders — as well as the Samaritan, all saw the man. Those who were considered "wise and intelligent" saw and passed by on the other side, going out of their way to create distance. But the Samaritan saw, was filled with pity, and went to the man, going out of his way to close the distance.

At the end of the parable, Jesus challenges the lawyer by asking him to answer his own question. The "neighbor" is the Samaritan who closed the distance between himself and the victim by bringing himself into the vicinity, into the neighborhood, of the one who had been mugged.

The lawyer was caught and had no other choice but to reply that the one who "did mercy" was the one who fulfilled the law. The lawyer, the priest, the Levite—all knew the law, were on the right road and saw the one lying by the roadside. But it was the foreigner, the alien, the Samaritan, who journeyed from merely seeing into acting with healing compassion.

■ **Is the gospel idea of "neighbor" (one who closes the distance) a new one to you? Describe some incident in which someone took the initiative and came to you as a neighbor. How did it affect your life?**

■ **Can you think of instances today when, in order to be a "neighbor," it might be necessary to be more concerned with mercy than with law?**

PRACTICE OF FAITH

PASSIONATE LOVE. On Saturday we keep the feast of St. Mary Magdalene, a passionate lover of Jesus. Though scripture scholars cannot confirm this, Christians have most often identified Mary Magdalene as the sinful woman who washed Jesus' feet at the home of Simon the Pharisee. Scripture does record that Mary Magdalene was one of the women who stayed with Jesus through his death and was the first to witness his resurrection. For this reason, she is called the apostle to the apostles. In the relationship between Jesus and Mary Magdalene, we see that Jesus was not afraid of passionate love but only interested that it be directed in ways that are life-giving and holy. Pray this week for the grace to love God with the same passion that Mary Magdalene had.

PRACTICE OF HOPE

TO RECONCILE ALL THINGS. Since 1989, the Crossroads program of the Greater Dallas Community of Churches has matched up more than 150 congregations across racial, ethnic and religious lines. Through worship, fellowship and dialogue, partner churches examine issues of justice and reconciliation and develop social action responses. The effort is building positive and creative partnerships in a diverse and divided community. Recently, a partnership produced a joint statement condemning the decision by an all-white jury to sentence a defendant to 10 years probation for his participation in the "skinhead" murder of an African American man.

PRACTICE OF CHARITY

TAKE CARE OF HIM. The suffering that accompanies an illness that leads to death can be substantial: Energy and resources can be drained; times of deep despair and anger can set in. It is important that people are available to support both the one dying and the family. This is a tough challenge, however, because our society is geared more toward promoting images of glamour and youthfulness than it is toward supporting and sustaining the dignity of the dying. We are invited by our God to stand with those in pain and to give them comfort and strength. Consider volunteering with your parish hospice program, or check your local phone book for the number of a hospice program in your area.

WEEKDAY READINGS **(Mo-Th) Exodus, chapters 1—3; (Fr) 11:10—12:14; (Sa) Mary Magdalene**

READING I *Genesis 18:1–10*

The LORD appeared to Abraham by the oaks of Mamre, as he sat at the door of his tent in the heat of the day. Abraham lifted up his eyes and looked, and behold, three men stood in front of him. When he saw them, he ran from the tent door to meet them, and bowed himself to the earth, and said, "My lord, if I have found favor in your sight, do not pass by your servant. Let a little water be brought, and wash your feet, and rest yourselves under the tree, while I fetch a morsel of bread, that you may refresh yourselves, and after that you may pass on—since you have come to your servant." So they said, "Do as you have said." And Abraham hastened into the tent to Sarah, and said, "Make ready quickly three measures of fine meal, knead it, and make cakes." And Abraham ran to the herd, and took a calf, tender and good, and gave it to the servant, who hastened to prepare it. Then he took curds, and milk, and the calf which he had prepared, and set it before them; and he stood by them under the tree while they ate.

They said to Abraham, "Where is Sarah your wife?" And he said, "She is in the tent." The LORD said, "I will surely return to you in the spring, and Sarah your wife shall have a son."

READING II *Colossians 1:24–28*

Now I rejoice in my sufferings for your sake, and in my flesh I complete what is lacking in Christ's afflictions for the sake of his body, that is, the church, of which I became a minister according to the divine office which was given to me for you, to make the word of God fully known, the mystery hidden for ages and generations but now made manifest to the saints. To them God chose to make known how great among the Gentiles are the riches of the glory of this mystery, which is Christ in you, the hope of glory, whom we proclaim, warning every one and teaching every one in all wisdom, that we may present every one mature in Christ.

GOSPEL *Luke 10:38–42*

As Jesus and his disciples went on their way, Jesus entered a village; and a woman named Martha received him into her house. And she had a sister called Mary, who sat at the Lord's feet and listened to his teaching. But Martha was distracted with much serving; and she went to Jesus and said, "Lord, do you not care that my sister has left me to serve alone? Tell her then to help me." But the Lord answered her, "Martha, Martha, you are anxious and troubled about many things; one thing is needful. Mary has chosen the good portion, which shall not be taken away from her."

REFLECTION

Jesus and the disciples were "on their way" (*poreuomai*, travelling — the journey theme), but then they went their separate ways. Jesus entered a village and was welcomed into Martha's house. Mary, Martha's sister, recognizing the presence of Jesus, sat at his feet and "heard the word" he spoke. But there was certainly much work to be done preparing refreshments and serving the honored guest. On hearing Martha's complaint, Jesus points out to her that she is worried and concerned, stirred up about many things. He continues by saying that just one thing is needed.

Luke was the only evangelist who considered this incident important enough to record. Why? In the context of Luke/Acts, concerned as the author was with the proclamation of the good news and the social implications of that news, it is not improbable that Luke wanted to present an image of Christian hospitality. Not only was this welcoming attitude part of the cultural tradition of the Middle East, it also became a trait of Christian communities.

The one necessity in welcoming others into one's home or community is being present to them — listening to what they have to say, as Mary does in this scene. Martha is caught up in the many demands put upon her by society's rules for serving guests. But really, there is little that is needed — or only one thing. Much of the anxiety and concern in serving has more to do with conforming to society's demands or with the desire of the host or hostess to shine as a model of accomplished and generous hospitality. Mary, disciple of Jesus and model of discipleship, has chosen the most important thing required in welcoming others — her presence and full attention, so that it is her guest who shines.

■ **The Greek word for hospitality is *philanthropia*, love of human beings, kindness. In the light of today's gospel reading, reflect on our attitudes regarding hospitality.**

■ **In your interactions with others, how do you balance the need to act and the need to listen? Is such a balance present in your life? If so, how?**

■ **Are you comfortable with listening while others do the talking? How do you try to let others shine?**

PRACTICE OF FAITH

HOSPITALITY. On Saturday we celebrate the feast of St. Martha and, coincidentally, today we hear the story of Jesus' visit to the home of Martha and her sister Mary. Though Jesus gave Mary credit for her quiet listening attitude, Christians have honored Martha as a patroness of Christian activism. In honor of Martha (who is also the patroness of cooks) and in imitation of Abraham, invite people into your home for a meal. If possible, bake bread or prepare something home grown. Let this meal be an invitation by the members of your household to others, and let your table be a place where Jesus is recognized in your generous breaking of the bread.

PRACTICE OF HOPE

MARY CHOSE THE GOOD PORTION. Dolores Mission Church in East Los Angeles houses a school and women's shelter in its parish hall. On Sundays, tortillas and *menudo,* a pungent soup, are served there after church.

The gospel reading one Sunday was the story of Jesus' visit to Mary and Martha. Father Greg Boyle asked the congregation, "Why do you think only men usually sat at Jesus' feet to listen and learn?" Seven year-old Miguel answered confidently, "Because the men don't know how to make *menudo.*"

Dolores Mission Church is a haven of hope amid poverty, illegal drug activity and gang violence. It is also a force for change, as women lead Bible studies and men get comfortable in the kitchen.

PRACTICE OF CHARITY

THAT YOU MAY REFRESH YOURSELVES. Our homes are places where we can be ourselves, unwind and shut out the cares of the day. But our homes cannot become places of isolation. With opened arms, Abraham and Sarah welcomed the messengers of God into their home. We are called to do the same. Do not let the summer go by without inviting neighbors over for an evening. Begin to extend hospitality to those who are new in your neighborhood or apartment complex. Then, God's messengers will find a place to refresh themselves and you will be refreshed by the strangers you welcomed.

WEEKDAY READINGS Exodus 14:5–18; 2 Corinthians 4:7–15; Exodus 16:1–15; 19:1–2, 9–11, 16–20; 20:1–17; 24:3–8

READING I *Genesis 18:20–32*

The LORD said to Abraham, "Because the outcry against Sodom and Gomorrah is great and their sin is very grave, I will go down to see whether they have done altogether according to the outcry which has come to me; and if not, I will know."

So the men turned from there, and went toward Sodom; but Abraham still stood before the LORD. Then Abraham drew near, and said, "Will you indeed destroy the righteous with the wicked? Suppose there are fifty righteous within the city; will you then destroy the place and not spare it for the fifty righteous who are in it? Far be it from you to do such a thing, to slay the righteous with the wicked, so that the righteous fare as the wicked! Far be that from you! Shall not the Judge of all the earth do right?" And the LORD said, "If I find at Sodom fifty righteous in the city, I will spare the whole place for their sake." Abraham answered, "Behold, I have taken upon myself to speak to the Lord, I who am but dust and ashes. Suppose five of the fifty righteous are lacking? Will you destroy the whole city for lack of five?" And the LORD said, "I will not destroy it if I find forty-five there." Again Abraham spoke to the LORD, and said, "Suppose forty are found there." The LORD answered, "For the sake of forty I will not do it." Then Abraham said, "Oh let not the Lord be angry, and I will speak. Suppose thirty are found there." The LORD answered, "I will not do it, if I find thirty there." Abraham said, "Behold, I have taken upon myself to speak to the Lord. Suppose twenty are found there." The LORD answered, "For the sake of twenty I will not destroy it." Then Abraham said, "Oh let not the Lord be angry, and I will speak again but this once. Suppose ten are found there." The LORD answered, "For the sake of ten I will not destroy it." And having finished speaking to Abraham, the LORD departed; and Abraham returned to his place.

READING II *Colossians 2:12–14*

You were buried with Christ in baptism, in which you were also raised with him through faith in the working of God, who raised him from the dead. And you, who were dead in trespasses and the uncircumcision of your flesh, God made alive together with Christ, having forgiven us all our trespasses, having canceled the bond which stood against us with its legal demands; this God set aside, nailing it to the cross.

GOSPEL *Luke 11:1–13*

Jesus was praying in a certain place, and when he ceased, one of his disciples said to him, "Lord, teach us to pray, as John taught his disciples." And Jesus said to them, "When you pray, say:

"Father, hallowed be your name. May your dominion come. Give us each day our daily bread; and forgive us our sins, for we ourselves forgive every one who is indebted to us; and lead us not into temptation."

And Jesus said to them, "Which of you will go to a friend at midnight, saying, 'Friend, lend me three loaves; for a friend of mine has arrived on a journey, and I have nothing to set out'; and the friend will answer from within, 'Do not bother me; the door is now shut, and my children are with me in bed; I cannot get up and give you anything'? I tell you, though the friend will not get up and provide anything because of the friendship, yet because of the neighbor's persistence the friend will rise and provide whatever is needed. And I tell you, Ask, and it will be given you; seek, and you will find; knock, and it will be opened to you. For every one who asks receives, and every one who seeks finds, and to everyone who knocks it will be opened. What father among you, if his son asks for a fish, will instead of a fish give him a serpent; or if he asks for an egg, will give him a scorpion? If you then, who are evil, know how to give good gifts to your children, how much more will the heavenly Father give the Holy Spirit to those who ask!"

REFLECTION

The gospel reading today again focuses on discipleship. Luke, of all the gospel writers, emphasizes the importance of prayer, both in the ministry of Jesus and in the life of a disciple. The first portion of the reading contains Jesus' instruction on the pattern suitable for all prayer. The second part of the reading highlights prayers of petition.

The instruction of Jesus contains the elements of prayer he learned from within his own religious tradition. The prayer opens with the recognition of the "otherness" of God and the sacredness of God's name. The second part of the prayer expresses the people's desire that the days of promise be fulfilled, that the kingdom of God appear. The next three elements are requests to fulfill needs.

There is ambiguity regarding the meaning of *epiousion*, translated as "daily" in our text. It is helpful to place this request within the context of the journey motif and the commissioning of the disciples. The meaning of *epiousion*, then, is nuanced by the disciples' trust that God will provide for them through others, on a day-to-day basis, as they continue their journey.

The next petition is a statement of the early Christian conviction that forgiveness of others was an essential part of Jesus' teaching and a prerequisite for any request for God's forgiveness. The verb used for forgive, *aphiemi*, means to cancel, leave behind, dismiss. The disciples hope for forgiveness because they forgive others.

The last request may be related to Jesus' testing in the wilderness: We are not to test God by doing irrational things, expecting to be bailed out by miracles. In this request, the disciple — like Jesus in the garden (22:39–42) — is to have a healthy reluctance to enter the process of testing or trial, a reluctance that arises from a clear awareness of human weakness.

■ **How would you describe prayer, from your own experience and in your own words?**

■ **In most religious traditions, there is public or communal prayer, and private or personal prayer. How would you compare the two forms, as you experience them in your life?**

PRACTICE OF FAITH

SAINTED SOLDIER. Tomorrow the church will remember a great saint who turned all his warriors' energy toward fighting ignorance and spiritual sloth. St. Ignatius of Loyola, born in the Basque region of Spain, experienced a conversion of heart during a long and painful recuperation from a war wound. Through his *Spiritual Exercises* and preaching, Ignatius increased both knowledge and fervor in the lives of others. Those who joined him became the nucleus of the Society of Jesus, the Jesuits. This prayer of St. Ignatius is one worth memorizing:

Take, O Lord, and receive my entire liberty,
my memory, my understanding
   and my whole will.
All that I am and all that I possess
   you have given to me.
I surrender it all to you to be disposed of
   according to your will.
Give me only your love and your grace;
with these I will be rich enough
   and desire nothing more.

PRACTICE OF HOPE

ASK, AND IT WILL BE GIVEN. Emma Dora Asher, an 85-year-old widow, lived alone in Dade City, Florida. She tended a large garden with hoe and rake and shovel. The day before Thanksgiving, she lost her balance and fell. She called long and hard, but no one heard.

After a while she stopped struggling and said, "Lord, you know I'm not one to wait 'til tomorrow to be thankful. Right down here, right in this dirt, I'm thankful. And if I die here, I'll die thankful. And if I'm not to die here, you'll have to get me up, 'cause there ain't nobody else to do it."

She explained, "The Lord sent it to me to just hook my large hoe around the fencepost and pull myself up by the handle. I knew since he told me to do it, it would work, and it did. For everything — no matter how great or small — I'm thankful."

PRACTICE OF CHARITY

GOOD GIFTS. Peer pressure among children and adults compels us to buy, buy, buy gifts for our children. But what exactly are good gifts?

A good gift teaches something about the world we live in — our respect for the environment, our respect for people, our respect for God's creation. A good gift will last, and can be recycled. A good gift is often one that brings people together to enjoy it. A good gift amuses, delights, and warms the heart.

The next time you are looking for a gift, think about what our gift-buying and giving are teaching our children.

WEEKDAY READINGS (Mo–We) Exodus 32:15 — 34:35; 40:16–21, 34–38; Leviticus 23:1–37; 25:1, 8–17

READING I *Daniel 7:9–10, 13–14*

As I looked,
thrones were placed
   and one that was ancient of days sat down,
whose raiment was white as snow,
   and the hear of whose head like pure wool,
whose throne was fiery flames,
   its wheels were burning fire.
A stream of fire issued
   and came forth from before the Ancient of Days,
who a thousand thousands served,
   and before whom ten thousand times ten
      thousand stood;
the court sat in judgment,
   and the books were opened.
I saw in the night visions,
and behold, with the clouds of heaven
   there came one like a human being,
and he came before the Ancient of Days,
   before whom he was presented.
And to the human being was given rule
   and glory and dominion,
that all peoples, nations, and languages
   should serve him;
the rule of this man of heaven is an everlasting rule,
   which shall not pass away,
and his dominion one
   that shall not be destroyed.

READING II *2 Peter 1:16–19*

For we did not follow cleverly devised myths when we made known to you the power and coming of our Lord Jesus Christ, but we were eyewitnesses of his majesty. For when Jesus our Lord received honor and glory from God, the Father, and the voice was borne to him by the Majestic Glory, "This is my Son, my beloved one, with whom I am well pleased," we heard this voice borne from heaven, for we were with Jesus on the holy mountain. And we have the prophetic word made more sure. You will do well to pay attention to this as to a lamp shining in a dark place, until the day dawns and the morning star rises in your hearts.

GOSPEL *Luke 9:28–36*

About eight days after these sayings Jesus took with him Peter and John and James, and went up on the mountain to pray. And as he was praying, the appearance of his countenance was altered, and his raiment became dazzling white. And behold, two men talked with him, Moses and Elijah, who appeared in glory and spoke of his departure, which we was to accomplish at Jerusalem. Now Peter and those who were with him were heavy with sleep, and when the wakened they saw his glory and the two men who stood with him. And as the men were parting from him, Peter said to Jesus, "Master, it is well that we are here; let us make three booths, one for you and one for Moses and one for Elijah" — not knowing what he said. As he said this, a cloud came and overshadowed them; and they were afraid as they entered the cloud. And a voice came out of the cloud, saying, "This is my Son, the chosen one; listen to him!" And when the voice had spoken, Jesus was found alone. And they kept silence and told no one in those days anything of what they had seen.

REFLECTION

The reading from 2 Peter can help us understand just how much the Transfiguration event meant to the Christian communities of the late first and early second centuries. Following a custom of the time, the author of 2 Peter writes as if he were Simon Peter, in order to add credibility to his work. He is writing to those already familiar with the synoptic accounts of the Transfiguration and is responding to those who contend that faith in the second coming of Jesus was based on a myth. Evidently there were already those who accused Christians of wishful thinking based on fantasy, which would explain why the author would want to use Peter's role as an eyewitness to the Transfiguration to strengthen his case.

The Transfiguration incident, recorded in all three synoptic gospels, was linked by all three to the coming of the kingdom in Jesus' exodus — his rising from the dead. The event was also a prophecy of the power and the coming (*parousia*, active presence, arrival) of the Lord. This prophetic word is reliable, firm and well-founded, because of its basis in the glimpse of glory that is given in the Transfiguration.

The author of 2 Peter then compares the event to a lamp, a small light shining (*phaino*, lighting up) in the dark and murky place that is our world until the day dawns. The synoptics and John often use "day of the Lord" to mean the coming of Jesus in glory. The morning star rises as dawn in the hearts of believers. (The word used for "hearts," *kardia*, connotes the inner self, the seat of physical vitality, the religious center to which God turns, and which determines moral conduct).

The Transfiguration, then, is a glimpse of life shining through the darkness of death. It is also, for the community of disciples throughout the ages, a prophetic lamp, a flickering vision of faith that relieves the murkiness of the unanswered questions until the brilliant dawn of Jesus' return in glory.

■ **Read the three synoptic accounts of the Transfiguration (Matthew 17:1–8; Mark 9:2–8; Luke 9:28–36), and compare the similarities and differences. This event held great significance for the early church, yet each evangelist described it differently. Why do you think that is? What does this tell you about the purposes of each gospel?**

■ **Do various interpretations and points of view strengthen or weaken the gospel message? Do they strengthen or weaken the church?**

PRACTICE OF FAITH

FULL GLORY. This year, the feast of the Transfiguration, which is always celebrated on the sixth of August, falls on a Sunday. This celebration gives us a glimpse into our future: In seeing Christ in his fullness, we are given a vision of the future glory God desires for all of us.

Unfortunately, on this very day history reminds us how far short we can fall in reflecting the glory of God in our actions. On this fiftieth anniversary of the bombing of Hiroshima, we must also be aware of the death and destruction of which we are capable. Fasting and prayer sometime during this week would be appropriate for all followers of the Prince of Peace.

PRACTICE OF HOPE

SHARING AMPLE GOODS. Dwelling House Savings and Loan, located in a primarily minority, low-income neighborhood in Pittsburgh, offers low-interest loans to borrowers who are considered high risks by other institutions. It is founded on the belief that home ownership is empowering, generating both financial stability and self-respect.

The organization recently responded to the economic hardships facing borrowers by voluntarily reducing interest rates on mortgages. In a rare choice to put people before profit, Dwelling House is "an institution that serves your need, not your greed."

PRACTICE OF CHARITY

HE WAS TRANSFIGURED BEFORE THEM. As we remember the anniversaries of the bombings of Hiroshima (August 6) and Nagasaki (August 9), we reflect on the horror of war. The massive destructive power of modern military technology is too great for us to imagine. And yet our nations continue to build weapons of war. First World countries continue to sell war technology to Third World countries who can ill afford it. It is time for a change in our country's foreign policy. We must shift our mode of thinking to recognize that real and lasting security comes not from nations arming themselves but from their being able to defend themselves against hunger, poverty, disease and illiteracy. Help our nation become transfigured. Write to your U.S. representative and senators. Enter a dialogue with them about our military expenditures and about more effective ways to ensure global security.

WEEKDAY READINGS (Mo–We) Numbers 11:4—14:35; 2 Corinthians 9:6–10; Deuteronomy 4:32–40; 6:4–13

READING I *Wisdom 18:6–9*

That night was made known beforehand
   to our forebears,
so that they might rejoice in sure knowledge of the
   oaths in which they trusted.
The deliverance of the righteous and the
   destruction of their enemies
were expected by your people.
For by the same means by which you punished
   our enemies
you called us to yourself and glorified us.
For in secret the holy children of the good people
   offered sacrifices,
and with one accord agreed to the divine law,
that the saints would share alike the same things,
both blessings and dangers;
and already they were singing the praises
   of the forebears.

READING II *Hebrews 11:8–17*

By faith Abraham obeyed when he was called to go
out to a place which he was to receive as an inheritance; and he went out, not knowing where he was
to go. By faith Abraham sojourned in the land of
promise, as in a foreign land, living in tents with
Isaac and Jacob, heirs with him of the same
promise. For he looked forward to the city which
has foundations, whose builder and maker is God.
By faith Sarah herself received power to conceive,
even when she was past the age, since she considered faithful the one who had promised. Therefore
from one man, and him as good as dead, were born
descendants as many as the stars of heaven and as
the innumerable grains of sand by the seashore.

   These all died in faith, not having received what
was promised, but having seen it and greeted it
from afar, and having acknowledged that they were
strangers and exiles on the earth. For people who
speak thus make it clear that they are seeking a
homeland. If they had been thinking of that land
from which they had gone out, they would have
had opportunity to return. But as it is, they desire a
better country, that is, a heavenly one. Therefore
God is not ashamed to be called their God, having
prepared for them a city.

[Complete reading: Hebrews 11:1–2, 8–19]

GOSPEL *Luke 12:32–40*

[At that time Jesus said,] "Fear not, little flock, for it
is your Father's good pleasure to give the dominion
to you. Sell your possessions, and give alms; provide
yourselves with purses that do not grow old, with a
treasure in the heavens that does not fail, where no
thief approaches and no moth destroys. For where
your treasure is, there will your heart be also.

   "Be dressed and ready, with your lamps burning, and be like those who are waiting for their
master to come home from the marriage feast, so
that they may open to him at once when he comes
and knocks. Blessed are those servants whom the
master finds awake when he comes; truly, I say to
you, he will have them sit at table and will dress
himself and come and serve them. If he comes in
the second watch, or in the third, and finds them so,
blessed are those servants! But know this: knowing
at what hour the thief was coming, the householder
would not have left the house to be broken into.
You also must be ready; for the Man of Heaven is
coming at an unexpected hour."

[Complete reading: Luke 12:32–48]

Tuesday, August 15, 1995

THE ASSUMPTION OF MARY

VIGIL

1 Chronicles 15:3–4, 15–16; 16:1–2 *David before the ark.*
1 Corinthians 15:54–57 *God gave us victory over death.*
Luke 11:27–28 *Blessed is the womb that bore you!*

DAY

Revelation 11:19; 12:1–6, 10 *A woman clothed in the sun.*
1 Corinthians 15:20–26 *Christ is the firstfruits of the dead.*
Luke 1:39–56 *He has raised the lowly to the heights.*

Now we keep the festival of Mary's passover. In time,
each one of us will be gathered into the reign of God,
shining like the sun with the moon at our feet.

REFLECTION

The first part of today's gospel has to do with the disciples' attitude regarding possessions. There should be a readiness to sell one's goods, give away what attracts thieves and focus the heart on what cannot be taken away. Luke later clarifies this teaching in Acts 4:32–37, where it is clear that the community advocated and practiced a sharing of goods yet allowed those who wished to do so to retain what they had. The principle was that no one should cling to possessions while others were in need.

The second admonition concerns the attitude of readiness. In early Christian communities, the second coming of Christ was expected in the not too distant future; the message in this passage is that disciples should keep their attention focused on the return of the master so that they will be awake to open the door when he returns.

Jesus' response to Peter's question is interesting for its use of the word *doulos* (slave) for steward: Even in his position of responsibility, the steward is in a state of dependency on the master. However, a different word is used for those beaten by the unfaithful steward. They are called *paidas,* or children. The steward and those who work for him are all "children" of one family. It is only in relation to the *kyrios,* the master, that they are *douloi,* slaves.

Those entrusted with positions of leadership are to be aware that they are, together with those in their care, equally *paidas* and equally servants of the one Lord.

■ Do scripture texts written during a time when Christ's return was thought to be imminent have meaning for us almost 2000 years later? How do you maintain an alert attitude while waiting for the coming of the Lord?

■ Reflect on the ideas of leadership, authority and power that are operative in our society. Compare these ideas with the image of the Christian leader that Jesus presents—a servant, brother or sister. Which models do our civic and religious leaders follow? Which model do you follow?

PRACTICE OF FAITH

LADY MARY. In a few days we will celebrate the solemnity of The Assumption of the Virgin Mary into Heaven. This celebration of Mary's full life in Christ has been a part of church life and belief since at least the sixth century. As this ancient feast of Mary approaches, pray this prayer, written in the fourth century by St. Athanasius.

It becomes you to be mindful of us, as you stand near him who granted you all graces, for you are the Mother of God and our Queen. Help us for the sake of the King, the Lord God and Master who was born of you. For this reason you are called full of grace.

Remember us, most holy Virgin, and bestow on us gifts from the riches of your graces, Virgin full of grace.

PRACTICE OF HOPE

ASSURANCE OF THINGS HOPED FOR. The day after the nation commemorated the 25th anniversary of the assassination of Martin Luther King, Jr., a young African American man hired to work with "at risk" students at North Carolina's Brevard High School was fired, causing many to cry discrimination.

Black students boycotted classes, while their parents and local pastors helped strategize a response.

Issues that had been simmering for years came to the surface. A task force was put into place, and five months later the school board agreed to a plan that included: hiring more minority teachers; offering a black history course; requiring training among staff to minimize prejudice; and implementing strict policies regarding racial slurs by staff and students. "Stick together and you can get some things accomplished," said community leader Selena Robinson. "And always keep God in front."

PRACTICE OF CHARITY

SEEKING A HOMELAND. The Statue of Liberty symbolizes our nation's willingness to welcome to its shores those escaping oppression and injustice. Yet how do we work with the complex issue of refugee immigration? How can we welcome our brothers and sisters fleeing injustice in their own lands? One small step we can take is to reevaluate our own prejudices and insecurities regarding immigrants. We can also keep ourselves informed on both the situation of refugees and our national policies. To learn more, contact: United States Catholic Conference—Migration and Refugee Services Department, 3211 Fourth Street NE, Washington DC 20017-1194; 202-541-3000.

WEEKDAY READINGS Deuteronomy 10:12–22; (Tu) The Assumption of the Virgin Mary into Heaven; Deuteronomy 34:1–12; (Th–Sa) Joshua, chapters 3 and 24

READING I *Jeremiah 38:4–6, 8–10*

The chieftains said to the king, "Let Jeremiah be put to death, for he is weakening the hands of the soldiers who are left in this city, and the hands of all the people, by speaking such words to them. For this man is not seeking the welfare of this people, but their harm." King Zedekiah said, "Behold, he is in your hands, for the king can do nothing against you." So they took Jeremiah and cast him into the cistern of Malchiah, the king's son, which was in the court of the guard, letting Jeremiah down by ropes. And there was no water in the cistern, but only mire, and Jeremiah sank in the mire.

Ebed-melech went from the king's house and said to the king, "My lord the king, these men have done evil in all that they did to Jeremiah the prophet by casting him into the cistern; and he will die there of hunger, for there is no bread left in the city." Then the king commanded Ebed-melech, the Ethiopian, "Take three men with you from here, and lift Jeremiah the prophet out of the cistern before he dies."

READING II *Hebrews 12:1–4*

Since we are surrounded by so great a cloud of witnesses, let us also lay aside every weight, and sin which clings so closely, and let us run with perseverance the race that is set before us, looking to Jesus the pioneer and perfecter of our faith, who for the joy that was set before him endured the cross, despising the shame, and is seated at the right hand of the throne of God.

Consider Jesus who endured from sinners such hostility against himself, so that you may not grow weary or fainthearted.

GOSPEL *Luke 12:49–53*

[At that time Jesus said,] "I came to cast fire upon the earth; and would that it were already kindled! I have a baptism to be baptized with; and how I am constrained until it is accomplished! Do you think that I have come to give peace on earth? No, I tell you, but rather division; for henceforth in one house there will be five divided, three against two and two against three; they will be divided, father against son and son against father, mother against daughter and daughter against her mother, and in-laws against one another."

REFLECTION

This short gospel reading is rich in meaning. Jesus states that he has come to cast fire upon the earth. Fire has several connotations. In the Hebrew Bible it was a sign of God's holiness and presence (see Exodus 13:21–22); God is described as a consuming fire (Deuteronomy 4:24), an irresistible force. Fire is also related to judgment (Genesis 19:24; Exodus 9:24; Leviticus 10:2; 2 Kings 1:10; Amos 1:4ff) and, in particular, to the Day of the Lord (Joel 2:20; Malachi 3:19).

In the New Testament, it is this last connotation that dominates — fire as a sign of the last days, of the end time. John the Baptizer had already pointed to the one who would baptize in the Holy Spirit and in fire (Matthew 3:11–12; Luke 3:9, 16–17), and in this passage Jesus connects fire and baptism. From this text, there emerges a sense of urgency and eagerness to enter into the final stage of the initiation of the messianic community.

What is this "fire" that Jesus is eager to cast upon the earth? In the context of Luke's narrative, the fire is a symbol of the "baptism" — the suffering, death and rising — of Jesus. It prefigures the sending of the Spirit in the form of tongues of fire (see Acts 2:17–21).

It is also clear from this text that the fire of the eschaton (the "last days," the age of the messianic community) would scorch a dividing line through the land. Elsewhere, Jesus speaks of peace, but here he makes clear that the peace he brings is not a peace built on false harmonies and passive acceptance; because Jesus' message often runs contrary to the norms of society, there will be division. Jesus comes bearing the good news to the poor and the marginalized, but this is not welcome news for those who oppose change. To accept the fire and the baptism is to be, like Jesus, in opposition to the way things are.

■ **Reflect on the paradox of peace and division in the life of a disciple. Describe someone you know or have read about who conveyed a sense of peace and gentleness while facing opposition or caused division by his or her adherence to principle.**

■ **As you read about the fire Jesus came to cast on the earth, where do you see this "fire" in the world today? Who are those, in your eyes, who are lighting up our world with God's presence?**

PRACTICE OF FAITH

KEEPING THE FEASTS. Many times throughout this book, you have encountered suggested ways for keeping the feasts of various saints. The tradition of remembering these heroes and heroines of holiness goes back to the earliest centuries of the church, when martyrs and other holy men and women were acclaimed by the local church to be saints. A list, or canon, of the saints of Rome is preserved in the first eucharistic prayer, the Roman Canon. The present process for official recognition of saints, or canonization, is relatively recent, dating only from 1588. In addition to celebrating the feast of those saints with universal significance, local churches often celebrate the memories of their own important saints. Do you know of the saints that are special to the church in America? To your local diocese? Spend some time this week learning more about the great cloud of witnesses surrounding you.

PRACTICE OF HOPE

SURROUNDED BY WITNESSES. A pastor of a small rural church was struggling with some difficult personal issues in her life. She stood one Sunday morning to read the words of the pastoral prayer: "O Lord, we don't know what to do. You alone can be our source of help...." Her voice broke and she was unable to continue. An awkward silence descended.

Then, from the congregation, a voice began, "And Jesus taught us to pray, 'Our father in heaven....'" The congregation spoke the prayer together while the pastor composed herself to continue, empowered by the grace of the moment to carry on.

PRACTICE OF CHARITY

RUN WITH PERSEVERANCE. Or if not run, how about walk? CROP Walk, sponsored by Church World Service, is an annual event dedicated to stopping hunger. The program is simple: Area churches organize their congregations to get pledges for every mile walked. The money raised is divided between the local community and Church World Service international projects. If you would like to participate, contact your local churches to see if they hold a CROP Walk, or contact: Church World Service, PO Box 968, Elkhart IN 46515; 800-456-1310.

WEEKDAY READINGS **Judges 2:11–19; 6:11–24; 9:6–15; Revelation 21:9–14; (Fr-Sa) Ruth—entire book**

READING I *Isaiah 66:18–21*

[Thus says the LORD:] "For I know their works and their thoughts, and I am coming to gather all nations and tongues; and they shall come and shall see my glory, and I will set a sign among them. And from them I will send survivors to the nations, to Tarshish, Put and Lud, who draw the bow, to Tubal and Javan, to the coastlands afar off, that have not heard my fame or seen my glory; and they shall declare my glory among the nations. And they shall bring all the children of Israel from all the nations as an offering to the LORD, upon horses, and in chariots, and in litters, and upon mules, and upon dromedaries, to my holy mountain Jerusalem, says the LORD, just as the Israelites bring their cereal offering in a clean vessel to the house of the LORD. And some of them also I will take for priests and for Levites, says the LORD."

READING II *Hebrews 12:5–7, 11–13*

Have you forgotten the exhortation which addresses you as if you were children?

"My child, do not regard lightly the discipline
    of the Lord,
nor lose courage when you are punished
    by the Lord.
For whom the Lord loves, the Lord disciplines,
and everyone whom the Lord receives
    is chastised."

It is for discipline that you have to endure. God is treating you as if you were children; for what child is there whose father does not discipline? For the moment all discipline seems painful rather than pleasant; later it yields the peaceful fruit of righteousness to those who have been trained by it.

Therefore lift your drooping hands and strengthen your weak knees, and make straight paths for your feet, so that what is lame may not be put out of joint but rather be healed.

GOSPEL *Luke 13:22–30*

Jesus went on his way through towns and villages, teaching, and journeying toward Jerusalem. And some one said to him, "Lord, will those who are saved be few?" And Jesus said to them, "Strive to enter by the narrow door; for many, I tell you, will seek to enter and will not be able. When once the householder has risen up and shut the door, you will begin to stand outside and to knock at the door, saying, 'Lord, open to us.' The householder will answer you, 'I do not know where you come from.' Then you will begin to say, 'We ate and drank in your presence, and you taught in our streets.' But the householder will say, 'I tell you, I do not know where you come from; depart from me, all you workers of iniquity!' There you will weep and gnash your teeth, when you see Abraham and Isaac and Jacob and all the prophets in the dominion of God and you yourselves thrust out. And the people will come from east and west, and from north and south, and sit at table in the dominion of God. And behold, some are last who will be first, and some are first who will be last."

R E F L E C T I O N

In today's gospel passage, Jesus brings out three major points concerning salvation. First, it involves a struggle; second, there are certain crucial moments; and third, belonging to a religious tradition does not guarantee entrance into the kingdom.

In the phrase, "Strive to enter by the narrow door," Luke uses the verb *agonizomai,* which is a more powerful expression than "strive." It involves conflict, fight and struggle, and in this text it implies an exertion and focus on a goal, on overcoming obstacles. This is borne out by Luke's use of the verb *ischyo,* translated as "able"; *ischyo,* in fact, emphasizes the qualities of strength and capacity. The message is now clearer: Those who struggle, who possess a certain staying power, will make it through the narrow door.

The second point Jesus makes here is that time and timing are extremely important. The occasion for action (the *kairos*) comes and is gone—a truth we have known all along but of which Jesus reminds us. When the occasion has passed, when the householder has shut the door, the moment is gone; it is too late, and no amount of knocking can bring the opportunity back.

The third point in Jesus' teaching about salvation is that even if people have firsthand knowledge of Jesus, this does not mean that Jesus will recognize them if they are workers (*ergatai,* active doers) of evil. Nor does membership in the people of the patriarchs and prophets guarantee against being shut out.

The passage ends with one of the clearest statements on the universal character of the kingdom. Jesus often said that he came first for the children of Israel; here he presents the familiar image of the kingdom as a banquet, with guests coming in from the four corners of the earth. Those called first may end up squeezing through the door, while those called last may be seated at the head table.

■ **How would you describe your own struggles as a disciple? Each day presents its small moments of *kairos,* opportune times to move into action. Review the day or days just passed. Can you find those moments and recall how you responded or did not respond?**

PRACTICE OF FAITH

AFRICAN SAINTS. If today were not a Sunday, the church would be observing the feast of St. Monica, mother of St. Augustine (whose feast is tomorrow). These two saints lived in North Africa and have had a profound influence on Christianity. St. Monica is honored for her perseverance in praying for her son's conversion. Her quiet, consistent and loving witness bore fruit for all the church: Augustine was baptized in 387 and became bishop of Hippo in North Africa less than ten years later. His writings and homilies show him to be one of the greatest intellects in the history of the church.

PRACTICE OF HOPE

GATHER ALL NATIONS AND TONGUES. In 1984, the Religious Task Force, a coalition of U.S. church and peace groups, sponsored its first "Children of War Tour." The tours have brought together young people from places as diverse as South Africa, Northern Ireland, Palestine and Cambodia to tell their stories.

Thirteen-year-old Richard Aguirre from Nicaragua said of the experience: "I learned that there is cruelty and suffering in other countries. That makes you feel good and bad. Bad, because almost all the world is suffering. But good, because we are not alone. And when some part of the world can solve its problems, maybe other parts of the world can follow the example, and maybe there will be peace in all the world."

PRACTICE OF CHARITY

MAKE STRAIGHT PATHS FOR YOUR FEET. The month of October is designated Respect Life Month. As such, it is a good time for further education regarding life issues. The United States Catholic Conference publishes a packet of material for Respect Life Month that addresses several life issues. You can enter into the dialogue by joining your parish social concerns group, by working on a Respect Life Month committee or by taking the time to read more about the issues. Every parish receives the Respect Life material in September. If your parish does not, write: Secretariat for Pro-Life Activities, National Conference of Catholic Bishops, 3211 Fourth Street NE, Washington DC 20017-1194. Or call 202-541-3070.

WEEKDAY READINGS 1 Thessalonians 1:1–10; Jeremiah 1:17–19; (We–Sa) 1 Thessalonians 2:9—4:11

READING I *Sirach 3:17–18, 20, 28–29*

Perform your tasks in meekness;
    then you will be loved by those whom
        God accepts.
The greater you are, the more you
        must humble yourself; so you will
        find favor in the signt of the lord.
Seek not what is too difficult for you,
    nor investigate what is beyond your power.
The mind of the intelligent appreciates proverbs,
    and an attentive ear is the desire of the wise.
Water extinguishes a blazing fire:
    so almsgiving atones for sin.

READING II *Hebrews 12:18–19, 22–24*

You have not come to what may be touched, a blazing fire, and darkness, and gloom, and a tempest, and the sound of a trumpet, and a voice whose words made the hearers entreat that no further messages be spoken to them. But you have come to Mount Zion and to the city of the living God, the heavenly Jerusalem, and to innumerable angels in festal gathering, and to the assembly of the firstborn who are enrolled in heaven, and to a judge who is God of all, and to the spirits of the just made perfect, and to Jesus, the mediator of a new covenant.

GOSPEL *Luke 14:1, 7–14*

One sabbath when Jesus went to dine at the house of a ruler who belonged to the Pharisees, they were watching him.

Now Jesus told a parable to those who were invited, when he marked how they chose the places of honor, saying to them, "When you are invited by a certain man to a marriage feast, do not sit down in a place of honor, lest someone more eminent than you be invited by him; and he who invited you both will come and say to you, 'Give place to this guest,' and then you will begin with shame to take the lowest place. But when you are invited, go and sit in the lowest place, so that when your host comes he may say to you, 'Friend, go up higher'; then you will be honored in the presence of all who sit at table with you. For they who exalt themselves will be humbled, and they who humble themselves will be exalted."

Jesus said also to the one who had invited him, "When you give a dinner or a banquet, do not invite your friends or your brothers or your kin or rich neighbors, lest they also invite you in return, and you be repaid. But when you give a feast, invite those who are poor, who are maimed, who are lame, who are blind, and you will be blessed, because they cannot repay you. You will be repaid at the resurrection of the just."

Friday, September 8, 1995

THE BIRTH OF THE VIRGIN MARY

Micah 5:1–4 *She who is to give birth is born!*
or
Romans 8:28–30 *We share the image of Christ.*

Matthew 1:1–16, 18–23 *Of her, Jesus was born.*

The words mother, *mater,* and material things, matter, are one and the same. In September, Mother Earth gives forth in fruitful abundance our material sustenance. Mother Mary is born, who knit together in her own fruitful body earth and heaven.

R E F L E C T I O N

The setting for Jesus' teaching in today's gospel reading is a meal at the home of one of the leaders of the Pharisees. As has occurred before (5:27–39, at Levi's home, and 7:36–50 and 11:37–54, at the homes of Pharisees), the meal becomes an occasion for a confrontation. Luke notes in verse 1 that "they," presumably the Pharisees, were watching him. The verb *paratereo* connotes a close scrutiny — the now-familiar attitude of the religious leaders who kept Jesus under close observation. Jesus, too, was alert, and Luke notes that Jesus gave close attention to the actions of those present. Jesus' carefully chosen remarks are directed first to the guests (verses 8–11) and then to his host (verses 12–14).

The first teaching is directed to the guests who were eager to get the best seats. A sense of honor or shame was very strong in the culture in which Jesus lived. The real lesson, however, is that it is God, not humans, who exalts. Those who lift themselves up over others will be brought down; those who regard themselves as among the "lowly," as human as anyone else, will be raised up. Raising up and exaltation belong to God; recognition of one's lowliness is the proper stance for human beings.

The second teaching goes against the accepted, normal practice of inviting only those who can be expected to return the favor in one form or another. Jesus reverses this norm: Do not invite to share a meal with you those who will some day reciprocate; instead, invite those who are never invited — the poor, the marginalized and those from whom no favors can be expected. The reading from Sirach expresses this same point of view: It is to the meek and gentle that God reveals secrets.

■ **It is a human tendency to seek honor, to show off. In your experience, is it difficult to follow the biblical teaching to be humble? To what extent do you think our culture makes it more difficult?**

■ **Do you help out "gratuitously" on a regular basis, without looking for thanks, publicity or even "feeling good about yourself"?**

PRACTICE OF FAITH

LABOR DAY. Monday we celebrate the gift of those who labor. Pray this prayer from *Catholic Household Blessings and Prayers* at the main celebratory meal of the day:

God our creator,
we are the work of your hands.
Guide us in our work,
that we may do it, not for self alone,
but for the common good.
Make us alert to injustice,
ready to stand in solidarity,
that there may be dignity for all
in labor and in labor's reward.
Grant this through Christ our Lord. Amen.

PRACTICE OF HOPE

TO THE MEEK ARE REVEALED THE SECRETS. Several years ago, I was on a bus heading home for my grandfather's funeral. I was feeling faint and overwhelmed with grief. With 38 empty seats from which to choose, an elderly woman wearing a bright-red knit stocking cap tottered down the aisle and fell into the seat next to mine, exclaiming, "Praise God, what a *beautiful* day!"

I was trying to figure out how I could get around her to change my seat, when she took my hand, gazed into my eyes, and asked, "Why are you so sad?" Suddenly I was telling this stranger all about my grandfather. After a while she said, "How good of God to give you such a gift!" And before long — thanks to an unexpected guardian angel — my sorrow had turned to gratitude.

PRACTICE OF CHARITY

TAKE THE LOWEST PLACE. What did Jesus have in mind when he spoke these words to his disciples? Could it not be seen as a mandate from Jesus for us to treat one another with equality, dignity and respect, to recognize that all carry the divine presence within them? We have one suggestion. This week do a mental check on how you interact with those you encounter. Be resolved to extend acts of kindness to all who are of service to you in your daily life.

WEEKDAY READINGS 1 Thessalonians 4:13–18; 5:1–11; Colossians 1:1–8; 1:9–14; (Fr) The Birth of the Virgin Mary; Colossians 1:21–23

READING I *Wisdom 9:13–18*

What human being can learn the counsel of God?
Or who can discern what the Lord wills?
For the reasoning of mortals is worthless,
and our designs are likely to fail,
for a perishable body weighs down the soul,
and this earthly tent burdens the thoughtful mind.
We can hardly guess at what is on earth,
and what is at hand we find with labor;
but who has traced out what is in the heavens?
Who has learned your counsel,
    unless you have given wisdom
and sent your holy Spirit from on high?
And thus the paths of those on earth were set right.

READING II *Philemon 9–10, 12–17*

I, Paul, an ambassador and now a prisoner also for Christ Jesus — I appeal to you for my child, Onesimus, whose father I have become in my imprisonment. I am sending him back to you, sending my very heart. I would have been glad to keep him with me, in order that he might serve me on your behalf during my imprisonment for the gospel; but I preferred to do nothing without your consent in order that your goodness might not be by compulsion but of your own free will.

Perhaps this is why Onesimus was parted from you for a while, that you might have him back for ever, no longer as a slave but more than a slave, as a beloved brother, especially to me but how much more to you, both in the flesh and in the Lord. So if you consider me your partner, receive him as you would receive me.

GOSPEL *Luke 14:25–33*

Great multitudes accompanied Jesus; and he turned and said to them, "They who come to me and do not hate their own father and mother and spouse and children and brothers and sisters, yes, and even their own life, cannot be my disciples. Those who do not bear their own cross and come after me, cannot be my disciples. For which of you, desiring to build a tower, does not first sit down and count the cost, whether there is enough to complete it? Otherwise, when the foundation has been laid, and the building cannot be finished, all who see it begin to mock the builder, saying, 'This person began to build, and was not able to finish.' Or what king, going to encounter another king in war, will not sit down first and take counsel whether he is able with ten thousand to meet him who comes against him with twenty thousand? And if not, while the other is yet a great way off, he sends an embassy and asks terms of peace. So therefore, whoever of you does not renounce all possessions cannot be my disciple."

Thursday, September 14, 1995

THE HOLY CROSS

Numbers 21:4–9 *Whoever gazed on the serpent received life.*

Philippians 2:6–11 *He accepted death on a cross.*

John 3:13–17 *God so loved the world…*

As the darkness of another autumn lowers around us, we lift high the shining cross. The means of the execution of a criminal has become the means of entering into eternal life. The wood of the cross is the ark that rescues us and the tree that feeds us.

R E F L E C T I O N

Jesus was accused by his enemies of many things, but no one could ever accuse him of drawing people to himself with false promises. Luke makes clear that Jesus had a large following among the common people. But unlike many popular figures, Jesus does not measure discipleship in numbers but in the willingness to place commitment to discipleship above all else. Today's text consists of a statement and a summary sentence.

Luke's choice of strong language is significant. He chose the word "hate" to express the importance of a clear, absolute preference for following Jesus. The "hate" has nothing to do with feelings and everything to do with a deliberate choice: To be a disciple is to prefer following Jesus above all else, even above one's own life. This preference will often be the cause of divisions. The reference to bearing the cross is a very active and deliberate one.

After the two parables, Luke concludes by summarizing Jesus' teaching in one sentence: Everyone who does not say farewell to all possessions is not able, does not have the capability, to be a disciple. The call to discipleship is no invitation to a position of prestige, ease or enhanced social status; it is a call to treat all "possessions" as marginal in a life focused on the journey.

■ **Jesus' teaching on the disciples' attitude toward possessions is one of Luke's favorites. How do you view your possessions? How do you relate to things: "more is better" or "only what I need"?**

■ **Making difficult, deliberate choices is sometimes required of a true disciple. Is the effort to live as a disciple the focus of your life? What difficult choices have you been faced with because of your beliefs? How did you respond?**

PRACTICE OF FAITH

CROSS OF GLORY. On Thursday we celebrate the feast of the Triumph of the Cross. Tradition has it that St. Helena, the mother of Emperor Constantine, discovered the true cross in Jerusalem in the fourth century. There, with the help of her son, she built the Basilica of the Holy Sepulchre over the site of the tomb of Jesus. During the seventh century, Jerusalem was captured by the Persians and the relic of the cross was taken from the basilica. Emperor Heraclius defeated the Persians and on September 14 returned the fragment of the cross to Jerusalem. This feast celebrates both the finding and the return of this important relic. Remember this feast by lighting candles near a cross or crucifix during prayer.

PRACTICE OF HOPE

RENOUNCE ALL POSSESSIONS. When Archbishop Janis Matulis of Latvia was dying, he asked a visitor to sing an old spiritual for him: "When I am alone, give me Jesus." When asked why he had requested the song, he explained that war had ravaged his homeland three times, killing two-fifths of its citizens. His church had been burned down and his wife had been taken away, never to be seen again. He realized then that he had only Jesus Christ.

"From that moment on," he said, "I learned how to use whatever came my way—little bits of medicine left over, a piece of coal, apples, spices—so that somehow the sacrament of God's love would be shared with the larger community because of Jesus Christ."

PRACTICE OF CHARITY

SAVED BY WISDOM. There is a Haitian proverb that says, *"Nou we kote nou kanpe,"* meaning, "We see from where we stand." In the work of charity we know this to be true. What an impact working with the homeless, persons living with AIDS or the working poor can have in someone's life. Volunteer Ministries in Haiti is concerned with engaging people to see with new eyes. Through their various programs in Haiti, the Catholic Diocese of Richmond is helping people to expand their view of the world. If you would like to begin an outreach ministry in your diocese or would like to participate in VMH, further information is available from the Haitian Ministry Commission, Diocese of Richmond, 811 Cathedral Place, Richmond VA 23220-4801; 804-359-5661.

WEEKDAY READINGS (Mo-We) Colossians 1:24—3:11; (Th) The Holy Cross; Hebrews 5:7-9; 1 Timothy 1:15-17

READING I *Exodus 32:7–11, 13–14*

The LORD said to Moses, "Go down; for your people, whom you brought up out of the land of Egypt, have corrupted themselves; they have turned aside quickly out of the way which I commanded them; they have made for themselves a molten calf, and have worshiped it and sacrificed to it, and said, 'These are your gods, O Israel, who brought you up out of the land of Egypt!' And the LORD said to Moses, "I have seen this people, and behold, it is a stiff-necked people; now therefore let me alone, that my wrath may burn hot against them and I may consume them; but of you I will make a great nation."

But Moses besought the LORD his God, and said, "O LORD, why does your wrath burn hot against your people, whom you have brought forth out of the land of Egypt with great power and with a mighty hand? Remember Abraham, Isaac, and Israel, your servants, to whom you swore by your own self, and said to them, 'I will multiply your descendants as the stars of heaven, and all this land that I have promised I will give to your descendants, and they shall inherit it for ever.'" And the LORD repented of the evil which the Lord thought to do to the chosen people.

READING II *Timothy 1:12–17*

I thank Christ Jesus our Lord, who has given me strength for this, because he judged me faithful by appointing me to his service, though I formerly blasphemed and persecuted and insulted him; but I received mercy because I had acted ignorantly in unbelief, and the grace of our Lord overflowed for me with the faith and love that are in Christ Jesus. The saying is sure and worthy of full acceptance, that Christ Jesus came into the world to save sinners. And I am the foremost of sinners; but I received mercy for this reason, that in me, as the foremost, Jesus Christ might display his perfect patience for an example to those who were to believe in him for eternal life. To the Sovereign of ages, immortal, invisible, the only God, be honor and glory for ever and ever. Amen.

GOSPEL *Luke 15:1–10*

The tax collectors and sinners were all drawing near to hear Jesus. And the Pharisees and the scribes murmured, saying, "This man receives sinners and eats with them."

So Jesus told them this parable: "Among you, which man, having a hundred sheep, if he has lost one of them, does not leave the ninety-nine in the wilderness, and go after the one which is lost, until he finds it? And having found it, he lays it on his shoulders, rejoicing. And coming home, he calls together his friends and his neighbors, saying to them, 'Rejoice with me, for I have found my sheep which was lost.' Just so, I tell you, there will be more joy in heaven over one sinner who repents than over ninety-nine righteous persons who need no repentance.

"Or what woman, having ten silver coins, if she loses one coin, does not light a lamp and sweep the house and seek diligently until she finds it? And having found it, she calls together her friends and neighbors, saying, 'Rejoice with me, for I have found the coin which I had lost.' Just so, I tell you, there is joy before the angels of God over one sinner who repents."

[Today's gospel continues with the parable of the prodigal son, Luke 15:11–32, which is also the gospel we read on the Fourth Sunday of Lent this year. See page 62 for this parable.]

REFLECTION

All three readings today form a unified whole with one message: repentance and conversion. In the first reading, the people are given yet one more chance to turn to the Lord, thanks to the prayer of Moses. In the letter to Timothy, Paul prays in thanksgiving for the mercy he received, recognizing that "Christ Jesus came into the world to save sinners." And in the three gospel parables, the saving mercy of God is brought out most clearly.

On the Fourth Sunday of Lent, we saw the context in which Luke places these parables. The shepherd, the woman and the father are all images of the God of relentless mercy, and these parables are told from that point of view. In the parallel version in Matthew 18:12–14, the sheep "goes astray." Here, Luke says that the man lost one of the sheep, using the word *apollymi* ("suffers the loss") to convey a keener sense of loss. He goes after the one sheep *until* he finds it (in Matthew, the phrase is "*if* he finds it"), returns rejoicing (*chairon*) and asks those gathered to rejoice with him. Jesus adds that there will be joy in heaven because of the repentant sinner.

Luke's second narrative, which features a woman, is a parable unique to his gospel. This image of God lighting a lamp, sweeping the house and carefully seeking until the coin is found is a very powerful one. The pattern in this parable is the same as in the first one, ending with the woman calling her friends and neighbors together in joy.

In both of these parables, as in the long narrative that follows, the joy explodes into a party. The shepherd calls his friends, the woman calls hers, the father prepares a feast; even in heaven there is the image of a community rejoicing. Luke presents in these narratives one of the essential aspects of the mission of Jesus — to seek and find what had been lost.

■ **How does the description of the shepherd God differ from your own image of God? What image would you choose to describe this God in a society that is unfamiliar with shepherds?**

■ **Reflect on the nature of discipleship as a continuous process of spiritual development. How would you react if, next Sunday, one or several paroled criminals were publicly and ritually welcomed back into the community?**

PRACTICE OF FAITH

TAX MAN. This Thursday we celebrate the feast of Saint Matthew. Scripture records that Matthew was at his tax post when Jesus called him to become one of his disciples. Besides being among the Twelve, Matthew is revered because of the gospel that is attributed to him. Scholars agree that Matthew's gospel was written for Jewish Christians, perhaps as late as 85–90 CE, sometime after the destruction of the temple in 70 CE. In the gospel reading for Matthew's feastday, we hear of the Pharisees' dismay at Jesus' choice to eat with outcasts. In honor of Matthew, take food to a homeless shelter, an AIDS hospice or some other place where you can participate in table fellowship with those who are marginalized in our society.

PRACTICE OF HOPE

REPENTANCE AND RECONCILIATION. On September 15, 1963, at 10:22 a.m., a bomb exploded at Sixteenth Street Baptist Church in Birmingham, Alabama — the work of the Ku Klux Klan in response to the desegregation of Birmingham's schools. Four schoolgirls — Denise McNair, Addie Mae Collins, Cynthia Wesley and Carole Robertson — were killed instantly. A week later, the Southern Baptist Convention's executive committee failed to pass a resolution to express grief and solidarity.

Thirty years later, the Baptist Peace Fellowship of North America chose to hold its annual conference in Birmingham. Thousands of people signed the "Birmingham Confession," which acknowledged "historic complicity with racism" and called the failure of leaders to speak out 30 years before "not simply an administrative mistake but a sin against the Holy Spirit." As an act of repentance and reparation, BPFNA executive director Ken Sehested presented a check to Rev. Christopher Hamlin of the church, along with a pledge to continue to work against racism.

PRACTICE OF CHARITY

APPOINTING ME TO HIS SERVICE. Whatever our works of charity, we regularly need to discern the guiding hand of God in our lives. Autumn is a traditional time for people to renew their parish commitments and to try new areas of service. It is a good time for the parish to offer a volunteer or ministry fair to help parishioners match their gifts to the needs within the parish and community. One idea is to set aside a Sunday during autumn as Ministry Sunday. Work with your pastoral associate or parish priest to set one up in your parish.

WEEKDAY READINGS (Mo–We) 1 Timothy, chapters 2—3; Ephesians 4:1-13; (Fr–Sa) 1 Timothy, chapter 6

READING I *Amos 8:4–7*

Hear this, you who trample upon the needy,
  and bring the poor of the land to an end,
saying, "When will the new moon be over,
    that we may sell grain?
And the sabbath,
    that we may offer wheat for sale,
that we may make the ephah small
    and the shekel great,
    and deal deceitfully with false balances,
that we may buy the poor for silver
    and the needy for a pair of sandals,
    and sell the refuse of the wheat?"
The LORD has sworn by the pride of Jacob:
    "Surely I will never forget any of their deeds."

READING II *1 Timothy 2:1–8*

First of all, I urge that supplications, prayers, inter-cessions, and thanksgivings be made for everyone, for rulers and all who are in high positions, that we may lead a quiet and peaceable life, godly and respectful in every way. This is good, and it is acceptable in the sight of God our Savior, who desires all humankind to be saved and to come to the knowledge of the truth. For there is one God, and there is one mediator between God and humankind, Christ Jesus, the human being, who gave himself as a ransom for all, the testimony to which was borne at the proper time. For this I was appointed a preacher and apostle (I am telling the truth, I am not lying), a teacher of the Gentiles in faith and truth.

I desire then that in every place the community should pray, lifting holy hands without anger or quarreling.

GOSPEL *Luke 16:1–13*

Jesus said to the disciples, "There was a rich man who had a steward, and charges were brought to him that this man was wasting his goods. And the rich man called the steward and said to him, 'What is this that I hear about you? Turn in the account of your stewardship, for you can no longer be stew-ard.' And the steward said to himself, 'What shall I do, since my master is taking the stewardship away from me? I am not strong enough to dig, and I am ashamed to beg. I have decided what to do, so that people may receive me into their houses when I am put out of the stewardship.' So, summoning his master's debtors one by one, the steward said to the first, 'How much do you owe my master?' He said, 'A hundred measures of oil.' And the steward said to him, 'Take your bill, and sit down quickly and write fifty.' Then the steward said to another, 'And how much do you owe?' He said, 'A hundred mea-sures of wheat.' The steward said to him, 'Take your bill, and write eighty.' The master commended the dishonest steward for his shrewdness; for the children of this world are more shrewd in dealing with their own generation than the children of light. And I tell you, make friends for yourselves by means of unrighteous mammon, so that when it fails they may receive you into the eternal habitations.

"Whoever is faithful in a very little is faithful also in much; and whoever is dishonest in a very little is dishonest also in much. If then you have not been faithful in the unrighteous mammon, who will entrust to you the true riches? And if you have not been faithful in that which is another's, who will give you that which is your own? No servant can be slave to two masters; for either you will hate the one and love the other, or you will be devoted to the one and despise the other. You cannot serve God and mammon."

Friday, September 29, 1995

ARCHANGELS MICHAEL, GABRIEL AND RAPHAEL

Daniel 7:9–10, 13–14 *A thousand thousand wait upon God.*
  or
Revelation 12:7–12 *The warrior Michael defeated the dragon.*

John 1:47–51 *You will see heaven open, and angels descend.*

Michael defeats the dragon, Gabriel announces the king-dom, and Raphael heals the wounded.

REFLECTION

Luke, a practical man, shows the call to discipleship through the world of economics. This is not a creation of Luke, however, but is the prophetic teaching of Jesus in line with the tradition of earlier prophets such as Amos.

In today's gospel the rich man had a steward (*oikonomos*, manager, treasurer) who was accused (rightly so, in the light of what follows) of wasting money. The pattern of this parable, found only in Luke, follows that of the prodigal son in 15:13–19. Both the son and the manager had wasted (*diaskoptizo*; the same verb in each case) goods entrusted to them, and then each one reflected on a course of action to get out of the predicament. The manager was then praised for his practical sense in making provision for the day he would be out of a job.

The conclusion to this parable, to make friends with the mammon of unrighteousness, is a puzzling one. The word "mammon" (*mamonas*, money, wealth, property) is not found in the Hebrew Bible but is found in other Jewish writings. The Greek word is apparently a derivation from an Aramaic root meaning "that in which one trusts." Luke's conclusion, then, is to not to place one's trust in earthly goods—because they inevitably fail—but only to use them and be on friendly terms with them. The final section highlights the inner attitude of reliability and trustworthiness that ought to be evidenced in even the smallest things, in dealings with earthly goods belonging to others.

The final verses contain an emphatic insistence on the need to lead a focused life. The disciple must choose to serve God, and merely use mammon. If not, it will be a case of serving mammon and "using" God.

■ **We are often presented with a spiritualized, ethereal version of religion. How do Amos and Luke amend this for us?**

■ **Take a good look at our economic system and its values: individualism, competition and the stockpiling of assets. How does this system, and how do its values, measure up against the values of human solidarity, justice and God's concern for the poor and the oppressed?**

PRACTICE OF FAITH

ANGELS AND ARCHANGELS. This week we keep the feast of the archangels, and next week we remember guardian angels. In honor of these heavenly beings, read this poem by Hildegard of Bingen on September 29 and October 2:

Angels that guard the nations
(the form of them gleams in your faces),
Archangels that welcome
souls of the just,
Thrones, dominations, princedoms,
    virtues, powers,
reckoned in the mystic five,
And cherubim, O seraphim,
seal upon the secret things of God:
All praise! you behold in the fountain
the place of the everlasting heart.

PRACTICE OF HOPE

TO THOSE WHO TRAMPLE THE NEEDY. The Festival of Shelters, a biblical observance that got lost in the early church, relates the goodness of God the Creator at harvest time to the freedom of God the Liberator. While in the wilderness, the people of God ate manna and lived in shelters, signs of God's provision and of their liberation from Pharaoh's slavery.

Members of the Open Door Community join Jewish sisters and brothers in marking the festival. They keep a vigil in downtown Atlanta among the homeless—proclaiming, with hope, that housing should be a human right for all people.

PRACTICE OF CHARITY

LIFTING HOLY HANDS WITHOUT ANGER OR QUARRELLING. Holy hands would not injure or abuse. If we all believed that our hands are indeed holy, what a different world it would be. One day this week, observe everything that you do with your hands from the time you wake up in the morning until you go to bed at night. Periodically reflect on the phrase, "these are holy hands." See if there is a difference in the way that you go about tasks or in the way that you touch. Come to appreciate the gift of your holy hands, and resolve to take the hand of another and share the insight.

WEEKDAY READINGS Ezra 1:1–6; 6:7–20; 9:5–9; Haggai 1:1–8; (Fr) Michael, Gabriel, and Raphael; Zechariah 2:5–15

AUTUMN ORDINARY TIME

Behold! The harvest!

God brings us back to Zion,
we are like dreamers,
laughing, dancing,
with songs on our lips.

Other nations say,
"A new world of wonders!
The Lord is with them."
Yes, God works wonders:
Rejoice! Be glad!

Lord, bring us back
as water to thirsty land.
Those sowing in tears
reap, singing and laughing.

They left weeping, weeping,
casting the seed.
They come back singing, singing,
holding high the harvest.

—Psalm 126

What tears you cry,
sower God, over us all.
But how you laugh in amazement
and what songs you sing
when there is some harvest.
Your saints from Adam and Eve,
from Moses and Miriam,
from Mary and Joseph,
until our own grandparents and parents,
and we too,
need your tears
and long to hear your laughter.
Harvest us home to sing your praise
forever and ever.

—Prayer of the Season

READING I *Amos 6:1, 4–7*

[Thus says the LORD:] "Woe to those who are
    at ease in Zion,
  who lie upon beds of ivory,
    and stretch themselves upon their couches,
and eat lambs from the flock,
    and calves from the midst of the stall;
who sing idle songs to the sound of the harp,
    and like David invent for themselves instruments
      of music;
who drink wine in bowls,
    and anoint themselves with the finest oils,
    but are not grieved over the ruin of Joseph!
Therefore they shall now be the first of those
    to go into exile,
  and the revelry of those who stretch themselves
shall pass away."

READING II *1 Timothy 6:11–16*

But as for you, who are of God, shun all this; aim at righteousness, godliness, faith, love, steadfastness, gentleness. Fight the good fight of the faith; take hold of the eternal life to which you were called when you made the good confession in the presence of many witnesses. In the presence of God who gives life to all things, and of Christ Jesus who in his testimony before Pontius Pilate made the good confession, I charge you to keep the commandment unstained and free from reproach until the appearing of our Lord Jesus Christ; and this will be made manifest at the proper time by the blessed and only Sovereign, the Ruler of rulers and Lordof lords, who alone has immortality and dwells in inapproachable light, whom no one has ever seen or can see, to whom be honor and eternal dominion. Amen.

GOSPEL *Luke 16:19–31*

[At that time Jesus said,] "There was a rich man, who was clothed in purple and fine linen and who feasted sumptuously every day. And at his gate lay a poor man named Lazarus, full of sores, who desired to be fed with what fell from the rich man's table; moreover the dogs came and licked his sores. The poor man died and was carried by the angels to Abraham's bosom. The rich man also died and was buried; and in Hades, being in torment, he lifted up his eyes, and saw Abraham far off and Lazarus in his bosom. And he called out, 'Father Abraham, have mercy upon me, and send Lazarus to dip the end of his finger in water and cool my tongue; for I am in anguish in this flame.' But Abraham said, 'Child, remember that you in your lifetime received your good things, and Lazarus in like manner evil things; but now he is comforted here, and you are in anguish. And besides all this, between us and you a great chasm has been fixed, in order that those who would pass from here to you may not be able, and none may cross from there to us.' And the rich man said, 'Then I beg you, father Abraham, to send Lazarus to my father's house, for I have five brothers, so that he may warn them, lest they also come into this place of torment.' But Abraham said, 'They have Moses and the prophets; let them hear them.' And the man said, 'No, father Abraham; but if someone goes to them from the dead, they will repent.' Abraham said to him, 'If they do not hear Moses and the prophets, neither will they be convinced if someone should rise from the dead.'"

R E F L E C T I O N

The parable of the rich man and Lazarus reflects Luke's motif of the overturning of conventional value judgments. The rich man feasted (the word used is *euphrainomenos*, made merry) every day. In contrast, Lazarus, one of the *ptochos*, the poor, lays at the rich man's gate. Presumably, he was in a crippled or weakened state, unable even to fend off the dogs. Despite their disparate fortunes, both men die, the one carried home to Abraham, the other buried.

Luke makes clear that the time for change, for repentance, is over. Yet Abraham addresses the rich man as "child" (*teknon*), and indeed, the rich man's concern for the conversion of his five brothers still alive shows that he belongs to the people, is a child of Abraham and has the decency to want to help others.

Luke concludes the parable by pointing once more to the importance of listening. The parable would seem to indicate that listening comes more easily to the "lowly," to those who are ready and open for change. The parable also continues Jesus' teaching on the place of possessions in the life of a disciple and highlights the abomination of the contrasting fortunes of two people of the same religious tradition, both children of Abraham.

■ **Read the texts chosen for the first and second readings. Are they of a piece with the gospel? Why do you think the prophets, Jesus and the early Christian communities were so hard on the rich? What does this mean for us today?**

■ **Reflect on why there are so many Christian movements today "taking the side" of the poor and marginalized. What do you think of this? What is your response?**

PRACTICE OF FAITH

BLESSED PETS. St. Francis of Assisi, whose feast we celebrate Wednesday, has always been known as one who praised God through all creation. A tradition has sprung up of blessing pets and other animals on his feastday. You can use this prayer from *Catholic Household Blessings and Prayers*:

O God,
you have done all things wisely;
in your goodness you have made us in your image
and given us care over other living things.
Reach out with your right hand
and grant these animals may serve our needs
and that your bounty in the resources of this life
may move us to seek more confidently
the goal of eternal life.
We ask this through Christ our Lord. Amen.

PRACTICE OF HOPE

AIM AT GENTLENESS. North of San Francisco, children whose lives will be short play among blackberry bushes and apple orchards. They are children with AIDS who live in an old farmhouse-turned-hospice run by Starcross Community, a group of Catholic lay monastics. The children are loved and honored, rocked and cuddled, and celebrated.

In January 1991, Starcross launched a sister effort in Romania for orphans with AIDS. Here too, the joy of childhood resounds. "We must somehow recognize," says Starcross founder Brother Tolbert McCarroll, "that there is a beauty even in these short lives."

PRACTICE OF CHARITY

AIM AT RIGHTEOUSNESS. Today is Respect Life Sunday. We are asked to take a hard look during this month at where we stand on the issues of life and our willingness to allow the words of Jesus to transform us. The sin of the rich man in today's gospel reading wasn't his wealth; it was the idol he created of his wealth and his exclusion of Lazarus. What idols keep you from standing for life? Name them and then work to smash them. It may be a life-long task, but we must start today to begin the process of walking in righteousness.

WEEKDAY READINGS Exodus 23:20–23; Zechariah 8:20–23; Nehemiah 2:1–8; 8:1–12; Baruch 1:15–22; 4:5–12, 27–29

READING I *Habakkuk 1:2–3; 2:2–4*

O LORD, how long shall I cry for help,
  and you will not hear?
Or cry to you "Violence!"
  and you will not save?
Why do you make me see wrongs
  and look upon trouble?
Destruction and violence are before me;
  strife and contention arise.
And the LORD answered me:
"Write the vision;
  make it plain upon tablets,
  so that whoever reads it may run.
For still the vision awaits its time;
  it hastens to the end—it will not lie.
If it seems slow, wait for it;
  it will surely come, it will not delay.
Behold, those whose soul is not upright within
  shall fail,
but the righteous shall live by their faith."

READING II *2 Timothy 1:6–8, 13–14*

I remind you to rekindle the gift of God that is within you through the laying on of my hands; for God did not give us a spirit of timidity but a spirit of power and love and self-control. Do not be ashamed then of testifying to our Lord, nor of me his prisoner, but share in suffering for the gospel in the power of God.

Follow the pattern of the sound words which you have heard from me, in the faith and love which are in Christ Jesus; guard the truth that has been entrusted to you by the Holy Spirit who dwells within us.

GOSPEL *Luke 17:5–10*

The apostles said to the Lord, "Increase our faith!" And the Lord said, "If you had faith as a grain of mustard seed, you could say to this sycamine tree, 'Be rooted up, and be planted in the sea,' and it would obey you.

"Will any one of you, who has a servant plowing or keeping sheep, say, when the servant has come in from the field, 'Come at once and sit down at table'? Will you not rather say to the servant, 'Prepare supper for me, and gird youself and serve me, till I eat and drink; and afterward you shall eat and drink'? Do you thank the servant because the servant did what was commanded? So you also, when you have done all that is commanded you, say, 'We are unworthy servants; we have only done what was our duty.' "

[Monday, October 9 is Thanksgiving Day in Canada. See page 156 for scripture citations.]

REFLECTION

Today's gospel continues Jesus' advice to his disciples, but it is the letter to Timothy that will be the focus of our reflection. The selection made for us omits the personal note in verses 3–5 that names two early Christian women: Timothy's mother, Eunice, and his grandmother, Lois. The selection also omits verses 9–12, a moving passage recognizing the gratuity of grace and salvation.

Paul reminds Timothy to fan the flame of the gift (*charisma*) given by God through the laying on of hands, a gesture with significant ritual meaning (see, for example, 1 Timothy 4:14; Mark 10:16; Acts 6:6; 8:17; 13:3 and 19:6). The Spirit that is given to the Christian is one of power, love and self-control. The power of God is also given for endurance, because bearing witness (*martyrion*) will mean a share in suffering for the sake of the good news. The last two verses can be translated with a slightly different emphasis: Timothy is urged to "protect," to care for, the good treasure through the Holy Spirit living in us.

This letter, if not directly from Paul's hand, clearly bears the mark of Paul and shows his personal concern for Timothy. The message to Timothy is above all a reminder of the gift of the Spirit, the holy calling and "the pattern of sound words" that has been placed in Timothy's care. The enthusiasm of the moment of conversion grows into self-discipline for the pastor Timothy. The warm welcome given the good news leads to suffering for that news, and the gift entrusted to Timothy will be "guarded " by the Spirit living within the community.

■ **Read all of 2 Timothy. Its personal tone provides a more practical vision of life in an early Christian community. How does your own parish community compare? What are some similarities? What are some differences?**

■ **In early Christian writings, there is a keen sense of the power — the dynamism — of the Spirit in the community. Are there ever moments in your parish when you can "feel" the Spirit at work? When is it most difficult for you to sense the Spirit within your community?**

PRACTICE OF FAITH

DAILY FORGIVENESS. The church's daily rhythm of prayer includes an opportunity to ask and receive forgiveness every day. During Night Prayer, we have the opportunity to examine our conscience and to ask God to reveal those sins we may have committed during that day. This also affords us the chance to forgive others whatever wrongs they may have committed against us. The beginning pages of this book contain a simple order for night prayer that you can use. Be sure to leave time for an examination of conscience. You may also wish to include a prayer of contrition or sorrow, as well as a prayer of forgiveness of others. Praying Night Prayer in this way makes forgiveness, which Jesus identifies as a duty of his disciples, a daily joy rather than a wrenching chore.

PRACTICE OF HOPE

REKINDLE THE GIFT OF GOD. Poet Maya Angelou was mute for five years after being raped at the age of seven. As an African American woman, she has known her share of suffering and discrimination. But she stood tall before the nation in January 1993, on stage at the presidential inauguration. She showed us the strength of a rock, a river, a tree. And she offered an invitation that we should take to heart each morning: "Here, on the pulse of this new day/You may have the grace to look up and out/And into your sister's eyes, and into/Your brother's face, your country/And say simply/Very simply/With hope/Good morning."

PRACTICE OF CHARITY

WE HAVE ONLY DONE OUR DUTY. Or have we? Twenty percent of all children in the United States live in poverty. Worse yet, almost 50 percent of all African American children live in poverty. A vast majority of these children live in single-parent homes. What can be done? For one, we must support programs like Head Start, Job Corps, and WIC (food program for women, infants and children). We must also support legislation that opens up avenues out of the cycle of poverty. It really is our duty.

WEEKDAY READINGS **(Mo–We) Jonah—entire book; (Th) Malachi 3:13– 20; (Fr) Joel 1:13–15; 2:1–2; (Sa) 4:12–21**

READING I *2 Kings 5:14–17*

Naaman went down and dipped himself seven times in the Jordan, according to the word of Elisha, the man of God; and his flesh was restored like the flesh of a little child, and he was clean [of his leprosy].

Then Naaman and his company returned to the man of God, and he came and stood before him, saying, "Behold, I know that there is no God in all the earth but in Israel; so accept now a present from your servant." But Elisha said, "As the LORD lives, whom I serve, I will receive none." And Naaman urged Elisha to take it, but Elisha refused. Then Naaman said, "If not, I pray you, let there be given to me, your servant, two mules' burden of earth; for henceforth your servant will not offer burnt offering or sacrifice to any god but the LORD."

READING II *2 Timothy 2:8–13*

Remember Jesus Christ, risen from the dead, descended from David, as preached in my gospel, the gospel for which I am suffering and wearing fetters like a criminal. But the word of God is not fettered. Therefore I endure everything for the sake of the elect, that they also may obtain salvation in Christ Jesus with its eternal glory. The saying is sure:

> If we have died with Christ, we shall also live
>   with Christ;
> if we endure, we shall also reign with Christ;
> if we deny him, he also will deny us;
> if we are faithless, he remains faithful—
> for Christ cannot deny himself.

GOSPEL *Luke 17:11–19*

On the way to Jerusalem Jesus was passing along between Samaria and Galilee. And entering a village he was met by ten people who had leprosy, who stood at a distance and lifted up their voices and said, "Jesus, Master, have mercy on us." Seeing them Jesus said to them, "Go and show yourselves to the priests." And as they went they were cleansed. Then one of them, when he saw that he was healed, turned back, praising God with a loud voice; and he fell on his face at Jesus' feet, giving him thanks. Now he was a Samaritan. Then said Jesus, "Were not ten cleansed? Where are the nine? Was no one found to return and give praise to God except this foreigner?" And Jesus said to the Samaritan, "Rise and go your way; your faith has made you well."

REFLECTION

Today's readings have to do with remembering: Naaman remembered to thank Elisha for his cure, and one of the ten lepers cured by Jesus remembered to turn back and thank his healer. It is in the passage from the second letter to Timothy, however, that remembering is placed center stage.

Paul speaks again of being a prisoner. In the passage read last week, he spoke of himself as being a prisoner of the Lord. Today we hear how he connects his suffering (*kakopatheo,* to experience something that comes from outside) with the gospel. An alternative translation for verse 8 reads, "the gospel *in* which I suffer ill under bonds as an evildoer." Paul's ministry is literally bound up in his calling as a prisoner of the Lord and in "being bound" in the preaching of the good news. The suffering of Paul, as that of Jesus, is inseparable from the ministry of proclaiming the good news.

Within the good news and its proclamation is a dynamic that provokes a reaction among those who hear it. But if the reaction is one of rejection and the preacher is silenced or imprisoned, the word itself remains unfettered and has not been bound. The poetic insert in verses 11–13 may well be from an early Christian hymn and contains the rhythmic paradoxes of dying and living, enduring and reigning. There is an equation here: If we deny Christ, he will deny us. But there is also a contrast: Even if we are faithless, God remains faithful.

The final statement of this passage, though not selected for our reading, is a magnificent description of a Christian pastor — one who has no need to be ashamed because of the work of "cutting straight the word of truth." The verb used, *orthotomeo,* means to cut a straight path and is used only here and in Proverbs 3:6 and 11:5. Timothy is urged to speak the word of truth and not to be like those engaged in empty, endless theological discussions and fruitless debate.

■ Do you think it is easy to know for certain exactly what a particular passage in scripture is saying? In other words, is it even possible to engage in debates that begin with "the Bible says"?

■ Carefully read the remainder of the second chapter of 2 Timothy, paying particular attention to the writer's use of the word "truth." What questions does this reading raise for you?

PRACTICE OF FAITH

THE PHYSICIAN. This Wednesday we celebrate the Feast of St. Luke, the evangelist. It is particularly appropriate to keep his feastday because this is the year we read from his gospel at Mass. It is recorded in the letter to the Colossians and elsewhere in the New Testament that Luke was a physician as well as a disciple and friend of St. Paul. Luke was a companion to Paul on two missionary journeys and was with Paul during his imprisonment in Rome. About 15 to 20 years later, Luke, a Gentile Greek Christian, wrote his account of Jesus and the church for other Gentile Greek converts. Tonight during your prayer time, read your favorite story from Luke's gospel. Give thanks for the compassionate and healing image of Jesus that Luke presents.

PRACTICE OF HOPE

HAVE MERCY ON US. Mary Williams' daughter, Rolveatta, disappeared for a year. She turned up in a Washington, D.C., hospital with AIDS. Mary quit her job, brought Rolveatta home, and cared for her and her 11-year-old daughter. Sometimes Mary would not eat when there wasn't enough food for all three of them.

After Rolveatta's death on her 30th birthday, Mary went to work at Joseph's House, a ministry of the Church of the Saviour for homeless men with AIDS. She said of those she serves, "They need understanding. They need love. They need to be touched; people are afraid to touch them.... And nobody needs to die alone." Joseph's House is a place of hope for those too often labeled today's "lepers." And Mary Williams is a bearer of compassion and mercy.

PRACTICE OF CHARITY

MET BY TEN PEOPLE WHO HAD LEPROSY. If Jesus were walking on the road today, he might meet ten persons living with AIDS. The number of people contracting the HIV virus and dying from AIDS is staggering. It has become a worldwide epidemic and rightly motivates calls for intensified efforts to find a solution. It also calls for an attentive response to the victims. Many larger communities have groups working to educate people about HIV and AIDS. There are also many fund-raising events to provide assistance to persons with AIDS, hotlines to answer questions and training programs to help people to live with and care for people with AIDS. To help, contact your local AIDS organizations or: National Catholic AIDS Network, c/o Executive Director, PO Box 422984, San Francisco CA 94142; 415-565-3613.

WEEKDAY READINGS Romans 1:1–7; 1:16–25; 2 Timothy 4:10–17; Romans 3:21–30; 4:1–8; 4:13, 16–18

READING I *Exodus 17:8–13*

Amalek came and fought with Israel at Rephidim. And Moses said to Joshua, "Choose for us men, and go out, fight with Amalek; tomorrow I will stand on the top of the hill with the rod of God in my hand." So Joshua did as Moses told him, and fought with Amalek; and Moses, Aaron, and Hur went up to the top of the hill. Whenever Moses held up his hand, Israel prevailed; and whenever he lowered his hand, Amalek prevailed. But Moses' hands grew weary; so they took a stone and put it under him, and he sat upon it, and Aaron and Hur held up his hands, one on one side, and the other on the other side; so Moses' hands were steady until the going down of the sun. And Joshua mowed down Amalek and his people with the edge of the sword.

READING II *2 Timothy 3:14 — 4:2*

As for you, continue in what you have learned and have firmly believed, knowing from whom you learned it and how from childhood you have been acquainted with the sacred writings which are able to instruct you for salvation through faith in Christ Jesus. All scripture is inspired by God and profitable for teaching, for reproof, for correction, and for training in righteousness, that the people of God may be complete, equipped for every good work.

I charge you in the presence of God, and of Christ Jesus who is to judge the living and the dead, and by Christ's appearing and dominion: preach the word, be urgent in season and out of season, convince, rebuke, and exhort, be unfailing in patience and in teaching.

GOSPEL *Luke 18:1–8*

Jesus told them a parable, to the effect that they ought always to pray and not lose heart. He said, "In a certain city there was a judge who neither feared God nor regarded the people; and there was a widow in that city who kept coming to him and saying, 'Vindicate me against my adversary.' For a while the judge refused; but afterward he said to himself, 'Though I neither fear God nor regard the people, yet because this widow bothers me, I will vindicate her, or she will wear me out by her continual coming.'" And the Lord said, "Hear what the unrighteous judge says. And will not God vindicate God's own elect, who are beseeching day and night? Will God delay long over them? I tell you, God will vindicate them speedily. Nevertheless, when the Man of Heaven comes, will he find faith on earth?"

REFLECTION

All three readings today deal with the attitude of insistence and persistence. In the reading from Exodus, a weary Moses is helped by Aaron and Hur to keep his drooping hand aloft so that Israel's victory is assured. In the gospel reading, a judge who fears neither God nor the people is worn down by a pesky widow who finally gets what she wants. But it is the second reading, a continuation of the pastoral advice to Timothy, that reveals the importance of persistence for every Christian.

The Christian life is a continual journey of moving deeper into what has been learned. This "learning" is related to experience and understanding, to accustoming oneself to a way of life — it is not an abstract, intellectual kind of learning. It is the learning that leads to firm belief because of the trust placed in the one who shared this understanding and introduced the believer to the meaning of the sacred writings of the Hebrew Bible.

Because of the importance of the scriptures, Timothy is "charged" with preaching the word. The word translated as "preach," *kerysso,* has a much stronger, more vigorous meaning. *Kerysso* is to proclaim, to announce, to cry out loud. The advice to Timothy, then, is that this proclamation must be made in season and out. The attitude of the persistent announcer of the good news, like that of Moses, Aaron, Hur and the widow, is one of unfailing patience and urgent persistence.

The message contained in all three of today's readings is clear: Patience and steadfastness in no way exclude a sense of urgency, insistence and persistence.

■ **How large a role does scripture play in your life as an individual and as a parish member?**

■ **Read the rather lengthy Psalm 119, substituting "the Word" where it talks about the law. Does such a reading make sense to you?**

PRACTICE OF FAITH

CEASELESS PRAYER. It is hard for many of us to imagine how one can persevere in prayer so that prayer becomes unceasing. One form of prayer that has been a part of our tradition is called the Jesus prayer. One prays the phrase "Lord Jesus Christ, Son of the living God" while inhaling a breath, and then the phrase "have mercy on me" while exhaling. In this form of prayer, one inhales the sacred name of Jesus and exhales a plea for mercy. At first, most of us need to sit quietly and concentrate on our breathing. If we are persistent, every breath will become a prayer and every moment of our life an offering of praise.

PRACTICE OF HOPE

PREACH THE WORD. Rev. Lynne Blankenship, a United Methodist pastor, was leaving a church after five years. She was bidding farewell to close friends and heading across North Carolina to begin a new pastorate, wondering if her new place could ever feel like home.

The day she arrived, she walked into the sanctuary. She looked up at the pulpit and smiled, her eyes growing moist. One of her new parishioners had already built a platform for this five-foot preacher to stand on for her sermons.

PRACTICE OF CHARITY

UNFAILING IN PATIENCE AND IN TEACHING. Part of the call to justice involves educating ourselves, gaining practical wisdom concerning current issues. This is also known as the virtue of prudence. Without it, our works of charity can become empty, misguided gestures. *The Other Side* magazine offers stories of the faith and compassion of real people who have encountered injustice. It challenges your mind and heart to join in the work for lasting change in our world. It is a magazine of hope and vision for those willing to deepen their commitment to peace and social justice. To subscribe, write: The Other Side, 300 West Apsley Street, Philadelphia PA 19144-4221. A one-year subscription is $29.50.

WEEKDAY READINGS Romans 4:20 – 25; 5:12 – 21; 6:12 – 18; 6:19 – 23; 7:18 – 25; Ephesians 2:19 – 22

READING I *Sirach 35:12–14, 16–18*

The Lord is the judge,
  with whom is no partiality.
The Lord will not show partiality in the case
    of one who is poor,
  and will listen to the prayer
    of one who is wronged.
The Lord will not ignore the supplication
    of the orphan,
  nor the widow when she pours out her story.
They whose service is pleasing to the Lord
    will be accepted,
  and their prayer will reach to the clouds.
The prayer of the humble pierces the clouds,
  and they will not be consoled until it
    reaches the Lord;
they will not desist until the Most High visits them,
  and does justice for the righteous,
    and executes judgment.

READING II *2 Timothy 4:6–8, 16–18*

I am already on the point of being sacrificed; the time of my departure has come. I have fought the good fight, I have finished the race, I have kept the faith. Henceforth there is laid up for me the crown of righteousness, which the Lord, the righteous judge, will award to me on that Day, and not only to me but also to all who have loved his appearing.

At my first defense no one took my part; all deserted me. May it not be charged against them! But the Lord stood by me and gave me strength to proclaim the message fully, that all the Gentiles might hear it. So I was rescued from the lion's mouth. The Lord will rescue me from every evil and save me for the dominion of heaven. To the Lord be the glory for ever and ever. Amen.

GOSPEL *Luke 18:9–14*

Jesus told this parable to some who trusted in themselves that they were righteous and despised others: "Two men went up into the temple to pray, one a Pharisee and the other a tax collector. The Pharisee stood and prayed thus with himself, 'God, I thank you that I am not like the rest of these people, extortioners, unjust, adulterers, or even like this tax collector. I fast twice a week, I give tithes of all that I get.' But the tax collector, standing far off, would not even lift up his eyes to heaven, but beat his breast, saying, 'God, be merciful to me a sinner!' I tell you, this man went down to his house justified rather than the other; for all those who exalt themselves will be humbled, but they who humble themselves will be exalted."

Wednesday, November 1, 1995

ALL SAINTS' DAY

Revelation 7:2–4, 9–4 *The crowd stood before the Lamb.*

1 John 3:1–3 *We shall see God.*

Matthew 5:1–12 *How blest are the poor in spirit.*

We welcome the winter with a harvest homecoming. All the people of God are gathered into the new Jerusalem to begin the supper of the Lamb. The poor, the mourning, the meek and the lowly remove their masks and see themselves as they truly are: the beloved children of God, the saints of heaven.

Thursday, November 2, 1995

ALL SOULS' DAY

Daniel 12:1–3 *The dead will rise to shine like stars.*

Romans 6:3–9 *Like Christ, we will live a new life.*

John 6:37–40 *No one who comes will I ever reject.*

In the northern hemisphere, nature shows forth the awesome beauty of the harvest. Yesterday we rejoiced in the harvest of the saints. Today we reflect on what made this harvest possible: self-sacrifice, completed labors and death.

REFLECTION

Today's gospel is the familiar parable of the Pharisee and the tax collector. It is also an illustration of one of Luke's favored themes, the reversal brought about by the coming of the Messiah. And it is a powerful story for our own day.

Luke notes at the beginning that Jesus directed this parable to a particular kind of people: those who were law-abiding in their own eyes but who looked down on everyone else. The Pharisee, a member of the group of the righteous, prayed "with himself" (*pros eauton*, to himself, facing toward himself), and the whole prayer he gives is focused on himself and his good works. He shines in his own eyes, especially as he compares himself to the tax collector, a member of a despised group.

In contrast, at a great distance (the same expression used in Luke 16:23 to describe the chasm between Lazarus and the rich man) the tax collector stood. A great distance separates these two people, not only physically but in their status in society and in their attitudes. The focus of the tax collector's prayer is on God and God's mercy.

The conclusion Jesus draws from the story is that judgment belongs to God. This is expressed in Luke's use of sharply contrasting verbs: *hypsoo*, which connotes heights and high places, and *tapeino*, the basic meaning of which is low, lowly, insignificant. The contrast is further sharpened by Luke's use of the word *anthropos*, human being, member of the human race. Two *anthropoi* went up to pray, and the Pharisee thanked God that he was not like the rest of humanity (*anthropoi*). But to be a member of the human race is just that — to belong to a humanity that of itself is lowly, weak and poor. To set oneself apart from "the rest," Luke tells us, is to go home unjustified, unapproved and ungraced by God.

■ As you read this parable, do you see any connection between its message and the prevalent attitudes within our own Christian communities? Within our society?

■ Re-read Luke 1:46–55 and 4:16–19 in the light of today's gospel. Do you see any indications in these three readings of Luke's special theme?

PRACTICE OF FAITH

EL DIA DE LOS DIFUNTOS, EL DIA DE LOS MUERTOS. Throughout the church we celebrate All Saints Day and All Souls Day on November first and second, respectively. In the southwestern states, Hispanic Catholics keep these feasts in a particularly festive way. Whole families will visit family cemeteries, transforming them into colorful gardens filled with flowers. There will be prayer and storytelling, reminding those present of who they are as a family. In some communities special sweet breads are blessed at Mass, taken home and shared in a festive meal. There are many ways to celebrate our connection to the communion of saints. Burn candles before the pictures of friends and family members who have died, and pray that one day we may all enjoy the fullness of heaven together.

PRACTICE OF HOPE

THE LORD HEARS SUPPLICATIONS. Rev. Ralph Eanes served the United Methodist church on the Cherokee reservation in western North Carolina for six years. Twenty years later, Rev. Pat Freeman was appointed the first Native American pastor at the church.

At a gathering of Methodist clergy, Eanes said, "I prayed for this man for 20 years before I knew his name. Now I know his name." He than offered a blessing for his clergy brother in Cherokee.

PRACTICE OF CHARITY

ALL DESERTED ME. Prisoners who are awaiting execution must feel utterly abandoned. Use of the death penalty appears to be on the rise in this country. Catholics Against Capitol Punishment is a non-profit organization, based in Washington, D.C., dedicated to building and strengthening the pro-life attitude of the Catholic tradition and committed to promoting a consistent ethic of life. To subscribe to their monthly newsletter ($25 per year) or to make a donation, write: Catholics Against Capital Punishment, PO Box 3125, Arlington VA 22203.

WEEKDAY READINGS (Mo–Tu) Romans 8:12–25; (We) All Saints; (Th) All Souls; Romans 9:1–5; 11:1-2, 11–12, 25–29

READING I *1 Wisdom 11:22–12:1*

The whole world before you is like a speck that tips
the scales,
and like a drop of morning dew that falls upon
the ground.
But you are merciful to all, for you can do all things,
and you overlook the sins of human beings, that
they may repent.
For you love all things that exist,
and have loathing for none of the things which
you have made,
for you would not have made anything if you had
hated it.
How would anything have endured if you had
not willed it?
Or how could anything not called forth by you
have been preserved?
You spare all things, for they are yours, O Lord,
lover of the living.
For your immortal spirit is in all things.

READING II *2 Thessalonians 1:11–2:2*

To this end we always pray for you, that our God
may make you worthy of the call, and may fulfill in
power every good resolve and work of faith, so that
the name of our Lord Jesus may be glorified in you,
and you in him, according to the grace of our God
and Lord Jesus Christ.

Now concerning the coming of our Lord Jesus
Christ and our assembling to meet him, we beg
you, dear people, not to be quickly shaken in mind
or excited, either by spirit or by word, or by letter
purporting to be from us, to the effect that the day
of the Lord has come.

GOSPEL *Luke 19:1–10*

Jesus entered Jericho and was passing through.
And there was a man named Zacchaeus who was a
chief tax collector, and rich. And he sought to see
who Jesus was, but could not, on account of the
crowd, because he was small of stature. So he ran
on ahead and climbed up into a sycamore tree to
see Jesus, who was to pass that way. And having
come to the place, Jesus looked up and said to him,
"Zacchaeus, make haste and come down; for I must
stay at your house today." So Zacchaeus made
haste and came down, and received Jesus joyfully.
And when they saw it they all murmured, "He has
gone in to be the guest of a man who is a sinner."
And Zacchaeus stood and said to the Lord, "Behold,
Lord, the half of my goods I give to the poor; and if
I have defrauded any one of anything, I restore it
fourfold." And Jesus said to Zacchaeus, "Today salvation has come to this house, since Zacchaeus also
is a child of Abraham. For the Man of Heaven came
to seek and to save the lost."

Thursday, November 9, 1995

THE DEDICATION OF THE LATERAN BASILICA IN ROME

Ezekiel 47:1–2, 8–9, 12 *The water from the temple brings
forth life.*

1 Corinthians 3:9–11, 16–17 *You are God's holy temple.*

John 2:13–22 *Zeal for God's house consumes me.*

Human flesh is God's dwelling place. In November, a
season of ingathering, we assemble in the Spirit. Our
own flesh and blood is becoming God's holy temple.
All creation is becoming Jerusalem.

REFLECTION

Zacchaeus (a name occurring only here in the New Testament) is featured in this incident recorded only in the Gospel of Luke. This event is important because it shows that while Luke most often speaks of the good news to the poor (*ptochos*, economically disadvantaged) and the lowly, he is also careful to point out that no one is excluded from the possibility of salvation. Zacchaeus was a "chief" tax collector, a type of collaborator despised by the people. And he was rich. In a sense, Zacchaeus could be counted as one of the lowly—literally—because he was small of stature and was one of the marginalized.

There are two sets of parallel words in this account. First of all, Zacchaeus *sought* to see who Jesus was. Later, Jesus states that the Man of Heaven came to *seek* and save the lost. There is in this parallel an image of the process of conversion and salvation, a major focus in Luke. The human being who is trying to see—who is open—and the Messiah, who is seeking what is lost—encounter one another. The second set of parallels is in the use of the word "today." Jesus calls to Zacchaeus, who is perched in the sycamore tree, saying that he must stay at Zacchaeus's house "today." And at the end of the narrative, Jesus declares that "today" salvation has come to the house of Zacchaeus. Luke's use of the word "must" is also significant. We have already noted that the word for "must," *dei* (an important word for Luke) conveys an element of necessity that is very strong.

This is a narrative filled with Luke's joyful news that Jesus seeks out those who are "sinners," that salvation is offered to all and that Zacchaeus—"even he"—is a child of Abraham.

■ **For other significant uses of the word "today," see Luke 2:11; 4:21; 5:25; 23:43.**

■ **Are there "Zacchaeuses" in our communities? Are we inclined to follow Jesus in seeking them out?**

PRACTICE OF FAITH

DEDICATION. On Thursday, the church celebrates the dedication of the Basilica of St. John Lateran in Rome. Why do we celebrate the dedication of a building? Because we are a community surrounded and supported by signs and symbols. Keeping the feast of this dedication is a sign that we are the living stones that comprise the dwelling place of God. Find out when your parish or diocese celebrates its dedication and how you can participate in the festivities. If there is not a local celebration, encourage your pastoral council or liturgy commission to plan one.

PRACTICE OF HOPE

FULFILL EVERY GOOD WORK. After floods devastated the Midwest in the summer of 1993, Steve Hartington initiated a "sister city" relationship between Brevard, North Carolina, and Ellwood, Kansas. Ellwood was all but washed away by the floods. While Hartington was receiving donations of food, clothing and household items, a five-year-old boy gave him a paper bag with his name, Nathaniel, written on it. Inside was a green toy bus. He explained that he wanted it to go to a child who "lost all his toys in the flood."

Ellwood Mayor Glenda Kelly was so touched by his gesture that she had Hartington track down Nathaniel, whose last name, he eventually learned, is Wetli. She asked Brevard Mayor Katherine Anderson to pay him a visit, with a certificate of gratitude from Ellwood and a Pony Express pin.

PRACTICE OF CHARITY

I MUST STAY AT YOUR HOUSE TODAY. Families are sometimes displaced from their homes while a family member receives specialized care in a hospital. Ronald McDonald House offers a home-like environment where families can give each other support and understanding. The houses are located near major medical facilities and are owned and operated by local not-for-profit organizations that depend on community funding for support. The houses also welcome volunteers to help with household chores, to provide simple meals and to assist in various other ways. A child in the hospital is greatly comforted just knowing that his or her parents are close by. Parents can come and go as they need to and get the rest that they need when facing a difficult situation. Find out where the nearest Ronald McDonald House is located and contact them to see what their needs are. Or write: Ronald McDonald House, 500 North Michigan Avenue, Suite 200, Chicago IL 60611.

WEEKDAY READINGS (Mo–We) Romans 11:29—13:10; (Th) The Dedication of the Lateran Basilica in Rome; (Fr–Sa) Romans 15:14—16:27

READING I 2 Maccabees 7:1–2, 9–14

It happened that seven brothers and their mother were arrested and were being compelled by the king, under torture with whips and cords, to partake of unlawful swine's flesh. One of them, acting as their advocate, said, "What do you intend to ask and learn from us? For we are ready to die rather than transgress the laws of our forebears."

When the second brother was at his last breath, he said, "You accursed wretch, you dismiss us from this present life, but the Sovereign of the universe will raise us up to an everlasting renewal of life, because we have died for the laws of God."

After him, the third brother was the victim of their sport. When it was demanded, he quickly put out his tongue and courageously stretched forth his hands, and said nobly, "I got these from Heaven, and because of God's laws I disdain them, and from God I hope to get them back again." As a result the king himself and those with him were astonished at the young man's spirit, for he regarded his sufferings as nothing.

When he too had died, they maltreated and tortured the fourth in the same way. And when he was near death, he said, "One cannot but choose to die at human hands and to cherish the hope that God gives of being raised again by God. But for you there will be no resurrection to life!"

READING II 2 Thessalonians 2:16—3:5

Now may our Lord Jesus Christ himself, and God, our Father, who loved us and gave us eternal comfort and good hope through grace, comfort your hearts and establish them in every good work and word.

Finally, my dear people, pray for us, that the word of the Lord may speed on and triumph, as it did among you, and that we may be delivered from wicked and evil people; for not all have faith. But the Lord is faithful, who will strengthen you and guard you from evil. And we have confidence in the Lord about you, that you are doing and will do the things which we command. May the Lord direct your hearts to the love of God and to the steadfastness of Christ.

GOSPEL Luke 20:27–38

There came to Jesus some Sadducees, those who say that there is no resurrection, and they asked him a question, saying, "Teacher, Moses wrote for us that if a man's brother dies, having a wife but no children, the man must marry the woman and raise up children for his brother. Now there were seven brothers; the first married a woman, and died without children; and the second and the third married her, and likewise all seven left no children and died. Afterward the woman also died. In the resurrection therefore, whose wife will the woman be? For she was wife to all seven."

And Jesus said to them, "The children of this age marry and are given in marriage; but those who are accounted worthy to attain to that age and to the resurrection from the dead neither marry nor are given in marriage, for they cannot die any more, because they are equal to angels and are children of God, being children of the resurrection. But that the dead are raised, even Moses showed, in the passage about the bush, where he calls the Lord the God of Abraham and the God of Isaac and the God of Jacob. Now the Lord is not God of the dead, but of the living; for all are alive to God."

REFLECTION

Today's first reading describes the faith and endurance of the Maccabees. The gospel presents a debate on the question of resurrection between the Sadducees — who represented mainstream belief — and Jesus. The absurd argument, intended to stump Jesus, leads to a reaffirmation that "all are alive to God," who is the God of the living. It is in the Second Letter to the Thessalonians, written to calm the anxiety of those awaiting an imminent return of Christ, that we will find matter for today's reflection.

The text is actually a prayer and an exhortation, assuring the Thessalonians that the God of encouragement and good hope will keep them going until the day the Lord returns — whenever that may be. Having spoken of hope, the author then speaks of faith. Because not all have faith, the Thessalonians and Paul will face opposition. But God is faithful and will guard them in faith, confidence and trust. Paul himself has confidence that the Thessalonians will continue in the way he has shown them.

The final prayer is that "the Lord direct your hearts to the love of God." The word *eis* has a meaning closer to "into" and here would imply not a vague "to the love of God" but a clearly imaged "into God's love" — as into an ocean. The prayer is that Christians enter into the love of God and remain in it with the endurance that in the early Christian churches was considered necessary and characteristic.

■ **Read 2 Maccabees 7:1–42. Though it pre-dates Christianity, it reads like some of the stories of early Christian martyrs and exemplifies the endurance and hope presented to the Thessalonians as ideals.**

■ **Describe some people in our own day who exemplify the same endurance and hope. What is it that they are enduring? Is their struggle worthwhile?**

PRACTICE OF FAITH

GOD OF THE LIVING AND THE DEAD. Winter is approaching as we move to the end of the liturgical year. Both the icy winds of winter and the readings at Mass invite us to reflect upon our own mortality. St. Nicholas of Flue wrote this prayer of dedication to our God, who sustains us now in life and will sustain us through death to everlasting life:

My Lord and my God,
remove far from me
whatever keeps me from you.
My Lord and my God,
confer upon me
whatever enables me to reach you.
My Lord and my God,
free me from self
and make me wholly yours.

PRACTICE OF HOPE

THE LORD GUARD YOU FROM EVIL. In May 1992, at about four o'clock one afternoon, Serbian mortar fire killed 22 people standing in line outside a bakery in Sarajevo, in the former Yugoslavia. For the next 22 days, Vedran Smailovic, a cellist in the Sarajevo Symphony, brought a chair and his cello to that deserted spot at four o'clock. With Serbian shells crashing around him, he played Albinoni's "Adagio" to honor each person who had died. In a situation of utter tragedy and grief, the martyrs were not forgotten.

PRACTICE OF CHARITY

COMFORT YOUR HEARTS. This time of year often stimulates us to reflect on our own death. Liturgy Training Publications offers a resource designed to help us plan our own funeral. Those left behind to mourn would certainly find comfort in knowing that the funeral liturgy speaks a message that we wanted to share. This resource, *Now and at the Hour of Our Death,* includes practical information about death and burial as well as legal and financial information. It can be obtained by contacting Liturgy Training Publications, 1800 North Hermitage Avenue, Chicago IL 60622-1101; 1-800-933-1800.

WEEKDAY READINGS Wisdom 1:1–7; 2:23—3:9; 6:1–11; 7:22—8:1; 13:1–9; (Sa) 18:14–16; 19:6–9

READING I *Malachi 3:19–20*

For behold, the day comes, burning like an oven, when all the arrogant and all evildoers will be stubble; the day that comes shall burn them up, says the Lord of hosts, so that it will leave them neither root nor branch. But for you who fear my name the sun of righteousness shall rise, with healing in its wings.

READING II *2 Thessalonians 3:7–12*

You yourselves know how you ought to imitate us; we were not idle when we were with you, we did not eat any one's bread without paying, but with toil and labor we worked night and day, that we might not burden any of you. It was not because we have not that right, but to give you in our conduct an example to imitate. For even when we were with you, we gave you this command: Those who will not work, neither should they eat. For we hear that some of you are living in idleness, mere busybodies, not doing any work. Now such persons we command and exhort in the Lord Jesus Christ to do their work in quietness and to earn their own living.

GOSPEL *Luke 21:5–19*

As some spoke of the temple, how it was adorned with noble stones and offerings, Jesus said, "As for these things which you see, the days will come when there shall not be left here one stone upon another that will not be thrown down." And they asked him, "Teacher, when will this be, and what will be the sign when this is about to take place?" And Jesus said, "Take heed that you are not led astray; for many will come in my name, saying, 'I am the one!' and, 'The time is at hand!' Do not go after them. And when you hear of wars and tumults, do not be terrified; for this must first take place, but the end will not be at once."

Then Jesus said to them, "Nation will rise against nation, and country against country; there will be great earthquakes, and in various places famines and pestilences; and there will be terrors and great signs from heaven. But before all this they will lay their hands on you and persecute you, delivering you up to the synagogues and prisons, and you will be brought before rulers and governors for my name's sake. This will be a time for you to bear testimony. Settle it therefore in your minds not to meditate beforehand how to answer; for I will give you a mouth and wisdom, which none of your adversaries will be able to withstand or contradict. You will be delivered up even by parents and family and kin and friends, and some of you they will put to death; you will be hated by all for my name's sake. But not a hair of your head will perish. By your endurance you will gain your lives."

Monday, October 9, 1995 (Canada)
Thursday, November 23, 1995 (USA)

THANKSGIVING DAY

Deuteronomy 8:7–18 *When you eat, you must bless the Lord.*

1 Timothy 6:6–11, 17–19 *Be rich in good works.*

Luke 12:15–21 *There was a man who had a good harvest.*

God has given us the earth to be our homeland, a land flowing with milk and honey. Yet along with this gift, we have been given the command to show our thankfulness by being wise and selfless stewards of the earth, by proclaiming God's peaceable dominion and by sharing our own gifts with one another.

R E F L E C T I O N

Today's gospel reading can be viewed as a summation of all Jesus' teachings on discipleship.

The passage begins with a prophecy of the destruction of the Temple. Jesus tells those who admired the Temple and its adornments that what they were seeing would one day be destroyed and overthrown—a familiar theme of Luke. Jesus also repeats a warning about listening to the false claims and dire predictions that were sure to come. He affirms that there will be world-shaking catastrophes and that his disciples will follow the path he endured.

The disciples will be seized, persecuted, delivered and led away to face those in power. Even family members will betray them. Some will suffer death and will be hated "by all." Jesus contrasts the many who will "come in my name" bearing false claims with the disciples' suffering "for my name's sake." As Jesus was rejected and handed over because of the "name" he claimed, so will those who honor that name be subjected to the same treatment. The passion, however, will turn into an occasion for testimony (*martyrion*, witness). At such times, the disciple is not to rehearse beforehand but is to depend on the speech and the wisdom that will be inspired from within.

The final verse is a summary of one of the core insights needed by a disciple: By patient endurance, steadfastness and perseverance, one will gain true life. The position of this particular teaching in Luke's gospel is no coincidence: It is in the next chapter that Luke's passion narrative begins.

■ **Read all of Luke 21. Reflect upon, and discuss with others, the difficulty we have in our culture of even considering patient, Christian endurance as a positive value.**

PRACTICE OF FAITH

THE PATRONESS OF MUSICIANS. On Wednesday we celebrate the feast of St. Cecilia, patroness of musicians. Most of what we know about her life is from unreliable legend, but she is remembered in the Roman Canon (Eucharistic Prayer I) as an early Christian martyr. Her feastday reminds us of the importance of music to our prayer. St. Augustine once said, "the one who sings, prays twice." Take time this week to thank the musicians of your parish who spend many hours at their art. Be open to your own musical gifts and to how you might share them with your community. Above all, honor St. Cecilia by using the voice God gave you to join fully in the sung prayer of the church.

PRACTICE OF HOPE

HEALING IN ITS WINGS. Arlene Kiely worked at Children's Hospital in Washington, D.C. She was asked by a teacher to help a child with some schoolwork. She didn't realize until she got there that he was on the burn unit, in pain and barely able to respond. She stumbled through the English lesson, ashamed at putting him through such a senseless exercise.

The next morning a nurse asked her, "What did you do to that boy?" Before she could finish apologizing, the nurse interrupted her: "You don't understand. His whole attitude has changed. It's as though he's decided to live." The boy explained later that he had completely given up hope until Kiely had arrived. With joyful tears, he said, "They wouldn't send a teacher to work on nouns and verbs with a dying boy, would they?"

PRACTICE OF CHARITY

DO NOT BE WEARY IN YOUR WELL-DOING. As we come to the end of the liturgical year, we can reflect on the past 12 months and wonder what charity is all about. However, we do not think you will wonder for long. The answer comes in so many ways: the new well dug for a village in Kenya; the nutrition class for mothers in Haiti; the smiling faces of the elderly at the local nursing home; the opportunity for further education for Native Americans; the warm clothes from your closet finding their way to those who would otherwise be cold. . . . When someone you know becomes burdened by the institutional sin in the world and wonders what kind of God would allow evil to happen, point them toward the many acts of charity that take place around us and ask them to fathom what kind of God would allow such *good* to continually transform and re-create our world each day.

WEEKDAY READINGS 1 Maccabees 1:10–15, 41–43, 54–57, 62–63; 2 Maccabees 6:18–31; 7:1, 20–31; (Th) Thanksgiving; 1 Maccabees 4:36–37, 52–59; 6:1–13

READING I *2 Samuel 5:1–3*

All the tribes of Israel came to David at Hebron, and said, "Behold, we are your bone and flesh. In times past, when Saul was king over us, it was you that led out and brought in Israel; and the LORD said to you, 'You shall be shepherd of my people Israel, and you shall be chief over Israel.'" So all the elders of Israel came to the king at Hebron; and he made a covenant with them at Hebron before the LORD, and they anointed David king over Israel.

READING II *Colossians 1:12–20*

Give thanks to the Father, who has qualified us to share in the inheritance of the saints in light. God has delivered us from the authority of darkness and transferred us to the dominion of the Son, the beloved of God, in whom we have redemption, the forgiveness of sins.

Christ is the image of the invisible God, the first-born of all creation; for in Christ all things were created, in heaven and on earth, visible and invisible, whether thrones or dominions or principalities or authorities — all things were created through him and for him. Christ is before all things, and in him all things hold together. Christ is the head of the body, the church; Christ is the beginning, the first-born from the dead, that in everything he might be preeminent. For in Christ all the fullness of God was pleased to dwell, and through Christ to reconcile to God all things, whether on earth or in heaven, making peace by the blood of his cross.

GOSPEL *Luke 23:35–43*

The people stood by the cross, watching; but the rulers scoffed at Jesus, saying, "He saved others; let him save himself, if he is the Christ of God, the Chosen One!" The soldiers also mocked Jesus, coming up and offering him vinegar, and saying, "If you are the King of the Jews, save yourself!" There was also an inscription over him, "This is the King of the Jews."

One of the criminals who were hanged railed at Jesus, saying, "Are you not the Christ? Save yourself and us!" But the other rebuked him, saying, "Do you not fear God, since you are under the same sentence of condemnation? And we indeed justly; for we are receiving the due reward of our deeds; but this man has done nothing wrong." And he said, "Jesus, remember me when you come into your kingdom." And Jesus said to him, "Truly, I say to you, today you will be with me in Paradise."

REFLECTION

On this last Sunday of the liturgical year, we celebrate the feast of Christ the King. Luke, the skilled artist, presents a strange picture of a king: Jesus, the prophet, the teacher and healer, hangs from a cross undergoing the death penalty meted out to criminals. The people stood watching (*theoreo,* as one would observe a public event). The rulers scoffed, the soldiers mocked, and one criminal railed.

Jesus spoke of salvation, healed, and even raised others from apparent death. Yet now he hangs on a cross in seeming powerlessness. One person in this narrative, one of the condemned criminals, recognizes Jesus' innocence and power and hears the blessed "today" that in Luke's writings conveys a sense of eschatological importance.

The portrait of the kingly messiah outlined in Colossians is more in accord with our usual post-Resurrection images of Christ the King. However, underlying the shining Christ is the blood of the cross.

Why such contrasting images? The key may be found in the nature of Christ's mission: The task of Christ is to reconcile all things to God and to establish a state of peace. Reconciliation has to do above all with change and exchange and involves movement and a reversal of the way things are. The kingdom initiated by God in Jesus is founded on change, and there can be no greater change than a crucified king.

The inauguration of the kingdom is watched as a spectator sport, is scoffed at and is mocked and railed at by those who only understand the language of power. Jesus is king and Christ by his endurance and acceptance of the consequences of his faithfulness to initiating the change necessary — the great reversal — that leads to peace and reconciliation.

■ The concept of "king" and "kingdom" are alien to us, yet they are at the core of the message of Jesus. Reflect on the inner reality behind these terms, translating them into concepts and terms that touch your life.

PRACTICE OF FAITH

ENDING THE YEAR. We have come full circle and close the liturgical year by proclaiming that Christ alone rules! Did you write any spiritual resolutions last year on the First Sunday of Advent? If you did, bring them out. Spend some time reviewing the past year. Pray in gratitude for those moments of growth, grace or revelation and ask forgiveness for times of sin. Be aware of the graces you wish to pray for in the new year. If you have kept a journal, put it away and get a fresh one to use beginning next week.

Remember to unpack your Advent wreath, purchase new candles and collect fresh greens so that you are ready for the new year to begin. May it bring many blessings!

PRACTICE OF HOPE

INHERITANCE OF SAINTS OF LIGHT. Hope was born HIV-positive, and much of her young life was spent in hospitals. As a toddler she loved "Alice in Wonderland," particularly the scene in which Alice stumbled onto an "un-birthday party." Hope exclaimed, "Everybody has a birthday, but we all can have 364 un-birthday parties a year!"

About once a week, her hospital room was decorated with balloons and she would ask visitors, "Would you like a piece of my un-birthday cake?" When she saw another patient in the hall struggling with a severely fractured leg, she said, "You need to have a party." And she threw him one. Hope died at the age of four, but she lived her life according to her name and left a legacy of joy to those around her.

PRACTICE OF CHARITY

THEY STOOD BY THE CROSS. Sometimes that is all we can do. When there are no words to speak, we can only stand by the cross of suffering, hopeful of offering comfort by our prayerful presence. The practice of charity does not always involve doing something or saying something or championing some cause. There are times when we must simply be present, times when we must stand by the cross of suffering and remain confident that Christ is King. Our presence can bring comfort and peace; it cannot take away the pain or suffering, but perhaps it can make it all a little more bearable. Be present to someone who is suffering this week. Stand by the cross in solidarity.

WEEKDAY READINGS **Daniel, chapter 1; 2:31–45; chapter 5; Romans 10:9–18; (Fr–Sa) Daniel, chapter 7**

Information On The License To Reprint From
At Home with the Word—*1995*

The low bulk-rate prices of *At Home with the Word 1995* are intended to make quantities of the book affordable. A single copy is $6.00; 2–99 copies are $4.00 each; 100 or more copies are $2.50 each. We encourage parishes to buy quantities of this book.

However, Liturgy Training Publications makes a simple reprint license available to parishes that would find it more practical to reproduce some parts of this book. Reflections (and questions), Practices, Prayers of the Season, and/or the holy day boxes can be duplicated for the parish bulletin or reproduced in other formats. These can be used every week or as often as the license holder chooses. The page size of *At Home with the Word 1995* is 8 x 10 inches.

The license granted is for the period beginning with the First Sunday of Advent— November 27, 1994—through the Solemnity of Christ the King—November 26, 1995.

Note also that the license does *not* cover the scriptures, psalms, or morning, evening and night prayer texts. See the acknowledgments page at the beginning of this book for the names and addresses of these copyright owners. Directions for obtaining permission to use these texts are given there.

The materials reprinted under license from LTP may not be sold and may be used only among the members of the community obtaining the license. The license may not be purchased by a diocese for use in its parishes.

No reprinting may be done by the parish until the license is signed by both parties and the fee is paid. Copies of the license agreement will be sent on request. The fee varies with the number of copies to be reproduced on a regular basis:

Up to 100 copies: $100
101 to 500 copies: $300
501 to 1000 copies: $500
More than 1000 copies: $800

For further information, call the reprint permissions department at 312-486-8970, ext. 38.